THE
NORMANS
IN IRELAND

THE NORMANS IN IRELAND

RICHARD LOMAS

First published in Great Britain in 2022 by
John Donald, an imprint of Birlinn Ltd

West Newington House
10 Newington Road
Edinburgh
EH9 1QS

www.birlinn.co.uk

ISBN: 978 1 910900 33 8

British Library Cataloguing-in-Publication Data
A catalogue record for this book is available on request from the British Library

Typeset by Biblichor Ltd, Edinburgh
Printed and bound in Malta by Gutenberg Press

Contents

Plates

Foreword

It is with pleasure that I write this foreword to Richard Lomas's book on a critical time in Irish history. Critical not only for the country as a whole but especially for my ancestor, Dermot MacMurrough, or as he was known in Middle Irish, Diarmait Mac Murchada. It is clear that he was a man prepared to commit acts of violence and take risks to further his ambition to be High King of Ireland, but we know from his other actions in promoting church reform that he was a moderniser who, had he accomplished his mission, may well have aimed at making the High Kingship less Irish and more European in style. I am pleased to give Dick Lomas my enthusiastic support, including access to my family records – which alas are few for his period, the early papers having been deposited in Dublin and lost in the Four Courts fire in 1916. I am equally pleased to become reacquainted with my ancestor, and wish the book every success.

Andrew MacMurrough Kavanagh

Preface

Turning points in history only become so when what they begin endures. By this obvious definition, Ireland has experienced three such moments. The earliest was the change from paganism to Christianity. It was a phase in the westward spread of this new religion following its adoption and promotion by the Roman Emperor Constantine I (312–37) and, with one exception, his successors. Their motives may not be entirely clear, but a perception of the advantages that could arise from alliance with an effective empire-wide network would, I believe, have been paramount. The change to Christianity in Ireland is particularly associated with two fifth-century foreign missionaries: Palladius, a Gaul, commissioned by Pope Celestine I (d. 432); and St Patrick (d. 461), a Briton, who was probably from the western end of Hadrian's Wall in what is now northern England. The third turning point was, of course, the achievement of Irish independence in 1922.

But it was the second that marked the onset of Ireland's entanglement with England (or, after 1707, Great Britain) – an entanglement that has taken many different forms and has been sustained, with varying degrees of intensity, until the present day. This second turning point began in the late 1160s with the alliance of two men. One was Irish: Diarmait Mac Murchada, King of Leinster (Irish = Laigin), a province comprising roughly the south-eastern quarter of Ireland. The other was an Anglo-Norman: Richard Fitz Gilbert de Clare, known then and ever since as Strongbow. Both were men on a mission: Diarmait to recover his kingdom, from which he had been driven out by Irish opponents, and Strongbow to gain lands and a title, having previously been deprived of both.

Their alliance was rewarded with success. Diarmait did recover Leinster, but did not live long enough to truly enjoy his restored kingship. This prize, though not the title, went to Strongbow, from whom it descended to his son-in-law, William Marshal, a remarkable man who had an indelible effect on both Ireland and England. The safekeeping of Leinster then passed successively in turn to his sons, until the family failed in the male line in 1245.

The area Strongbow and his family ruled was not the entire kingdom of Leinster, but only that part allocated to them by the kings of England, who intervened to devise and impose arrangements acceptable and convenient to themselves. What Strongbow and his descendants possessed was the liberty of Leinster. It comprised the modern counties of Carlow, Kildare, Kilkenny and Wexford, and parts of Offaly and Laois. What they were denied was Dublin and its county, which remained under royal control and included what became Co. Wicklow in the early seventeenth century.

The word 'liberty' may seem incongruous in this context, yet it encapsulates a concept with which we are all familiar: a franchise. A medieval liberty was a designated area in which some, but not all, of the functions of government were devolved by the crown upon an individual or institution, which then exercised them while retaining whatever profit accrued. Kings found them a useful and convenient way of governing a distant or troublesome province. The concept of the liberty was not new, nor was it unique to Ireland. There were several in England, the most durable being the Palatinate of Durham, a liberty ruled by the bishop of Durham.

The limits of time and space created by the liberty of Leinster provide me with a convenient context in which to explore the processes of conquest, migration, settlement and the introduction of alien social, economic and ecclesiastical forms and practices. This will be the substance of this book. All aspects of the subject have been researched at considerable length and depth since the publication of Goddard Henry Orpen's four-volume work *Ireland under the Normans*, now reissued as a single volume with an introduction by Sean Duffy (Dublin, 2005). His work is, and will continue to be, the foundation of and the starting point for scholars in future research. To the expanding body of knowledge on this subject has been added an artistic dimension in needlework and music: the Ros Tapestry. This splendid work has been produced in fifteen panels over many years by a group of women from the south-east of Ireland and beyond. The Ros Tapestry Suite is a musical work inspired by it, and together they tell the story of Strongbow's intrusive arrival in Ireland in 1170 – just as their famous counterpart in France, the Bayeux Tapestry, told the story of the invasion of England by William, duke of Normandy, in 1066.

The events in England in 1066 are a reminder that what happened in Ireland just over one hundred years later should not be seen as an in-house affair involving only the lands of the Atlantic archipelago. The men who came to Ireland after 1169 came from England and Wales, but were not basically English nor Welsh. Rather they were Anglo and Cambro-Normans, albeit one or two generations from their true homeland. In their invasion of Ireland they were in fact the latest participants in a remarkable phenomenon: the outspread in the eleventh and twelfth centuries of people from a very distinctive part of north-west France, who took control not only of these Atlantic islands but also created states in Italy and the Holy Land. In doing so, they achieved a wide dispersion of the French language which remained a distinguishing mark among the European elite until the twentieth century.

I have structured this book so as to bring together all aspects and facets of life and society within the framework and timespan of the liberty of Leinster, though where it is necessary and valid I have made use of later evidence. But the book is also intended as an introduction to the wider world of Western Europe. In particular, interest is focused on the emergence and development of the nation state and of its branch of the Christian Church in the twelfth and early thirteenth centuries and its impact on Ireland.

At the end of the book, I have listed the books and articles from which I have gained knowledge, insights and provocation of thought. They are but a representative sample of a much larger and expanding body of literature; time and constrictions of length unfortunately preclude a study in depth of any aspect I have discussed. And because I have tried to angle the book towards a general readership, I have favoured endnotes rather than footnotes for additional information and details of further reading. Consequently, my only attributions are in the text, and only where specific identification is essential.

Finally, on a personal note, I would like to add that my interest in the project has been fuelled by a growing acquaintance with the part of Ireland on which the book is focused; but also by the fact that my own academic work concerned with the far north of England and southern Scotland, showing the course of events there in the late eleventh and twelfth centuries, has parallels with the events in Ireland between 1167 and 1247.

No book is written that does not owe something – in some cases, perhaps, a great deal – to the help of others. This book is no exception and therefore I willingly and gratefully acknowledge the advice, help and encouragement given by my friends in Ireland, in particular Máire Dunne, Fran and Robert Durie, Ian Fox, Eithne Frost, Grace Hall, Jeremy Hill, Andrew and Morgan Kavanagh, Gerry Murphy, Connie Tantrum and New Ross Needlecraft Ltd. I give my special thanks to my daughter, Clare, for giving her time and expertise as a photographer; and to my wife, Joan, whose help and sage advice have been invaluable in bringing the book to fruition. It has been my pleasure to work with my copy editor, Camilla Rockwood, and I add my thanks to her for her meticulous editing. Finally, my thanks to managing director Hugh Andrew and academic editor Mairi Sutherland at Birlinn, who have patiently guided me through my worst excesses of 'academia'.

My advance acceptance of guilt for any errors that the book may contain is genuine and owes nothing to convention.

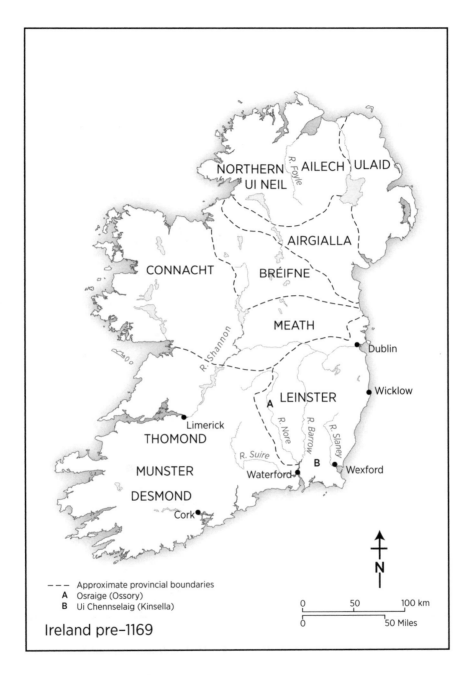

Ireland pre–1169

- - - Approximate provincial boundaries
A Osraige (Ossory)
B Ui Chennselaig (Kinsella)

All boundaries are approximate as they were constantly liable to change. The ancient province of Munster was forcibly divided by the High King of Ireland in 119 into two kingdoms, Desmond and Thomond. Every kingdom had several sub-kingdoms; those in Leinster that are important in this book have been labelled.

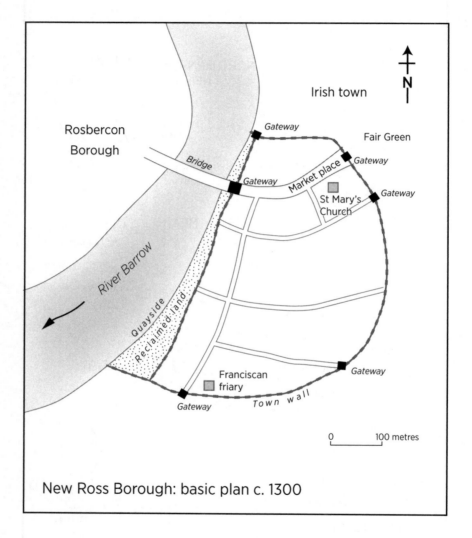

Irish town

Rosbercon
Borough

Fair Green

Gateway

Bridge

Gateway

Market place

Gateway

River Barrow

Gateway

St Mary's
Church

Quayside

Reclaimed land

Franciscan
friary

Gateway

Town wall

Gateway

0   100 metres

New Ross Borough: basic plan c. 1300

Source: Based on a plan from Avril Thomas, *The Walled Town of Ireland*, Vol. 2.

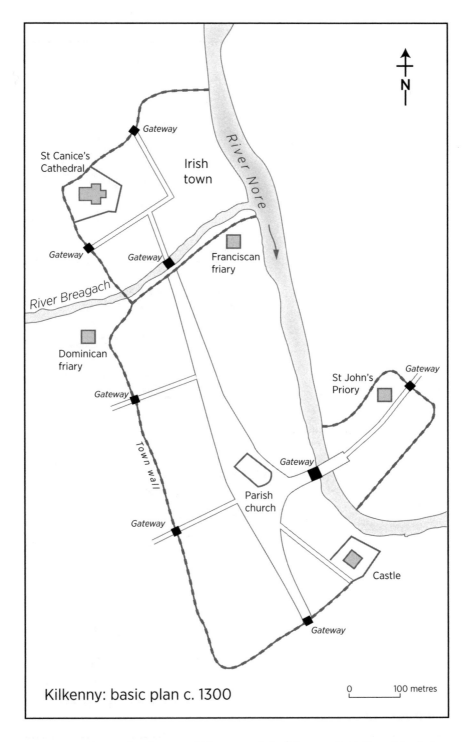

Gateway

St Canice's
Cathedral

Irish
town

River Nore

Gateway

Gateway

Franciscan
friary

River Breagach

Dominican
friary

St John's
Priory

Gateway

Gateway

Town wall

Gateway

Parish
church

Gateway

Gateway

Castle

Gateway

Kilkenny: basic plan c. 1300

0   100 metres

Source: Based on a plan from Avril Thomas and C. Ó'Drisceoill, *William Marshal in Ireland*.

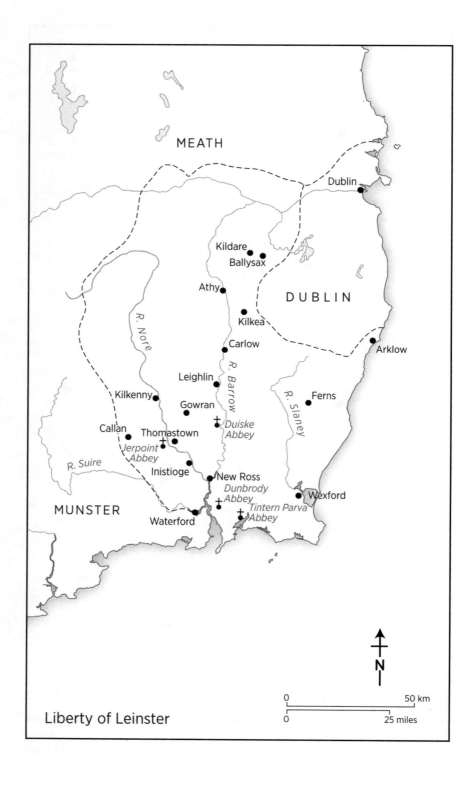

MEATH

Kildare
Ballysax

DUBLIN

Dublin

Athy

R. Nore

Kilkea

Carlow

R. Barrow

Leighlin

Arklow

Kilkenny

Gowran

R. Slaney

Ferns

Callan

Thomastown

✝ *Duiske Abbey*

Jerpoint Abbey

Inistioge

New Ross

✝ *Dunbrody Abbey*

✝ *Tintern Parva Abbey*

Wexford

MUNSTER

R. Suire

Waterford

N

0   50 km

0   25 miles

Liberty of Leinster

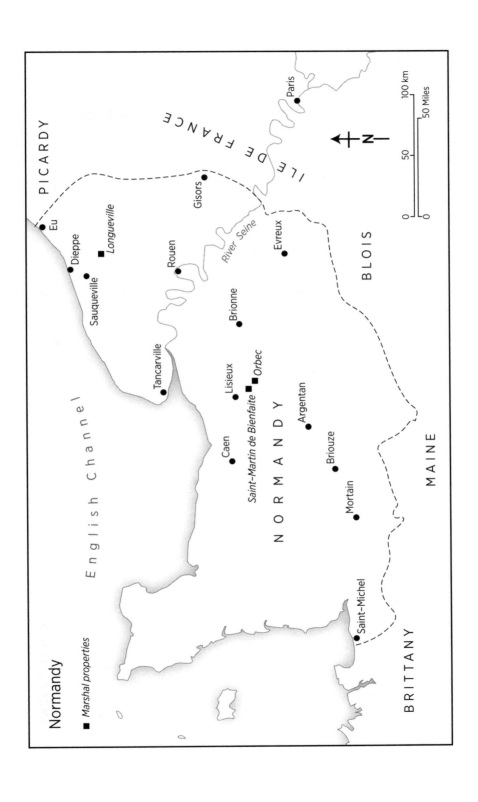

Normandy

■ *Marshal properties*

PICARDY

ÎLE DE FRANCE

Paris

Gisors

Eu

Dieppe

■ *Longueville*

Sauqueville

Rouen

River Seine

Evreux

BLOIS

English Channel

Tancarville

Brionne

Lisieux

■ *Orbec*

■

Saint-Martin de Bienfaite

Caen

Argentan

N O R M A N D Y

Briouze

Mortain

MAINE

Saint-Michel

BRITTANY

100 km

50 Miles

50

N

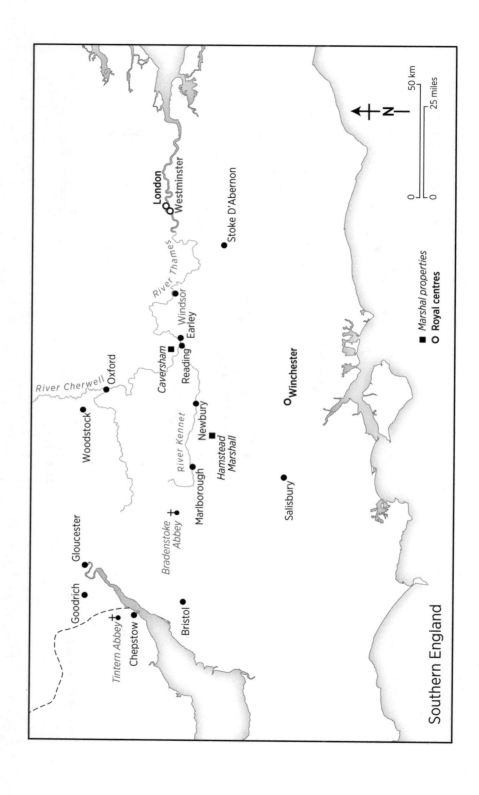

Southern England

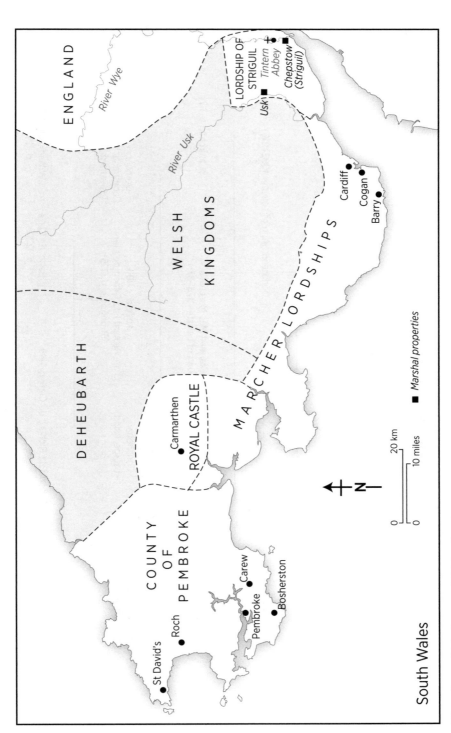

South Wales

Places from which there was Welsh migration

Mac Murchada Family

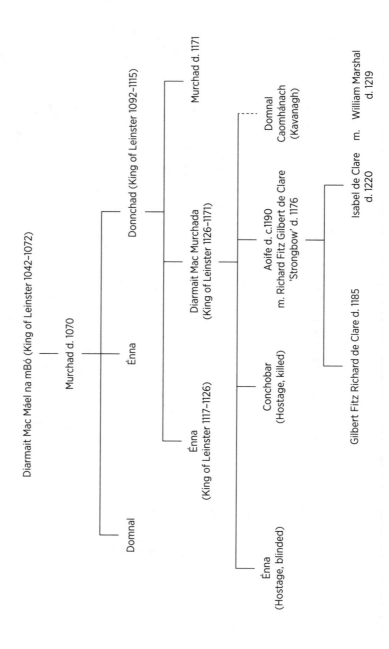

Diarmait Mac Máel na mBó (King of Leinster 1042-1072)

Murchad d. 1070

Domnal

Énna

Donnchad (King of Leinster 1092-1115)

Murchad d. 1171

Énna
(King of Leinster 1117-1126)

Diarmait Mac Murchada
(King of Leinster 1126-1171)

Énna
(Hostage, blinded)

Conchobar
(Hostage, killed)

Aoife d. c.1190
m. Richard Fitz Gilbert de Clare
'Strongbow' d. 1176

Domnal
Caomhánach
(Kavanagh)

Gilbert Fitz Richard de Clare d. 1185

Isabel de Clare   m.   William Marshal
d. 1220   d. 1219

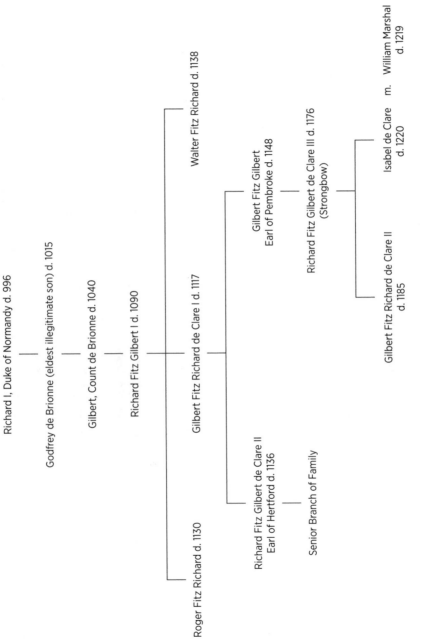

De Clare Family

Marshal Family

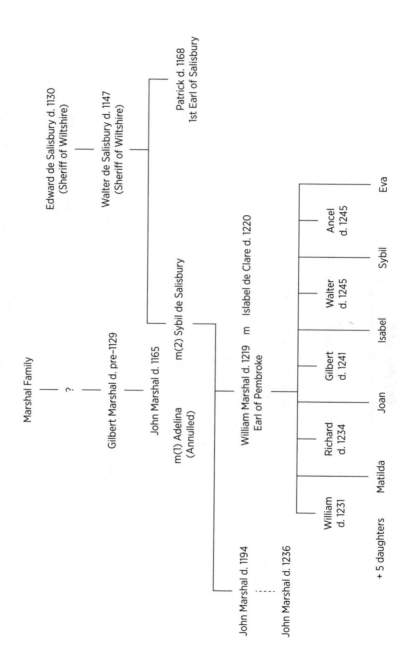

Marshal Family

?

Gilbert Marshal d. pre-1129

John Marshal d. 1165

Edward de Salisbury d. 1130
(Sheriff of Wiltshire)

Walter de Salisbury d. 1147
(Sheriff of Wiltshire)

Patrick d. 1168
1st Earl of Salisbury

m(1) Adelina
(Annulled)

m(2) Sybil de Salisbury

William Marshal d. 1219   m   Isabel de Clare d. 1220
Earl of Pembroke

John Marshal d. 1194

John Marshal d. 1236

+ 5 daughters

William
d. 1231

Matilda

Richard
d. 1234

Joan

Gilbert
d. 1241

Isabel

Walter
d. 1245

Sybil

Ancel
d. 1245

Eva

PART I: ROOTS

The reasons why in 1169 and the following years groups of Anglo-Norman and Cambro-Norman warriors came to Ireland are immediate and local. But there was an obvious geographical unity in that as an island it had long attracted previous adventurers, raiders and traders, like the Vikings, although, surprisingly, not the Romans. Within the confines of Ireland there were no formal boundaries but nine kingdoms with their own ruling kings, and no dynastic High King; this politically fractured society was almost inevitably warlike. The Normans, therefore, arrived at the end of a train of events stretching back over 200 years.

A balanced perspective requires an understanding of these events. As the story unfolds, the two chapters that follow will be of help in achieving this.

I

Viking Eruptions

Throughout the ninth century, Western Europe endured violent assaults at the hands of raiders from beyond its borders. From the steppes of western Asia came the Magyars, from across the Mediterranean came the Saracens of North Africa, and from Scandinavia came the Vikings or Northmen. It is with these last intruders that this book is concerned. The damage and rampaging disruption caused by their raiding intrusions could be, and was, made good. But their brutality and disruptive engagement against native societies destroyed kingdoms, so much so as to set the political development of many parts of Europe onto a new course.

Before looking at this, it is worth bringing the Vikings into better focus. The chroniclers who recorded their raids were rightly horrified by their savagery, barbarity and wanton violence. There is no validity in the common belief that they wore horned helmets, but these animal-skin-clad, hirsute, fearsome warriors, known by the Norse word *bersurker* (from which is derived the word 'berserk'), did indulge in pre-battle rituals which resulted in winding themselves up into a frenzy, which they then unleashed upon their enemies to devasting effect: in fact, they did run berserk. They were a cruel people who killed indiscriminately, possibly because there appears to have been no teaching of restraint in their religion, unlike Christian teaching – but here I am speculating through lack of firm evidence.

However, the Vikings had another side to them. They became excellent colonists; they were skilled craftsmen; and through their expertise in naval architecture, innovative shipbuilding and seamanship, they fostered an international commercial nexus that extended from Kiev to Limerick. It will, I hope, become apparent that what happened in Ireland after 1169 stemmed directly from the changes they made or introduced.

FRANCE

The kingdom of France takes its name from the Franks, a Germanic people who in the sixth century occupied the Roman province of Gaul. Once settled, they adopted the Romans' institutions and gradually their language. It has been said, mischievously, though with a basic truth, that the French language is 'a debased dialect of Latin'. In adopting this formula, the Franks were at one with all other Germanic peoples who took over Roman provinces.

Subsequently and through conquest, a Frankish empire was created, stretching from the river Ebro in Spain to the river Elbe in Germany. Its high point was the coronation of the Frankish king Charlemagne (Charles the Great) as Holy Roman Emperor by Pope Leo III, in St Peter's Church in Rome on Christmas Day 800. When Charlemagne died in 814 he was succeeded by his only surviving son, Louis, known as Louis the Pious. The empire survived intact until after Louis's death in 840. He left three legitimate sons, and consequently, according to custom, after his death in 843 the empire was divided between them. It was West Francia, or part of it, that was to develop into the kingdom of France.[1]

FRANCE AND THE FOUNDING OF NORMANDY

The history of the West Frankish kingdom was of political disintegration, so that by around 1100 it could be described as a failed state. The effective authority of the king gradually shrank to no more than that of the Île de France, a small area around Paris. The real power had been usurped by local or regional officials bearing the titles of count or duke. They were the descendants of royal officials appointed by the king and were theoretically answerable to him. The effective power of the French kings was gradually but massively eroded, although they retained one unique feature: sovereignty. They alone were crowned and anointed monarchs, a title and status that no count or duke could deny. In the end, this proved to be their priceless asset and the basis on which they were to rebuild their authority.

One of the major causes of the decline of French royal authority was the Viking raids that reached a crescendo in the late ninth century.[2] The task of organising defence measures to thwart or defeat these assaults proved to be beyond the ability of the crown and consequently it was shouldered by the counts and dukes. Inevitably, the forces they raised, mainly heavy cavalry, were used to substantiate their authority over their subjects as well as providing defence.

It was this situation that gave rise to the duchy of Normandy, which was to play such a crucial role in the history of Britain and Ireland. Its creation was an initiative of the French king, Charles III (895–929), who in 913 negotiated a treaty with a Viking leader, Rollo (or Rolf), whereby the latter was granted land along the Channel coast in return for his loyalty to the crown and conversion to Christianity.[3] In effect, Charles employed the tactic 'if you can't beat them, get them to join you'. Rollo would henceforth protect the French interior from his fellow Vikings. Over the following twenty years further grants of land were made, until Normandy extended in a direct line of about 80 miles (125 km) from Mont-Saint-Michel at the base of the Cotentin peninsula to Le Tréport. Its inland depth was 60 miles (90 km) at its maximum. One clue as to Charles III's thinking was that his Viking allies would control the mouth of the River Seine, one of the main points of access to the French interior used by the Viking raiders.

Without doubt, large numbers of Viking men and women migrated from the north to settle in Normandy, although the exact figures will never be known. This migration continued until after c. 960, when it gradually dried up. With the end of migration came assimilation, so that by the year 1000, Normans of whatever ethnic origin were speaking French.

FOUNDING OF BRITAIN: ENGLAND AND SCOTLAND

Britain was unlike France in several ways. In Britain three languages were spoken, the early versions of English, Welsh and Irish, broadly reflecting the island's ethnic and political divisions. The largest area was that occupied by English-speaking kingdoms, the products of invasions and migrations of Germanic people (Angles, Jutes and Saxons) from Europe between c. 450 and c. 600. By 850, the number of kingdoms had been reduced by warfare and conquest to four: Northumbria (Firth of Forth – river Humber); Mercia (river Humber – river Thames); Wessex (river Thames – south coast) and East Anglia. At this stage, there was no kingdom of England.[4] The nearest these kingdoms came to unity was the enforced acknowledgement that one of the kings was *Bretwalda* (ruler of Britain). It was a temporary and enforced acceptance without constitutional validity, akin to the situation in Ireland where there were multiple provincial kings, each striving to enforce superiority as High King.

The northern limit of English Britain was a line running from the Forth to the Clyde represented by a Roman wall: not Hadrian's Wall, but the one built by Hadrian's successor as emperor, Antoninus Pius (AD 138–161), now referred to as the Antonine Wall. To the north of this wall, which at that time would still have been substantially intact, lay two quite different kingdoms. The larger, in the east, was Pictavia, which occupied the fertile land between the Firth of Forth and the Dornoch Firth.[5] The Picts, who produced a distinctive but enigmatic art, almost certainly spoke Brittonic, a Celtic language common to the entire island of Britain from which the Welsh language developed.

To the west was the smaller kingdom of Dál Riata, which comprised territory on both sides of the North Channel. The Irish territory was essentially that which is now Co. Antrim, while the Scottish territories were comprised of the later counties of Argyll and Bute and included the islands of Arran, Islay, Jura and Mull. These kingdoms differed in several ways, the principal one being language. In Dál Riata, the spoken language was the other Celtic language, Goedelic, from which Irish and its Scottish offshoot, Gaelic, developed.

Finally, west of a line from the estuary of the river Dee to that of the river Severn, was the land roughly corresponding to present-day Wales. It was divided into four kingdoms but was homogeneous in language and culture.

The Vikings changed northern Britain in two profound ways. Vikings from Norway took control and colonised the Northern Isles of Orkney and Shetland, and the islands of the Outer Hebrides. From these bases they extended their control over those parts of the mainland covering the later counties of Caithness, Sutherland, Inverness, and Ross and Cromarty. In doing so they introduced another foreign language, Norse. Their impact was long-lasting, though not permanent: in the late fifteenth century (1472) the earldom of Orkney and the lordship of Shetland were annexed to the Scottish crown, and the lordship of the Isles was forfeited in 1493.

Arguably of greater significance was their impact on Pictavia and Dál Riata. It is unfortunate that the evidence for what happened, when and why is so sparse as to make certainty well-nigh impossible. That said, what has become clear to me is that between c. 840 and c. 890 the Gaelic-speaking kings of Dál Riata gained control of Pictavia, thereby bringing into existence a new, larger kingdom, Alba. Without doubt, this was a remarkable turnover of political power. Since the early years of the ninth century, the Pictish kings had exercised political hegemony over their western neighbour, which is not surprising given their disparity in size. Traditionally, responsibility for this turn of events has been attributed to one man, Cinead (Kenneth) Mac Alpin (d. 858), but this is now considered to be too simplistic. Instead, the basic and underlying reason is now thought to be the gradual weakening of the Pictavian state, brought about by Viking assaults to the point where it became vulnerable to a Dál Riatan takeover. Added to this was that Dál Riata too was vulnerable to Viking pressure, so that salvation must have seemed to lie in union with Pictavia. Change of political control was followed by language change: in ways and at a pace which are hidden from us, Brittonic gave way to Gaelic, which in the long run became the language of the northern Scottish mainland and Western Isles – though not Orkney and Shetland, where a Norse language known as Norn continued to be spoken until the eighteenth century.

On the English-speaking kingdoms the Viking impact was equally drastic. Between 865 and 878 a large Viking army effectively destroyed Northumbria, Mercia and East Anglia as states. Only Wessex, under its king, Alfred (871–99), did not succumb.[6] The Vikings were fought to a standstill and accepted peace terms, which included their conversion to Christianity.

In the course of the tenth century Alfred's successors, Edward (899–927), Aethelstan (927–39), Edmund (939–46), Eadred (946–55) and Edgar (955–75), gradually succeeded in imposing their rule over the Viking areas. They did not do so, however, to re-impose the *status quo ante* but to incorporate what had been Mercia, Northumberland and East Anglia into an enlarged Wessex. By 975, this name had become obsolete. A new kingdom had emerged and needed a new name: England.

In the following twenty-five years, the kings of Alba took over the most northerly parts of Northumbria so that by the year 1000, they had advanced their southern border to the river Tweed.[7] They had in effect converted Alba into the kingdom of Scotland. The two kingdoms into which Britain was and is divided were the consequence of Viking invasions.

IRELAND

Compared with France and Britain, the Viking impact on Ireland was not extensive, at least geographically.[8] As elsewhere, Viking activity began with annual raids during the early 830s which then became more widespread and penetrating in the middle decades, particularly with the introduction of over-wintering and fortified camps, called *longphorts* in Ireland. But there was no concerted attempt, as in England, at total conquest; nor as in France, to create a large province capable of attracting large scale immigration. At first glance, the Viking legacy appears to be little more than a few coastal settlements, the most important of which were Dublin, Waterford and Limerick; how large was the community, if established, will only be determined by ongoing archaeological research . The most these coastal towns were concerned to control were limited hinterlands, from which they could draw what they required by way of foodstuffs. Their primary interest was not conquest, but commerce.

It was through this that they drew Ireland into a wider economic world, and this was far-ranging. The Irish towns lay at the western limits of an international trade network. Far to the east it was anchored at Viking settlements at Novgorod and Kiev in what the Arabs called 'the land of Rus' (hence Russia). Using their naval skills, the Vikings used rivers such as the Dvina and the Dneipr to reach the Black Sea and Byzantium (Istanbul). It was a network that helped to bring the more backward west into contact, economically and culturally, with the more sophisticated Arab and Oriental worlds.

Closer to home, Ireland became engaged with the Norse sea world that encompassed the Isle of Man and the western islands and coasts of Britain. Here too Dublin was to the fore, particularly in the tenth century through its links to the Norse kingdom of York and increasingly in the eleventh century with the west coast towns of Bristol and Chester, while in Ireland, the smaller Viking towns of Cork and Wexford became more prominent.

Nevertheless, the political structure of Ireland remained fundamentally unaltered. The island was divided between nine kingdoms, each with its own ruling dynasty. From south to north there were: Laigin (Leinster), Munster (though this was divided into Thomond and Desmond), Connacht, Bréifne, Mide (Meath), Airgialla, Ailech and Ulaid. Every provincial king was faced with two permanent problems. One was to maintain control over the sub-kings within his province, of which there were about fifty in all. The other was the engagement in a contest to become High King of Ireland, or to resist the same ambition in a rival. As in England in the pre-Viking era, there was no recognised sovereign, as there was in France. To attain the High Kingship of Ireland a provincial king required military might, to enforce the acknowledgement by all other kings and to maintain that submission. It is clear, however, that the Viking towns had become participants in this kaleidoscope of political ambition. By 1169, control of Dublin had become key to the mastery of Ireland and it was on its way to becoming Ireland's capital.

At the beginning of the eleventh century, the far west of Europe exhibited two things that could be attributed to the Vikings. One was that a powerful French–Norse province, the duchy of Normandy, was well established along a stretch of the southern shore of the Channel. The other is that two new kingdoms, England and Scotland, had come into being in Britain, both formed by the union of smaller kingdoms, and both with ruling dynasties with accepted sovereignty. Beyond them to the west lay Wales and Ireland, each with its ethnic and linguistic homogeneity but still politically fragmented and thereby vulnerable to an aggressive predator. And by 1169, the Vikings had succeeded in forging links joining Ireland to Britain, Europe and the wider world. They were the precursors of their Frenchified descendants in Normandy, the main characters of this book.

Norman Eruptions

This title may seem exaggerated, and in simple numerical terms it is; but not if the impact Norman activity made on politics and the political structures of Europe between *c.* 1040 and *c.* 1140 is considered. In the course of those years, Normans created two new states and radically transformed two others.[1] Their outstanding achievements have occasioned much thought over many years in the search for an explanation, but none has been found wholly acceptable.

What I believe to be certain is that the Normans were aware of their origins and what made them distinctive; there was a characteristic self-awareness and pride in their achievements. They believed themselves to be distinct, and to some extent they were. France (Roman Gaul) had been taken over by Germanic peoples, who were already Christianised and who were seeking not only enrichment but also the benefits of being within what was still an essentially Roman world. The Normans, however, were Danes who came later and were heathens, although they did become Christian fairly quickly. Their numbers were insufficient to displace or swamp the indigenous inhabitants, but large enough to have a dominating influence.

As already noted, the Normans were different to a large extent because they believed themselves to be different. Believe it long enough and declaim it regularly, and it becomes an embedded characteristic. This self-assessment appears to have developed during the thirty-year rule of Richard II (996–1026), the first ruler to be styled Duke rather than Count, as the nascent 'Normandy' emerged from a long period of gestation in which native and migrant merged. But perhaps more important was that it was given a powerful literary impetus by 'histories', the first of which was written by Dudo, a man from St Quentin in Picardy who became Richard II's chaplain. Based largely on orally transmitted stories, the result, although incorporating undoubted facts, was what we would now consider myth. Myths, however, can be far more potent than fact.[2]

One dramatic example of how this could work is in the witness of their self-awareness in the speech made by Walter Espec (a nickname meaning 'woodpecker'), lord of Helmsley, on 22 August 1138 when addressing an army assembled on Cowton Moor in North Yorkshire to confront a large Scottish army led by its king, David I. Walter was one of the Anglo-Norman commanders, chosen on account of his stentorian voice to make the traditional pre-battle speech to arouse the courage, confidence and conviction of men about to face the possibility of death. He did so by reminding them of who they were and of the prowess of their ancestors. It worked: the Scots were defeated.

But myths alone do not explain how the Normans came to forge new lives for themselves in distant parts. There were more practical, and indeed more urgent, stimuli.

One was the need for room to expand, particularly when allied with the growing preference for male primogeniture as the principle governing succession to title and property. Here, the Normans, particularly younger sons, were at a disadvantage. They lived in a small state hemmed in by the Channel and, landward, by neighbours well capable of repelling attempts at expansion. Contrast this with the situation on the eastern borders of Germany or the southern borders of Castile and Aragon, where expansion by violence could be justified and in fact encouraged by religious belief. To dispossess, respectively, heathen Slavs and Moorish Muslims was construed as God's work; or so the perpetrators were ready to believe. Robbery with violence could masquerade as a crusade.

However, while instances of migration in search of better fortune can be adduced, so can examples of men exiled for political and behavioural reasons. Examples of both voluntary and enforced migration were crucial in driving certain Normans to migrate to Italy. Although difficult to prove, it would seem that the Normans' desire to move on into other lands in order to dominate them was hard-wired into their character.

At the same time, there is no evidence to suggest the Normans were superior militarily or in any other way to the people of the neighbouring duchies and counties, who were by turns their allies and enemies. What does stand out, however, in all the following four ventures is that they achieved success by self-confidence, fierce commitment, willing ruthlessness and a determination to exploit opportunities presented by the fluctuations of the then political world.

One further introductory point: not all participants in Norman ventures were from Normandy. Their ranks were swelled by men from across northern France, trained for war and eager for betterment. The fact that such men accepted Norman leadership shows that the Normans had already become an important part of the Frankish world.

Two of these ventures may be dealt with briefly, since they have no direct bearing on the matter of this book. But it would be wrong to leave them out, since this would leave the picture incomplete; whereas their inclusion adds greater awareness of the breadth of Norman activity. The first was the conquest of the far south of Italy and the island of Sicily, which they welded into a new kingdom. The second, a sequel, was the capture of one of the major cities of the Levant, Antioch, and its hinterland, which became a principality.

CREATION OF NEW STATES IN SOUTHERN ITALY, SICILY AND ANTIOCH

The Norman achievement in southern Italy was remarkable in that it brought together into a single political entity a number of small units that were diverse politically and culturally.[3] In the early eleventh century, the far south of the Italian mainland, the areas known as Apulia and Calabria, were a hotchpotch politically, ethnically and in religion. The northern parts comprised several small duchies, notably Salerno, Benevento, Capua and Naples, ruled by descendants of their ninth-century conquerors, the Germanic Lombards. In religion, they were Catholic Christian.

South of them were two outlying provinces of what remained of the Roman Empire, the bulk of which lay in the Balkans and Asia Minor. Ruled from Byzantium, they were Greek in language and were Christian but Orthodox, not Catholic. Between these two wings of the Christian faith no love was lost, since neither was prepared to cede primacy to the other.

Added to this mix was Sicily. Its native population was largely Catholic, but since the ninth century the island had been ruled by Muslim conquerors from North Africa.

Political fragmentation, compounded by cultural differences, was virtually an invitation to ambitious foreign intruders. It was Normans who were quick to seize the opportunity.

Who were these brisk, risk-taking Normans? Basically, there were two groups. The earlier arrivals were led by a certain Rainulf, a man banished from Normandy on account of his violent behaviour. He took service with the duke of Naples, who gave him the town of Aversa, and also his sister as his wife, and eventually Capua. The other group, who came to be dominant, were led by five sons of a middle-ranking Norman landowner, Tancred de Hauteville. The fact that Tancred produced twelve sons, all of whom grew to manhood, goes far to explain why some of them sought fame and fortune in Italy. Two of them were of prime importance. One of the earliest arrivals was the elder, Robert, nicknamed Guiscard ('crafty'), who was to succeed in conquering Apulia and Calabria. The last to come south from Normandy was Count Roger, the youngest but probably the most able of the brothers. He was assigned the task of subjugating Sicily, which he completed successfully by 1091, and is still remembered today in Sicily and Malta.

Thirty-seven years later, Roger's son, Roger II, united all the parts conquered by the previous generation of Normans into a single state and in 1130, he persuaded Anacletus II (1130–8), an unsuccessful claimant to the papal throne, to raise his title from duke to king. However, Anacletus's dubious status rendered the title nugatory. It was the victor in the papal contest, Innocent II (1130–43), who, albeit with great reluctance, conferred the royal title on Roger in 1140. A new kingdom, that of Sicily, had been created, and would last until absorbed into a united Italy in the late nineteenth century.

Roger's achievement was remarkable not only politically but socially, in that he permitted freedom of worship and eschewed enforced conversion of his Greek and Arab subjects. His purpose was simple: they possessed skills and talents the Normans lacked. Religious toleration made them loyal subjects and allowed him to employ them to the benefit of himself and his kingdom.

The second Norman venture took place about 1,250 miles (2,000 km) to the east, in Syria. But it can be seen as a continuation of the Hauteville family story, in that the central character, Bohemond (known from the place of his birth as Bohemond of Taranto), was Robert Guiscard's eldest son by his first wife, Alberada, who was Norman. After her death he remarried, his second wife being Sichilgaita, a Lombard, who also bore him a son, Roger. When Robert Guiscard died in 1085, his son and namesake was left the duchy of Apulia and Calabria. The second wife had outflanked her deceased predecessor. In doing what he did, Robert Guiscard did not flout the rules, since it was a widely accepted custom that a man was free to dispose as he wished of that he had won by his sword. All Bohemond was given was a small part of the Byzantine Empire on the eastern shore of the Adriatic Sea, to make of it what he could. This did not satisfy Bohemond; he was now a man looking for a better opportunity.

He found it by joining the expedition known as the First Crusade.[4] This was the brainchild of Pope Urban II (1088–99), which he launched in 1096 in a well-rehearsed speech to a large, receptive audience at Clermont in central France. Its purpose was to recover from Islamic control Jerusalem and other places sacred to Christians. These had been in Arab, therefore Islamic, hands since 634, but for most of that time Christians had been able to make their pilgrimages without undue danger or difficulty. This changed with the arrival from the steppes of Central Asia of another but far more warlike and less tolerant Islamic people, the Turks. They rapidly overran the Caliphate of Baghdad, which ruled Palestine and Syria, and in 1071 they inflicted a crushing defeat on a Byzantine army. Their victory enabled them to over-whelm most of Asia Minor (now Turkey) and threaten Byzantium itself.

Urban's call for a crusade was therefore prompted by an appeal for help which he had received from the Byzantine Emperor, Alexius I: though quite what help Alexius hoped to receive is not clear. But Pope Urban also had another, more astute local purpose in appealing for an armed exped-ition. The political fragmentation of France had resulted in constant warfare between its small principalities, which their rulers conducted with the use of heavily armed armoured cavalry known as knights. The activities of these warriors had devastating effects on civil society, and consequently Urban calculated that if they could be put to good use plying their trade far from home and to good purpose, European society would be lot a happier and more peaceful.

The response to the papal appeal was electric. From the central parts of Europe thousands set off to realise his ambition. Theirs was an act of folly: they were poorly trained and ill-prepared for the task, and as a result they either perished or were enslaved in the Balkans and Asia Minor. However, the expedition of the late 1090s did succeed and achieved its principal objective, although only after an arduous campaign lasting three years; it was driven by a smaller body of professional warriors composed of men drawn almost entirely from the Frankish world, and in contingents raised and financed by counts and dukes. These men formed a committee of command-ers, although with a papal legate as an *ex officio* chairman. By late 1097 they had reached the city of Antioch, which was too strong and strategically located to be bypassed. The only apparent way of taking it was by siege, and as they were without the necessary siege artillery, the assault dragged on well into 1098. In the end it was taken by devious means: Bohemond's collusion with a traitor inside the city. He then commanded a force that defeated a Turkish army sent to bring relief to the beleaguered city. Bohemond proceeded to claim Antioch as his prize, claiming that it had been agreed that the city should go to the person who had engineered its surrender.[5] Having secured what he had come for, Bohemond withdrew from the crusade, which carried on south to take Jerusalem the following year.

Another Norman, who was also to some extent a loser, commanded another contingent. He was Robert, duke of Normandy since the death of his father, William the Conqueror, in 1087. The Conqueror had three sons, Robert, William and Henry. To Robert he bequeathed his dukedom; to William he gave England, the kingdom he had won by conquest; and to Henry he left money but no land. As already noted, it was a division according to the rules: as the eldest son, Robert could not be denied what his father had inherited. England, which William had conquered, was his to bequeath as he as he saw fit, while his youngest son would have to make his own way in the world.

Robert, nicknamed by his father Curthose ('short stockings') on account of his lack of height, was an easygoing man, though an excellent soldier. It was typical of him that he should desert his responsibilities in Normandy for foreign adventure. He had no difficulty in recruiting a contingent of eager knights. His problem was how to pay them. This he solved by mortgaging his duchy for three years to his brother William II, king of England.

Robert performed well on crusade but had no intention of staying in Palestine. On his return, however, he found William II unwilling to return Normandy to him. Equally obdurate was his youngest brother, Henry, who became King of England in 1100 as a result of William II's death while hunting in the New Forest in Hampshire. This was the sort of dispute between royal siblings that could be settled only one way; by a battle, which was fought at Tinchebray in Normandy in 1106. Robert was defeated and spent the rest of his life as Henry's prisoner, dying in 1134, only a year before Henry himself.

CONQUEST OF ENGLAND

The armed intruders into Ireland were second- or third-generation Norman, Flemish or Breton settlers who came to Britain after 1066. It follows, therefore, that a rounded understanding of events in Ireland requires a knowledge of similar events in Britain one hundred years before. Perhaps the most basic point is the sharp contrast between the Norman conquest of England and the Norman ventures into Italy and Syria. The latter were private initiatives; the Norman invasion of England was not. It was a

carefully planned and ruthlessly executed assault by a head of state, William
II, duke of Normandy (1027–87). To fully understand why William committed himself to such a hazardous venture, we need to go back to the
closing years of the reign of Aethelred II (978–1016), who is commonly
described as 'the Unready'.[6] This is a mistranslation of the old English word
unraed, meaning 'without counsel'. By his first, English wife, Aethelred
had a son, Edmund, nicknamed Ironside. He reigned briefly after his
father's death in 1016. However, Edmund, like his father before him, faced
a full-scale invasion by Swein, king of Denmark, known as 'Forkbeard',
and after his death, by his son, Cnut. Edmund's premature death shortly
after that of his father led to a collapse of English resistance, the result of
which was that Cnut gained the English throne. This North Sea Empire
was short lived: King Cnut and the two sons who succeeded him all died
in quick succession between 1035 and 1042.

The way was then open for the return of the English royal dynasty,
although it is probably more accurate to call it the Anglo-Norman dynasty.
The new king of England was Edward, known as the Confessor because of
his interest in religion and ecclesiastical affairs: he was responsible for building the first Westminster Abbey. Edward was born possibly in 1005, to
Aethelred and his second wife, Emma, daughter of Duke Richard I of
Normandy (d. 996). When Cnut became king, Edward was still a boy and
so taken for safety to Normandy, where he spent his formative years. His
mother, however, remained in England, where as a widow, she married
Cnut, an arrangement politically advantageous to both parties. It made it
possible for Emma to secure the succession after Cnut's death for the son
born to them, and after his death, for Edward to succeed to the English
throne. In doing so, she was able to thwart the progeny of Edmund 'Ironside'.

And progeny there was, but living far away in Hungary, in the person
of Edmund's son Edward, known as the Aetheling (Prince) – a fair indication that he was aware of having been denied his right to the throne. In
adulthood, Edward the Aetheling married and had two children –
Margaret (b. 1047) and Edgar (b. 1052) – and in 1056, the family were
allowed to return to England. Edward the Aetheling died shortly after
landing; there is no evidence of foul play, only a lurking suspicion. With
his death, the title Aetheling, and with it the claim to the throne, passed
to his son, Edgar. The possibility of Edgar's claim being realised became
live on 5 January 1066, when Edward the Confessor died.

The question of who should succeed to the throne had to be answered
by the leading figures in English public life. Edgar had to be considered

but was ruled out on account of his age (he was only thirteen years old). Although being of royal kin counted for much, at this date male primogeniture had yet to become *de rigueur*, and the times were not propitious for having a king who could reign but not rule. The obvious English candidate was Harold Godwinson, earl of Wessex, whose family had dominated English political life for most of the Confessor's reign and who was a man of proven ability. His links to the royal dynasty were, however, tangential, amounting to no more than his sister's marriage to the Confessor, making him his brother-in-law. What clinched it for him was that the Confessor named him as his successor on his deathbed. A dying monarch's recommendation carried weight: Harold Godwinson became King Harold II.

Why, then, did William of Normandy decide to take a gambler's risk and bid for the English throne? The most obvious answer was that it was a prize worth winning: England was larger and wealthier than Normandy and was a kingdom, not a mere dukedom. But aside from his undoubted desire for wealth and power, William had a claim to the throne that did not lack substance: he was a peripheral member of the English royal family through Emma, his great-aunt. In addition, there is some evidence that earlier in his reign the Confessor had indicated to William that he intended to name him as his successor. This was reinforced by Harold taking an oath in support of William's claim while visiting Normandy in 1065. The event is depicted in the Bayeux Tapestry, which shows Harold taking the oath with outstretched hands, one apparently touching a Bible, the other on a reliquary. This later allowed William to claim that Harold was a perjured usurper and that all who supported Harold, or resisted William, were guilty of treason. But it was a tenuous argument; what William really needed was international backing. This he secured, at least in some measure, from the only two institutions qualified to give it: the Holy Roman Emperor (Henry IV, 1056–1109) and the Pope (Alexander II, 1061–73).

The Norman Conquest is generally seen as an event that lasted eighty-nine days, from the landing of the Norman army on the Sussex coast in September 1066 to William's coronation later in the year, on Christmas Day, in Westminster Abbey. It was, it seemed, mission accomplished, but this is an over-simplification: it took a further thirty years of hard work by armed men in the saddle to secure the new regime full acceptance. Arguably, the Norman Conquest was not fully achieved until 1095.

Conquest was followed by expropriation and redistribution of land. William's justification for this was on the grounds that all who resisted his just claim to the throne were guilty of treason, and thereby forfeit in life and land. This may be seen as a thin veneer of respectability; the brutal fact, however, was that the men who risked their lives to win William his throne did so for personal gain. The evidence of their success is written in the form of the Domesday Book of 1086.[7] This was the product of a detailed survey commissioned by William in 1085, aimed at providing him with an accurate picture of who possessed land *tempore regis Edwardi* (Latin: in King Edward's time) and who had it now. The evidence of the Domesday Book is that, apart from the land belonging to the King, almost all the land of England south of the river Tees was in the hands of men from Normandy or thereabouts. Most of the indigenous English had been ousted.

EXPANSION INTO WALES

By becoming king of England William inherited the perennial problem of Wales, which his English predecessors had never conquered or pacified.[8] Their policy was one of containment, exemplified by Offa's Dyke, the earthwork between the estuaries of the rivers Dee and Severn, constructed by Offa, king of Mercia (757–96) to act as a barrier against Welsh raids or expansionist attempts. Although homogeneous in language and culture, Wales was not a political entity but divided between three small kingdoms: Gwynnedd (North), Powys (Central) and Deheubarth (South), each seeking to dominate the others. There was a further problem facing the would-be conqueror: the mountainous nature of much of the terrain, which favoured defence.

Given all these problems, it is not surprising that William stuck with the policy of containment. To contain or repulse Welsh aggression and to act as bases for a westward expansion, he created three powerful earldoms along the border based upon castles at Chester, Shrewsbury and Hereford. He also licensed ambitious and adventurous Normans to try their hand at conquest. Such men were not in short supply, so that by 1090, much of the fertile lowland areas along the coasts had been conquered and turned into what were known as marcher lordships. These advances were particularly notable along the south coast, in areas now covered by the counties of Monmouth, Glamorgan, Carmarthen and Pembroke. However, the years after 1093 saw a Welsh revival and repossession of much of the land which had been lost.

This prompted royal intervention, which had the additional benefit of establishing crown control. The author of the new policy was Henry I, who built a royal castle and created a borough, at Carmarthen. This site was strategically important: the main road crossed the river Tywi close to where it was joined by two tributaries, the valleys of which gave access to the heartland of Deheubarth. Henry also increased the endowments of the bishopric of St David's to enhance its wealth and status and settled a substantial colony of Flemings in the *cantrefs* of Rhos and Dongleddau, close to the important port of Milford Haven. Flemings made good colonists – so much so that in an agreement Henry made with the count of Flanders in 1101, he had a clause inserted stipulating that the count would not hinder any of his subjects wishing to take service with the king of England. These Norman colonies and lordships in South Wales were to play notable roles in Ireland after 1169.

THE 'NORMANISATION' OF SCOTLAND

The last phase of the Norman takeover of Britain took place in the last decade of the eleventh century and the first third of the twelfth.[9] During these years, the far north of England was incorporated into the English state and the kingdom of Scotland conquered – though not by military from without, but by adaption from within. Although concerned with separate political regimes, these events were so interlinked that they need to be considered together.

I feel the starting point has to be 1066, when Edward the Aetheling's two orphans – Edgar (now himself the Aetheling) and his sister Margaret – were still living in England. The advent of William of Normandy rendered their continued residence ill-advised, and consequently they sought refuge at the court of the Scottish king, Malcolm III. In 1070, Malcolm married Margaret, now twenty-three years old – his first wife, Ingeborg, having either died or been set aside in Margaret's favour. It is said that he was captivated by Margaret's beauty, and perhaps he was. But the real reason for the match was genetic: any male offspring of their marriage would have a claim to the throne of England as well as that of Scotland. In this matter, Malcolm and Margaret produced an abundant harvest: at least one daughter and six sons, all of whom grew to adulthood. But what is significant is the names they gave to their sons. The first four were named after Margaret's closest English kin, Edward, Edmund, Aethelstan and Edgar, while for the two youngest, they chose names of the greatest kings of antiquity, Alexander and David; their daughter, they named Edith. Not one of their offspring was given a Gaelic name. Political ambition could not have been better advertised.

William I's actions in respect of the far north of England and Scotland amounted to no more than stop-gap expedients. In 1072 he led an army into

Scotland, not with the intention of conquest, but to force Malcolm III to swear allegiance and to give hostages. As he returned south, William installed a French cleric named Walcher as bishop of Durham, for whom he then built a castle, the motte of which still stands. Four years later, William deposed and executed for rebellion Waltheof, the English earl of Northumbria, who was married to William's niece and whose services William had retained: he then added the earldom to Walcher's burden. However, this did not last long: Walcher was murdered in 1080 during a native uprising against his rule. This brought down the Conqueror's wrath in the form of an armed expedition led by his son Robert, so bringing fire and sword upon the region. Subsequently, its cowed population was placed under the control of Normans: Robert de Mowbray as earl, and William of St Calais as bishop. The latter immediately disbanded the Community of St Cuthbert, founded on Lindisfarne in 635 by Aidan, an Irish monk, from Iona. This Community, for greater security, had twice moved south, ending in Durham in 995. They may well have harboured anti-Norman sentiments. St Calais, therefore, removed it as his cathedral chapter and replaced it with a Benedictine monastery. As he was himself a Benedictine monk, this meant that he could be abbot as well as bishop – a cunning doubling of his authority.

When William I died in 1087 the north of England was under Norman control but not integrated into the English state system, a fact clearly underlined by the omission of land north of the river Tees from the Domesday Book.

Incorporating the north fully into the English state, therefore, was left to William's son and successor, William II (1087–1100). He began in 1092 by annexing Cumbria, for many years part of the Welsh-speaking kingdom of Strathclyde, but dominated by the king of Scots. To give substance to this, he built a castle at Carlisle and brought colonists from the south to populate and develop its associated borough. Three years later, he deposed Earl Robert de Mowbray for rebellion, put the office of earl into abeyance and turned the land between the rivers Tweed and Tyne into a normal English county, Northumberland. The land between the Tyne and the Tees, Durham, was left as a liberty under the rule of its bishop.

Between those dates, a major shift in the balance of power took place between England and Scotland. Incensed by the annexation of Cumbria, Malcolm III launched an invasion of northern England. It was a catastrophe: his army was routed outside Alnwick in Northumberland and he and his eldest son, Edward, were killed. A few days later, on learning of their deaths and the military disaster, Queen Margaret died in Edinburgh;

perhaps of shock, or maybe she was ailing from a terminal illness, the news hastening on her death.

The Scottish throne passed very briefly to Duncan II, Malcolm's son by his first wife, and then to his brother, Donald III *bán* (fair), who was intent on restoring the Gaelic nature of the monarchy. Scotland was now no place for Malcolm's second family. Three of his sons, Edgar, Alexander and David, together with their sister, Edith, escaped to England to find sanctuary at the court of William II. Four years later, an English army invaded Scotland, overthrew Donald III and placed Edgar on the throne. The price was Edgar's sworn allegiance to the king of England: the king of Scots was to be a client king.

Four years later, in 1100, William II was killed and his younger brother succeeded as Henry I (1100–35). Almost immediately, Henry brought Edith from the nunnery, where she had been housed for safety, and married her. All that was required of her was to accept a change of name from Edith (which to Norman ears was outlandish) to Matilda, the fashionable name among high-born Norman ladies and, significantly, the name of Henry's mother. Marriage to the last surviving female member of the pre-conquest English royal house would add legitimacy to Henry's title. But, in addition, any male child born to them would have a claim to the thrones of both England and Scotland. Henry I had effectively stolen and turned upside down his father-in-law's strategy. Initially, it was a success in that Henry and Matilda had a son, William, named for his father. But it all came to nought: Matilda died in 1118 and their son was drowned at sea in 1120. Henry, however, had a reserve scheme in the person of David (b. 1085), Malcolm III and Margaret's youngest son. Through his upbringing at the English royal court among the other young aristocrats, David had been 'reprogrammed' as a Norman. He was then found a young widow to marry, who brought with her the earldom of Huntingdon: David had been transformed into an Anglo-Norman, and a member of the top echelon of the English nobility.

Henry's scheme came to fruition in 1124 when David became king of Scots, both his elder brothers having died without legitimate heirs (Edgar in 1107 and Alexander I in 1124). David's personal 'makeover' now became apparent, for he set about 'modernising' Scotland along Anglo-Norman lines. The church was reformed and economic development was stimulated by new urban foundations. Above all, he implanted Anglo-Norman barons in much of southern and eastern Scotland. Three were especially noteworthy: Guy Balliol, Robert Bruce and Walter Fitz Alan (progenitor of the Stewart family) – descendants of whom, in that order, became kings of

Scotland. Interestingly, only one, Robert Bruce, was of pure Norman provenance; Guy Balliol's roots were in Picardy and those of Fitz Alan were in
Brittany. But all came into Scotland as Anglo-Norman barons.

However, as well as being Henry's protégé, David was the son of
Malcolm III; and, therefore, in addition to developing Scotland along
Norman lines, he espoused the ambition of his Gaelic forebears to push
the boundaries of his kingdom southwards. In particular, he wished to
recover Cumbria and in the east, to move his frontier to the river Tyne,
or possibly to the river Tees. David's opportunity to implement his policy
came about in the 1130s, with the death of King Henry I in 1135 and
the contested succession between Henry's daughter, Matilda, and his
nephew Stephen, a younger son of the count of Blois. Stephen reacted
rapidly to the news of Henry's death and secured the crown with the
backing of the English baronage, whose leaders had sworn under duress
to accept Matilda as queen, but who did not relish the prospect of a
female monarch.

War broke out in England between the two rival factions in 1139. It
was to King David's advantage, because the price for reneging on his pledge
to support Matilda's claim and change to backing Stephen was that Stephen
ceded Cumbria and Northumberland to David. Scottish possession only
lasted until 1157. By then the world had changed: both Stephen and David
were dead; Scotland's king was a youth, David's grandson Malcolm IV;
and England, together with Normandy, Anjou and Aquitaine, was ruled
by Matilda's son Henry II. Henry demanded, and Malcolm conceded, and
returned Cumbria and Northumberland to England. Before his death,
Henry I had completed the task of consolidating the grip of the English
government on the far north of England. He carved the land of
Northumberland (except that belonging to the church) into twenty baronies, which he granted to his favoured Anglo-Normans. He also completed
the integration of Cumbria by securing papal consent to raise it to be the
diocese of Carlisle within the archbishopric of York, thereby thwarting the
ambitions of the bishops of Glasgow.

In light of these actions, it could be argued that the Norman conquest
of England was not completed until 1135 – only a generation before the
Anglo-Normans turned their attention to Ireland. It was more protracted
in Wales, where independence was not finally suppressed until 1284; and
in Scotland it lasted even longer, until 1266 and finally 1468, when the
kings of Norway ceded sovereignty over the Western Isles and then the
Northern Isles to the Scoto-Norman kings of Scots.

PART II:
CONQUEST, CREATION
AND CONTROL

Part II of this book is devoted to the creation and the break-up of the first Anglo-Norman colony in Ireland, the liberty of Leinster. It was initiated by Diarmait Mac Murchada, the Irish king of Leinster, who engaged the services of an Anglo-Norman baron, Richard Fitz Gilbert de Clare (known as Strongbow) to help him regain his kingdom and eventually to succeed him. After their deaths, the liberty passed into the hands of King Henry II of England and then his son, John. Later it reverted to Strongbow's heir and Mac Murchada's granddaughter, Isabel de Clare, and her husband, William Marshal. After they died, the liberty existed for another twenty-six years before ending with the death of their youngest son in 1245.

3

The Protagonists

The Norman intrusion into Ireland was not inevitable, although given the fragmented polity of the island and the Norman propensity to conquer, there was every chance it would happen sooner rather than later. That it began when it did, in 1169, was the outcome of events in Ireland and the reactions of three men: Henry II, king of England; the Irish king of Leinster, Diarmait Mac Murchada; and an Anglo-Norman baron, Richard Fitz Gilbert de Clare. Each had his own aims and ambitions, and these require careful examination if the course of events is to be properly understood.

KING HENRY II

Pride of place has to be given to Henry II. Although apparently peripheral, he was by far the most powerful: others might propose, but only he had the power to impose. In 1169, Henry was thirty-six years old and had been King of England since 1154. However, he was also duke of Normandy, count of Anjou and, in the right of his wife, duke of Aquitaine, therefore, he had a conglomeration of territories that extended from the Pyrenees to the Cheviots. This accumulation, which changed the political map of Western Europe, was recent and rapid; and the consequence of diplomatic, but especially military action.

Henry's father was Geoffrey, count of Anjou; his mother was Henry I's daughter, Mathilda. Their marriage was dynastic and no love match: Geoffrey was only fourteen years old, while Mathilda was twenty-five and a widow, her first husband, the Holy Roman Emperor, Henry V, having died in 1125. However, Geoffrey recognised the potential gains which might accrue, and his father-in-law, King Henry I of England, urgently needed a male heir. Until 1120, the problem did not exist, as Henry and his wife (also Mathilda) had a son and heir, William. But in that year disaster struck when their heir, William, was drowned at sea. He was amongst a large number of the royal court sailing across the Channel from Barfleur when their ship struck a rock and sank with the loss of all but one on board (because, it was alleged, both the crew and the passengers were drunk).[1] For Henry it was a double tragedy as he was already a widower, his wife having died two years earlier. It was now imperative that he beget a legitimate heir.

In haste he remarried, but his second wife bore him no children, which was ironic since he was reputed to have sired over forty illegitimate offspring. Therefore, Henry's only legitimate child was his daughter Mathilda. Desperate measures were now called into play: he required the leading men of his kingdom to swear an oath that they would accept Mathilda as their monarch after his death. Hopefully Mathilda and her husband, Geoffrey, would have sons, one of whom would succeed her on the throne.

The couple duly obliged when Mathilda gave birth to Henry in 1133, Geoffrey in 1134 and William in 1136. King Henry I died in 1135 believing that with grandsons, the succession was secured, albeit at one remove. His scheme did come to fruition – but only after an interval of nineteen years. The delay was caused by a usurper, Stephen, younger brother of Theobald IV, count of Blois-Champagne, one of the major powers within the French kingdom. These two men, together with their youngest brother, Henry, were nephews of King Henry I of England, their mother being Henry's sister, Adele. During his reign, Henry I had favoured both the younger brothers. Henry, who had already been launched on an ecclesiastical career, he made bishop of Winchester, the wealthiest diocese in England. To Stephen, a layman, he granted large estates in England as well as making him count of Boulogne.

The speed with which events moved after Henry I's death suggests that the nephews were well primed. On receiving news of Henry's demise Stephen immediately crossed from Boulogne to England and, in collusion with his brother, the bishop of Winchester, persuaded the leading members of the English baronage to break their oaths to accept Mathilda as monarch. Instead they supported Stephen to succeed Henry I on the English throne. It is unlikely the barons took too much persuading; the prospect of a female monarch for many of them may have been a leap in the dark with which they were not comfortable – indeed, a leap too far.

Almost inevitably, Stephen's *coup d'état* provoked turmoil and conflict. Immediately, Mathilda's husband, Geoffrey of Anjou, invaded Normandy in the interests of their infant son Henry (grandson of King Henry I), and by 1144 he had succeeded in securing the submission of its leading men. Meanwhile, in England in 1139, serious civil war had broken out with Mathilda's arrival in the country, together with her most effective supporter, Robert, earl of Gloucester (who, incidentally, was one of Henry I's many illegitimate children). Mathilda was very courageous and brave, but at the same time she was haughty, demanding and very conscious of her status as a former empress; these traits made her unlikable and made Gloucester's support even more invaluable.

The war did not provide a definitive outcome, however, and by 1150 it had ended in stalemate. The issue was finally settled in the early 1150s by a series of deaths (and a marriage). With Geoffrey's sudden demise in 1151, Henry – Geoffrey and Mathilda's eighteen-year-old son – became count of Anjou and duke of Normandy, and a claimant to the English throne. The following year Henry doubled the size of his empire when he married Eleanor of Aquitaine, who in her own right was duke of Aquitaine, the wedding having taken place soon after her divorce from King Louis VII of France. The divorce had been sanctioned by Pope Eugenius III, with much reluctance.

What hastened the denouement in England was the death of Eustace, King Stephen's heir, by all accounts a man not highly regarded. Stephen, by that time a widower, was not only old, tired and dispirited by the death of his son and heir, but also bereft at the loss of his wife, Matilda of Boulogne, who throughout their marriage had been his trusted help-mate, domestically and politically.[2] Under the circumstances, it was not too difficult for the two rival factions to come together in agreement. Stephen was to remain king, but was obliged to acknowledge Henry, count of Anjou, duke of Normandy, duke of Aquitaine and grandson of King Henry I, as his rightful heir. They did not have long to wait: with Stephen's death in November 1154, Henry added the title of King of England to his already ample portfolio of titles. Henry I's gamble had paid off after a long delay, albeit thanks to good fortune rather than good management.

Like most kings, Henry II had a hybrid pedigree. His genetic make-up included contributions from the English (Anglo-Saxon) and Scottish (Gaelic) royal families, as well as from Norman dukes and Angevin counts. Not so our other protagonist, Richard Fitz Gilbert de Clare.

RICHARD FITZ GILBERT DE CLARE

Known then and since as Strongbow, Richard Fitz Gilbert de Clare's ancestry was exclusively Norman.[3] His descent could be traced back to Godfrey, the eldest illegitimate son of Duke Richard I (d. 996) who gave Godfrey the lordship of Brionne, to which was later added the county of Eu by his successor, Duke Richard II (d. 1026). Godfrey's son, Gilbert, before his murder in 1041 had played a major role in securing the succession of Normandy for William, Duke Robert I's illegitimate eight-year-old son in 1035, when his father died while on a pilgrimage. Gilbert had two sons, Richard Fitz Gilbert and Baldwin Fitz Gilbert, both of whom were prominent in William's invasion of England in 1066. The brothers were well rewarded by William, as duke and then as king. The elder brother, Richard, who is of interest to us, was initially granted two estates in Normandy: Orbec and Saint-Martin-de-Bienfaite, situated 12.5 miles (20 km) south-east of Lisieux. Then, for his part in helping him to win England, William granted Richard the lordship of Clare in Suffolk, which also included estates in Essex, Surrey and Kent. William also arranged Richard's marriage to Rohese, sister of Walter Giffard (a nickname meaning 'chubby cheeks'), whose dowry included estates in Hertfordshire and Huntingdonshire. Finally, the archbishop of Canterbury, Lanfranc, invested him with the castle and manor of Tonbridge in Kent. The Domesday Survey of 1086 reveals Richard Fitz Gilbert as one of the richest men in England.

When Richard Fitz Gilbert died in 1090, his estate in Normandy and England was divided between his sons, Roger and Gilbert Fitz Richard. To Roger (probably the eldest of his five sons) went the estates in Normandy, while the English estates were inherited by Gilbert. Gilbert's estate was further enlarged by Henry I, possibly because of Gilbert's involvement with the death of Henry's brother and predecessor, King William II of England, while hunting in the New Forest in Hampshire. (This incident had been declared an accident, but suspicions suggest that it might not have been so; these arise from the fact that the fatal arrow was fired by Walter Tirel, who was Gilbert's brother-in-law, having married his sister, Adelize.) Immediately on becoming king, Henry I made generous grants to Gilbert Fitz Richard and his brothers. To Gilbert he gave his permission to conquer Ceredigion (Cardigan) in Wales, while his brother Walter was granted Netherwent, the land between the rivers Wye and Usk, in what is now Monmouthshire. It was based upon Striguil (now Chepstow), where

Walter built a castle; he also provided the land for the Cistercian abbey of Tintern, which later featured in Anglo-Norman Leinster.

Gilbert Fitz Richard died in 1117, leaving five sons. The only one of concern to us is the second of these, Gilbert Fitz Gilbert, who also bene-fited from Henry I's largesse and generosity – probably because Gilbert's wife, Isabel de Beaumont, was one of Henry's favourite mistresses. When Gilbert's uncle Roger died without heirs in 1130, Henry allowed him to inherit the Norman estates near Lisieux. Royal beneficence continued after Henry's death in 1135. When in 1138 another of Gilbert's uncles, Walter, died without heirs, Gilbert was allowed to inherit the Netherwent estate. King Stephen also granted to Gilbert the lordship of Pembroke, which had been in the hands of the crown for thirty-six years, and created him earl of Pembroke. This time, royal generosity was not fostered by lust but by Stephen's need to bolster support for his struggle against Mathilda.

As well as granting her favours to King Henry I, Isabel de Beaumont bore a son to Gilbert Fitz Gilbert. The baby, Richard Fitz Gilbert, was destined to become famous as Strongbow. When Gilbert Fitz Gilbert died in 1148, his title, earl of Pembroke, and his accumulated estates should have passed to Strongbow; however, he was under age, and it was not until he reached his majority in 1151 that he could inherit. Three years after that, Strongbow's fortunes changed for the worse. The new king, Henry II, deprived him of Pembroke, both title and estate; and Henry, as duke of Normandy, also confiscated from him his estates at Orbec and Saint-Martin-de-Bienfaite, instead bestowing them on his cousin. Strongbow did retain the Netherwent estate, and he was able to talk Henry into allowing him to retain the prestigious title of Earl, but not of Pembroke. Thereafter, Strongbow became widely known as 'earl of Striguil', although this was not a formally confirmed title. Henry's confiscation of Pembroke is readily explicable. Both Stephen and Mathilda had increased the number of earls from seven to twenty-three, made them hereditary and given them power over the counties of their title. Henry reversed this policy, rightly seeing it as a diminution of royal authority.

His reason for depriving Strongbow of his estates in Normandy, however, is not so clear-cut, but it might have been a punishment for his father's lingering support for Stephen. Whatever the reason, Strongbow, like Bohemond before him, was a man deprived of much of his inheritance. In consequence, he too was a man seeking the opportunity to restore his fortunes.

DIARMAIT MAC MURCHADA, KING OF LEINSTER

The third principal character in the drama was Diarmait Mac Murchada, king of Leinster (Irish: Laigin). His role was pivotal in that it was he who drew in the other two protagonists.[4] Without him, it is doubtful that Strongbow would have become involved in Irish politics at that time, although at a later time he may have seen Ireland as troubled waters in which he might profitably fish.

In the early years of his reign, Henry II had contemplated conquering Ireland in order to provide a kingdom for his youngest brother, William. Henry was encouraged in this by the English bishops, and also by the only English pope, Hadrian (or Adrian) IV (1154–9) – all of whom believed the Irish church was desperately in need of reform. However, in the end Henry's mother, the ex-Empress Mathilda, talked him out of becoming embroiled in this unnecessary venture. As already noted, Ireland's political structure at the time was inherently unstable, with the rulers of the nine major kingdoms having to struggle to keep their subordinate sub-kings under control while at the same time each striving to become High King of Ireland, or at least prevent any rival achieving this position. In this maelstrom, politics was largely conducted by violence.

For much of the tenth and early eleventh centuries, the dominant dynasty was the O'Briains, Kings of Munster. There was, however, an interlude between 1042 and 1072 when Diarmait Mac Murchada's great-grandfather, Diarmait Mac Máel na mBó, dominated southern Ireland, including the Norse town of Dublin, which was rapidly becoming key to the control of the island. It was after his death in battle that the O'Briain dominance was restored under Toirdelbach Ua Briain (d. 1086) who was followed by his son, Muirchertach Ua Briain (d. 1119).

But the early twelfth century saw the rise of a new power, the kingdom of Connacht, an area west of the river Shannon. The driving force was its king, Toirdelbach Ua Conchobair, whose reign of fifty years (1106–56) allowed him to put his ambitious plans into effect. In his early years as king, Toirdelbach was able to gradually engineer the weakening of Munster. A golden opportunity then arose in 1114, when Muirchertach Ua Briain fell seriously ill. Toirdelbach successfully invaded Munster in 1118 and divided it into two smaller provinces, Thomond and Desmond. By the time of Toirdelbach's death, Connacht had become Ireland's most powerful province, powerful enough for Toirdelbach's successor, his son, Ruardri, to bid for the High Kingship. However, there was always someone waiting in the wings to make a counter-bid, and the major obstacle to Ruardri's ambition on this occasion was Muirchertach Mac Lochlainn, king of Ailech, the dominant power in the northern third of Ireland. It was during these years of strife that Diarmait Mac Murchada became king of Leinster following the death of his father in 1127.

The kingship to which he succeeded was not an uncontested gift. His clan, the Uí Chennselaig (O'Kinsella), were dominant in southern Leinster, their power base being in what is now Co. Wexford. But they had rivals, the Uí Dúnlainge (O'Dowling), who were dominant in the north of Leinster and in fact had monopolised the kingship until the rise of Diarmait's great-grandfather, Diarmait Mac Máel na mBó, in 1042. While elevation to the kingship of Leinster was not strictly an election by one's peers, it was obvious that you had to show proven leadership qualities for your clan followers to make their choice. Of course, a hereditary claim to the title must have been a plus point too.

So Diarmait Mac Murchada became king of Leinster. He was a man of insatiable ambition, driven by great energy and with a pronounced ruthless streak. But he was also a man of contrasts. On the one hand, he was a moderniser in government and an active church reformer, founding six monasteries: two in Dublin, three in Kildare and one in his provincial capital, Ferns. He was a friend of St Malachy, and he backed the election of Lorcán Ua Tuathail (Laurence O'Toole) as archbishop of Dublin, both leading champions of church reform in Ireland.

But in complete contrast, there was a violent and cruelly brutish side to Diarmait's nature that allowed him to commit, without apparent compunction, savage atrocities in pursuit of his political aims. In 1132 he authorised his troops to rape the abbess of Kildare, the head of one of Ireland's leading monasteries. And, in 1152, he abducted Derbforgail, the wife of Tigernán Ua Ruairc, king of Bréifne, although she might have been complicit in his bravado because of the ill-treatment she received at the hands of her husband. In one of his displays of barbarity, Diarmait is known to have killed or blinded seventeen hostages his sub-kings had been obliged to deliver into his hands. In mitigation, however, it needs to be recognised that these were not always entirely gratuitous acts for the pleasure of inflicting pain, but that they had a serious political purpose despite the revolting barbarism employed to achieve their ends. Vicious though it was, barbarity seems to have been a common practice among the warring factions.

Diarmait's scope for doing as he pleased was in fact underpinned by the powerful Muirchertach Mac Lochlainn, with whom he was in alliance, which was fostered by their mutual hostility to Ruardri Ua Conchobair. Mac Lochlainn's death early in 1166 at the hands of Tigernán Ua Ruairc was a blow to Diarmait, as it tilted the balance of power in Leinster by fatally weakening Diarmait's position as king. It was now possible for Conchobair to deal with Diarmait, and he had no difficulty in assembling a fearsome military coalition of willing allies which included Ua Ruairc, eager to avenge his humiliation of 1152. The horde also included many others alienated from Diarmait Mac Murchada, for example, the king of Meath and the Norse of Dublin. The force Conchobair mustered had enough military power to easily overwhelm Leinster. Diarmait's only option was flight, and in August 1166, together with his wife, Mór, and their daughter, Aoife, he fled and took ship for Bristol to find refuge with its provost, his long-time friend Robert Fitz Harding.

Over the following twelve months, Diarmait busily sought a means of recovering his lost inheritance. To further this ambition, he went to visit King Henry II, with whom he was acquainted, despite the necessity of journeying to Aquitaine where Henry was engaged at the time. The purpose of his visit was to plead for Henry's support for a recovery expedition to Ireland. What he hoped Henry would offer is not entirely clear, but if it was the king's personal and direct military intervention, he was disappointed. Henry had more urgent problems to deal with and therefore adopted a policy of benevolent neutrality, merely permitting Diarmait to raise a body of troops from within his domains. With hindsight, this was a very shrewd decision on King Henry's part: let someone else pave the way, then move in yourself later – for that is just what happened.

Diarmait's other achievement was to meet Strongbow. Where they met is not known, but a likely venue would have been Strongbow's castle at Striguil (Chepstow). No matter where they met, it was a stroke of luck, for the outcome of the meeting was an agreement: Strongbow would raise sufficient forces for a successful campaign to restore Diarmait to the kingship of Leinster. In return, Diarmait promised Strongbow his daughter Aoife's hand in marriage and the kingship of Leinster after his death. On the face of it, Strongbow had driven a hard bargain by forcing Diarmait to accept his offer on humiliating terms; but frankly, it was an inevitable outcome because of Diarmait's weak negotiating position. On the other hand, Diarmait was an astute, cunning and practised politician who may have seen his situation in terms of *reculer pour le mieux* (retreat for a better leap). He possibly thought that he would use Strongbow's military strength to win back Leinster, then use him to further his desire to win the High

Kingship of Ireland. Strongbow would then be king of Leinster, but as his vassal – and should Strongbow and Aoife produce a male heir, the kingship of Leinster would revert back to the Mac Murchada family. We know enough about the wily and pragmatic Diarmait Mac Murchada to make this scenario credible. Like Henry I of England, he had the ability to think several moves ahead.

The planned agreement between Diarmait and Strongbow blatantly overlooked the existence of Diarmait's two legitimate sons, Énna and Conchobar, and their claims to the kingship. In the end, the trouble this may have caused the schemers was avoided by Diarmait's sons' unfortunate, but fortuitous removal from the scene for them, before Aoife and Strongbow were married in Waterford Cathedral in August 1170.

Énna, Diarmait's designated heir, did not leave Ireland with his parents in 1166, although whether by intent or by accident is not known. Unfortunately, he fell into the hands of Diarmait's long-time enemy, the king of Osraige (Ossory). Two years later, in 1168, as will be explained shortly, the Osraigan king had Énna blinded, thereby ensuring that he would be unable to succeed his father as king of Leinster.

Diarmait's return was early and hasty, since he did not wait to bring with him the Norman troops promised by Strongbow. His return, in fact, brought him fresh humiliation. Ruardri Ua Conchobair, now recognised as High King, assembled a military coalition and invaded Leinster. Powerless to resist, Diarmait acknowledged Ruardri as High King and gave hostages, including his second son and heir, Conchobar. When, following the arrival of the early Norman contingents from Wales, Diarmait launched his campaign to regain control of Leinster, it was astonishingly bad timing for Conchobar Mac Murchada, and he suffered his inevitable fate: being put to death by Ruardri Ua Conchobair, so ending the legitimate Mac Murchada male line.

Diarmait did have a third son, Domnal; but he was illegitimate. However, the law governing succession to kingship in Ireland at that time was still fluid enough for bastardy not to be an insuperable obstacle. In fact, as will become apparent later, Domnal was to pioneer an illustrious family.

INVASIONS AND MILITARY EVENTS

I will not attempt a blow-by-blow account of all the warfare in Leinster in the twenty-four months between 1169 and 1171, since there were many similar battles and skirmishes, making it confusingly disjointed.[5] Instead, I will attempt to identify the main episodes and the eventual outcome of the conflict. However, before proceeding, it is worth remarking that what happened in Ireland had echoes of earlier Norman ventures elsewhere: a ruler fighting to regain what he believed to be rightfully his; the involvement of mercenary troops, who relished combat but who were also looking for substantial gain; and the advantage to the intruders in operating in a politically disunited situation. Another illustration of the Normans seizing the main chance.

The first Normans to enter the fraught political world of Ireland were the mercenary troops recruited by Diarmait Mac Murchada in 1167 and 1168. They were a small group of Cambro-Normans from South Wales, and as it proved, were insufficient in number. At their core were two distinct types of warrior. More prominent were the knights, who belonged to the elite stratum of twelfth-century society socially and militarily, although not necessarily economically. A knight was the product of a long, demanding and rigorous apprenticeship, which will be explained later. The result was a finely honed warrior, heavily armoured, who could skilfully wield formidable weapons, principally the sword and lance. Although knights could and did fight on foot, they were most formidable when mounted: a coordinated charge of a squadron of fearless mounted knights was almost unstoppable. But knights were equally most effective when operating in conjunction with archers: the archer's longbow too was a fearsome weapon, mastered only by years of practice.

Landing at Bannow Bay, the first to arrive in Ireland were the Cambro-Normans on 1 and 2 May 1169. They numbered thirty-seven knights and 500 hundred other troops. They formed, however, two distinct groups. By far the larger, consisting of thirty knights and 300 other men, were those recruited and led by Robert Fitz Stephen. He belonged to a very particular group – particular in that all of them could trace their ancestry back to one of the most interesting, and presumably most alluring, Welsh women of the late eleventh century. Her name was Nest (or Nesta), and she was the daughter of Rhys ap Tewdwr, king of Deheubarth, the dominant political force in South Wales. In the course of her fertile years Nest gave birth to five sons by three different Anglo-Normans: her husband, Gerald of Windsor, Constable of Cardiff Castle; and two lovers, King Henry I and Stephen, Constable of Cardigan. It was the son of the latter, Robert Fitz Stephen, who was recruited by Diarmait Mac Murchada to raise and lead the force that landed at Bannow Bay on 1 May.

Fitz Stephen had accepted Diarmait's offer as a means of securing his release from captivity. He was a prisoner in the clutches of Rhys ap

Gruffydd, the grandson of Rhys ap Tewdwr, who in the 1160s was intent on making himself the dominant man in South Wales. It was in the course of his re-conquest of Cardigan that he captured Robert Fitz Stephen, the price for his release from captivity being that he should take up arms against the English king, Henry II. Fighting in Ireland would seem to have been an acceptable alternative. Prominent among those Robert recruited were Meiler Fitz Henry, grandson of Henry I's liaison with Nest, and Miles Fitz David, son of the bishop of St David's – whose father, Maurice, was one of the offspring of Nest's marriage to Gerald of Windsor. These formed a group with close affinity, which allows us to refer to them as the Geraldines.[6]

The smaller group, who landed the following day (2 May 1169), were equally but differently distinctive. They were recruited by Maurice de Prendergast, a man of Flemish descent whose following was almost certainly composed of men drawn from the Flemish communities Henry I had settled around Milford Haven.[7]

There was with them, however, a man who belonged to neither group: Hervey de Montmorency. He was Strongbow's paternal uncle and the son of the second marriage of Adeliz, the widow of Richard Fitz Gilbert, who died in 1117. Montmorency's presence at the outset, and his subsequent appearances at crucial moments, is significant. He has been unanimously described as Strongbow's spy or reporter, but there are grounds for according him a higher status as Strongbow's political adviser – the man he entrusted with a watching brief over the activities of those who were ostensibly fighting for Diarmait Mac Murchada, but ultimately for Strongbow.

In the course of the campaigning season of 1169 the relatively small group of Cambro-Norman troops from South Wales had considerable success. They began by securing the submission of Wexford, largely by negotiation and with very little bloodshed. The town of Wexford and the other Norse towns, Waterford and Dublin, were prime targets. Not only did they control the main points of entry to Ireland, but their trading generated wealth and they also possessed a core of effective fighting men. Without a strong presence in those towns, there could not be a fully effective control of Leinster. Their other success was achieved only with considerable bloodshed, however, when they defeated Domnal Mac Gilla Pátraic, king of Osraige. The kingdom of Osraige covered all of what is modern Co. Kilkenny and part of Co. Laois, and was the largest sub-kingdom of Leinster. Because of this defeat, Mac Gilla Pátraic resisted and resented domination by Mac Murchada. In fact, the Mac Gilla Pátraic dynasty had never accepted being subordinate to the king of Leinster and did so only under duress. Consequently, as already noted, they seized the opportunity of Diarmait's ill-advised premature return to Leinster in 1168 to blind his eldest son and heir, Énna, who had fallen into their hands; and they joined Ruardri Ua Conchbair's invasion of Leinster, which resulted in Diarmait Mac Murchada's second son, Conchobar, becoming a hostage and later killed. It was indeed a savage revenge on Diarmait Mac Murchada.

But once he had the services of an adequate force of Cambro-Norman mercenaries, Diarmait set about crushing Osraigan pretensions. Twice he led devastating raids into Osraige that resulted in heavy defeats for the Osraigan army. The first of Diarmait's raids produced a harvest of 220 severed heads, many previously attached to leading members of Osraigan society. Diarmait is said to have been so delighted that he celebrated by biting off the noses and ears of some of the heads. This heinous act of savage barbarity disgusted the Norman troops, but no doubt Diarmait Mac Murchada saw it as avenging his son, Énna: these were savage, brutal times. After this defeat, Domnal Mac Gilla Pátraic remained king of Osraige, but his capacity to wage war had been seriously degraded.

However, it was not all success for Diarmait. One setback was the decision by Maurice de Prendergast to leave Diarmait's service, claiming he had not been adequately rewarded. When Diarmait blocked his departure from Wexford, Maurice promptly offered his services to Mac Gilla Pátraic. This was not readily accepted by the Osraigan leaders and so Prendergast contrived to extricate himself and his followers, via Waterford.

A more serious incident was the subsequent invasion of Leinster by the High King, Ruardri Ua Conchobair, who was concerned by Diarmait's growing success. He was joined in this expedition by Tigernán Ua Ruairc, king of Bréifne, who was seeking recompense from Diarmait for the abduction of his wife in 1152. Again, Diarmait bought peace by giving hostages and paying Tigernán off with 100 oz of gold to compensate for his dishonour. What stands out is Ruardri Ua Conchobair's reluctance to give battle. Instead, in believing that he had secured Diarmait's meaningful submission by the giving of hostages and making a promise not to invite any more foreigners to Leinster, Conchobair badly misjudged his man. Shortly after giving his promise, Diarmait welcomed the belated arrival of Maurice Fitz Gerald with a force of ten knights and 130 archers, whose combat potential probably exceeded that of the departed Flemings. Moreover, as a son of Gerald of Windsor and Nest, Maurice was a Geraldine, which gave a cultural homogeneity to the Cambro-Norman army in Mac Murchada's service.

With his military capacity enhanced, Diarmait decided to bring the campaigning season to a close with a last raid into north Leinster, the prime objective being Dublin, the most important of the Hiberno-Norse towns. He succeeded, though only up to a point. The Dublin leaders accepted him as king, but not to the extent of admitting a garrison of his troops; Diarmait accepted the half-measures for the moment.

The Cambro-Norman victories of 1169 had exposed the nature, strengths and weaknesses of Irish armies, and these matters were doubtlessly reported back to Strongbow by his uncle, Hervey de Montmorency. What Montmorency may also have conveyed was the need for a much larger force if complete success was to be achieved. By the spring of 1170, this had been assembled.

But before Strongbow embarked his main force, he despatched a vanguard to prepare for his coming. It comprised ten knights and seventy archers under the command of Raymond Fitz William – then and since, because of his considerable girth, known as Raymond *le Gros*. He was a son of William Fitz Gerald, lord of Carew, in Pembrokeshire, the elder brother of Maurice Fitz Gerald. Raymond, therefore, was one of the younger generation of Geraldines. He must have been seen as a knight of great promise, since he had been recruited by Strongbow and entrusted with command of the vanguard.

Raymond arrived in May, landing at Dun Domnail, about 8 miles (12 kilometres) east of Waterford, where he was joined by Hervey de Montmorency with three knights. His first task was to build a fortified camp, which became known as *Baginbun*, after the names of the two ships that had brought them from Wales. This was to be the base camp of operations for the main force; meanwhile, it acted as the corral for a large herd of cattle which Raymond had rounded up from the surrounding countryside to feed Strongbow's army.

As soon as the Norse community in Waterford became aware of the threat to them, they allied with the king of the neighbouring kingdom of Dèise to form a force intent on ejecting the intruders. Their army is said to have numbered 3,000, and in the face of such numbers Raymond might well have considered surrender – but he did not. What saved him from annihilation was a stampede of the herd of cattle he had rounded up; whether this was deliberate or accidental is not clear, but the result was that 500 attackers were killed and no further attempts were made to remove the small Cambro-Norman force. Strongbow and the bulk of his Anglo-Norman troops were able to land unopposed on 23 August 1170 and combine forces with Diarmait's Irish troops.

The following day, Waterford was taken in an assault led by Raymond *le Gros*. It was a bloody affair in which fierce street fighting resulted in the death of seven hundred defenders, followed by the execution of their captured leaders. Victory was followed almost immediately by Strongbow's marriage to Aoife. What appears as indecent haste, I speculate, may have stemmed from Strongbow's concern for public affirmation of his status as Diarmait's heir. With Wexford and Waterford now in their possession, Strongbow and Diarmait agreed that there was enough of the campaigning season left for them to make an attempt on Dublin. Of the three Norse towns in Ireland, Dublin was the most important and control of it was a prerequisite for mastery of Leinster and indeed Ireland. But for Diarmait there was an additional, personal reason: revenge for his father, killed by the Dubliners in 1115.

Their intention was soon known to Arsculf Mac Turkil, the leader of Dublin's Norse community. Consequently, he alerted Ruardri Ua Conchobair, the High King, who rapidly put together yet another coalition force that included the kings of Bréifne, Meath and Airgialla. Their aim was to protect Dublin by blocking the approach of Strongbow and Diarmait. He was foiled by Diarmait's local knowledge; instead of taking the lowland route, the joint Anglo-Norman and Irish army was led through the Wicklow Hills via Glendalough. When they came down onto the plain, Ruardri found that they were between him and the town he had come to protect. Yet again, he refused to settle the issue by battle, but retreated westwards.

With the break-up and departure of the High King, Strongbow and Diarmait were able to lay siege to Dublin. In the hope of avoiding bloodshed and with Strongbow and Diarmait's agreement, Lorcán Ua Tuathail, the archbishop of Dublin, undertook to negotiate with the defenders. Whether he would have succeeded in persuading them to capitulate peacefully will never be known, since some of the Anglo-Norman troops lost patience with the inaction and, on 21st September, stormed the town. They were led by Milo de Cogan, who was to prove himself the most dashing of Strongbow's commanders. Although from Wales (Cogan is now an area of Penarth, near Cardiff), de Cogan was not a Geraldine. Whether he acted entirely on his own initiative when storming the town or whether he had a nod of approval from Strongbow, I cannot tell; but it may be significant that he chose to surrender the town to him rather than to Diarmait. However, de Cogan's victory was incomplete in that Arsculf Mac Turkil and the other leaders of the Norse community managed to avoid capture by escaping in their ships. They headed for the Isle of Man and the Norse communities along the western seaboard of Scotland, from which they expected to be able to recruit a force of fighting men large enough to retake Dublin.

The year 1171 proved to be pivotal, with a sequence of events that could have led either to crushing defeat for Diarmait and Strongbow or, as it happened, to Strongbow's triumph. It began with a major disruption when, at the age of sixty-one, Diarmait Mac Murchada died at Ferns, his capital. His death raised a number of questions, all fundamental and all urgent. Would Diarmait's family – particularly his brother, Muirchertach, and his only surviving (though illegitimate) son, Domnal Caomhánach (Kavanagh) – accept Strongbow as successor to the kingship of Leinster? Domnal took his name from Cill Chaomain, now Kilcavan, near Gorey, Co. Wexford, the place where he was fostered. Would the petty kings of Leinster also accept him as their lord? How would the High King, Ruardri Ua Conchobair, react to having a 'foreigner' as king of Leinster and thereby a potential threat to his position? And how would King Henry II respond to seeing one of his subjects become king of Leinster, perhaps with the ambition to become king of Ireland? Rather surprisingly, the internal questions about Leinster were solved without significant bloodshed. Typically, the king of Osraige, Domnal Mac Gilla Pátraic, made his submission after a show of force and the threat of being charged with treason against the late Diarmait Mac Murchada. It is possible that Domnal Mac Gilla Pátraic's capacity for waging war had not fully recovered from the defeats of 1169.

Peaceful solutions were also found to the family problems. Muirchertach Mac Murchada's reaction to Diarmait's death was to proclaim himself king of Uí Chennselaig, his family's native territory. In this role, he took up arms in support of the High King's attempt to dislodge the Anglo-Normans from Dublin. Had this venture succeeded, Muirchertach would have become king of Leinster. His failure placed him at Strongbow's mercy. Instead of exacting revenge, however, Strongbow played a clever hand and confirmed him as king of Uí Chennselaig, winning his submission and acceptance. In contrast, Domnal Mac Murchada Kavanagh was from the outset loyal to Strongbow, who rewarded him with a new office: that of Chief Justice, responsible for Strongbow's Irish subjects. Both of these appointments were politically astute, although they also make clear that Strongbow's situation was far from secure.

The Dublin problem proved, however, to be far more serious and was solved only by considerable violence and bloodshed. In the end, the Anglo-Normans succeeded in defeating two attempts to dislodge them from Dublin, though neither victory was easily won. The first attempt on Dublin was led by Arsculf Mac Turkil, with the force he had been able to recruit from the Norse communities of the Isle of Man and Scotland. It appears to have been much larger than the Dublin garrison under Milo de Cogan's command. However, in a hard-fought contest, the Anglo-Normans prevailed against unfavourable odds. Many Norse warriors were killed in the battle and during the flight to get to their ships. This time, Arsculf Mac Turkil did not escape and was executed after deigning to plead for his life. The second attack on Dublin was on an even larger scale, being orchestrated from within Ireland by Ruardri Ua Conchobair, who again was able to summon up help from the provincial kings. They set up camp at Castleknock with the intention of starving the Anglo-Norman garrison into surrender. Yet again, Ua Conchobair chose to avoid battle. This may have been the wisdom of generals, who knew that the outcome of a battle is never predictable; in his case, however, it is hard not to conclude that there was an element of fear and timidity in Ruardri, and perhaps he was a man who hoped to win by making a display of force rather than actually using it. The Dublin garrison by this time had certainly been enlarged by the arrival of Strongbow and Raymond *le Gros*. Despite this, Ua Conchobair's tactic almost worked, its failure only due to him overplaying his hand. With food stocks dwindling, Strongbow decided that he had to negotiate. He sent the archbishop of Dublin, Lorcán Ua Tuathail, to Ruardri Ua Conchobair with the offer of a deal: it was suggested that Strongbow be allowed to retain Leinster, but as the High King's vassal. Ua Conchobair, concluding that victory was within his grasp, refused and offered Strongbow only the three Hiberno-Norse towns.

These were humiliating terms that Norman pride could not accept. Instead, it aroused their determination to fight. Three groups were assembled, each of 200 and each including a body of knights: twenty with Milo de Cogan, who led the vanguard; thirty with Raymond *le Gros* in the centre; and forty with Strongbow commanding the rear. The small army moved out on a late October afternoon in 1171, guided by a man with local knowledge. They crossed the river Liffey and headed for the enemy camp at Castleknock. It is testimony to the inadequacy of Ua Conchobair as a commander that his camp was not fortified; nor had he posted scouts to alert him of an attack. The result was that the Anglo-Norman force completely surprised Conchobair's army. At the moment Strongbow launched his attack, Ua Conchobair was taking a bath in the river – he was fortunate not to be captured. The outcome was an overwhelming Anglo-Norman victory: 1,500 Irish troops were killed without a single Anglo-Norman fatality. Moreover, the haul of booty was immense and included a much-needed supply of food.

Any triumph Strongbow may have felt, however, was marred by news of a setback to one of his trusted commanders, Robert Fitz Stephen. He had been left in command of a limited force based at the small fort at Carrick, in order to keep a watchful eye on the situation in Wexford. Deceived into believing that Strongbow had been defeated and killed in the Dublin debacle, he had surrendered. He was a prize captive. The following year his Wexford captors tried to use him to ingratiate themselves with King Henry II, but without success.

INTERVENTION OF KING HENRY II

By late 1170, the situation in Ireland was of sufficient concern to convince Henry II that he needed to discover for himself what was happening and how it could be brought under his control.[8] Meanwhile, to prevent further escalation, he placed an embargo on ships leaving English ports for Ireland and ordered all his subjects there, to return to England by Easter 1171, on pain of forfeiture of their estates and enforced exile.

Two deaths added urgency. The earlier was the murder in Canterbury Cathedral on 29 December 1170 of Archbishop Thomas Becket. Pope Alexander III (1150–81) immediately despatched two legates to investigate the extent of King Henry's complicity, and if warranted, to impose appropriate penalties. By going to Ireland Henry would put a greater distance between himself and the papal legates. Because of the embargo on shipping, the journey of the legates would be extended, thereby delaying their meeting with the king. This was followed in May 1171 by the death of Diarmait Mac Murchada and the succession of Strongbow to the kingship of Leinster. Strongbow at that time was heavily involved in the struggle to defend Dublin, Waterford and Wexford and his imposition of authority on Leinster's petty kings. He therefore sent Raymond *le Gros* and Maurice Fitz Gerald to meet with Henry, who was then at Chinon in Touraine, to assure him of his loyalty and that he had no ambition to become king of Ireland. This did not work. Strongbow then sent his uncle, Hervey de Montmorency, with the same message, to meet King Henry, who was by then at Argentan in Normandy. Again the journey was made without success. On his return, Hervey met Strongbow at Wexford with an unambiguous message: if Strongbow crossed the sea and met with the King on *his* ground, it would signal loyalty and submission; but if the King had to cross to Ireland to compel a meeting, it would be taken as obduracy.

Strongbow took the obvious step and crossed St George's Channel to meet with King Henry at Pembroke. It could be seen as a courtesy that Henry chose to travel to the furthest edge of his kingdom for the meeting. But his choice of venue was also pointed: it was the administrative centre of the earldom he had taken from Strongbow fifteen years earlier. Their meeting was, or gradually became, cordial and concluded with a nicely balanced compromise: Henry confirmed Strongbow's possession of Leinster, but without the three Norse towns of Dublin, Waterford and Wexford.

This arrangement sat well with the belief that a man should not be deprived of that which he had won by the sword. Had Henry flouted this custom, he would have aroused fears and suspicions among his baronage, as his son, John, would later discover. On the other hand, Henry could claim with some justification that Strongbow was in contempt for his earlier crossing to Ireland contrary to the initial royal request. But being deprived of the three towns was more than a slap on the wrist: all three, especially Dublin, were too valuable economically and too important strategically to be left out of direct royal control.

While this meeting was taking place, a royal army comprising 500 knights and 4,000 other troops was mustering at Newnham, in Gloucestershire. Brought to Milford Haven, they embarked on 16 October and landed the following day on the section of the river Suir east of Waterford, known as the Passage. On 18 October the king and his army entered Waterford, where Strongbow formally surrendered Leinster to him. Henry then invested Strongbow with Leinster (less the three Hiberno-Norse towns) as his vassal, for the service of one hundred knights – but excluding also from the grant most of what is now Co. Dublin and the littoral as far south as Arklow.

Henry and his impressive and intentionally daunting entourage then proceeded northwards to Dublin, arriving on 11 November 1171. As they travelled through the provinces, the various Irish kings through whose lands they passed came to submit and swear fealty to King Henry II. A notable exception was Ruardri Ua Conchobair, king of Connacht, the self-styled High King. Henry chose not to react to what was a deliberate act of defiance, but merely sent two emissaries, Hugh de Lacy and William Fitz Audelin, with a message requesting that he and Ruardri meet on the border of his kingdom, the river Shannon. There Ruardri Ua Conchobair made a token submission, but without swearing fealty to King Henry. Five years later, Henry would regularise their relationship.

Henry's stay in Dublin was protracted, lasting five months. Monarchs and great nobles engaged on royal service with dispersed estates led peripatetic lives, and did not stay long in one place. King Henry was endowed with abundant energy; he was constantly on the move with a huge entourage to do his bidding. The fact that he had an extended visit to Ireland, however, was partly due to the risks of sailing during the winter, but it did allow him time to impose two changes of government. One concerned Dublin, and it was drastic. The Norse population was removed to a new settlement close to St Mary's Abbey, on the north bank of the river Liffey, where it developed into Oxmantown. The area they had vacated was handed over to Bristol to be repopulated with migrants from outside Ireland, who were to enjoy the same rights and privileges as their parent town. This new Dublin proved to be a strong magnet. A late twelfth-century survey revealed that the newcomers came from sixty-two places, forty-three in England and a further twelve in Wales. The total was made up from places in France and three places in Scotland.

The other change of arrangement was, or would be in time, for the whole of Ireland. The key figure, however, was not Strongbow, but Hugh de Lacy, whose English estates were around Ludlow and Weobley on the Welsh border. He was granted the lordship of Meath (which he would have to subjugate) for the service of fifty knights. He was also made constable of Dublin Castle with a garrison of twenty knights, four of whom (Milo de Cogan, Meiler Fitz Henry, Milo Fitz David and Maurice Fitz Gerald) were drawn from Strongbow's army, thereby weakening it by depriving him of the service of four of his best men. Finally, de Lacy was appointed *custos* (keeper) of Ireland, in effect Henry's representative. This office was the embryo from which the viceroyalty would grow. Waterford and Wexford created arrangements similar to those for Dublin: Waterford a garrison of thirty knights under the command of William Fitz Audelin, and Wexford forty knights under Robert Fitz Bernard.

When King Henry departed from Wexford on 17 April 1172, he left behind an arrangement that was clearly intended to restrict Strongbow's freedom of action. He had also put an end to the endless Irish strife for the title of High King. Henceforth, the ultimate authority in Ireland would not be an Irish high king but the king of England, as *Dominus Hiberniae*.

Fate allowed Strongbow, as lord of Leinster, a mere four years in which to stamp his authority. Among its petty kings the most obdurate was Diarmait Ua Dimmisaig, King of Uí Failge. The problem was exacerbated by the inability of the High King, Ruardri Ua Conchobair, to exercise control over the kings of Déise, Desmond and Thomond from the Munster province. Dealing with these problems required Strongbow's full attention but this was made impossible by King Henry's request, as his feudal lord, for military assistance in putting down widespread and serious rebellions in Normandy, Anjou and England. The root cause of these rebellions was the discontent of his eldest son, Henry, who at the age of fifteen had been crowned king so as to proclaim his status as the designated heir. The Young King, as he was known, became frustrated at having status and title without power, and his discontent was further fanned by two of Henry's enemies: King Louis VII of France and Henry's own wife, Queen Eleanor, from whom he was estranged. Although most of the fighting took place in Normandy, two English earls, Leicester and Norfolk, also took the opportunity of rebelling, while King William I of Scotland (known as William the Lion) invaded northern England hoping to regain the earldom of Northumberland (which Henry II had obliged his predecessor, his brother King Malcolm IV, to return to English control).

Strongbow's role in helping his king was to command the vital fortress of Gisors, situated on the eastern border of Normandy and controlling the road between two capitals, Paris and Rouen. He discharged his duty faithfully, thereby earning a royal reward. This was the reinstatement of the Norse town of Wexford and the castle at Wicklow, to the liberty of Leinster. Strongbow had done enough to return to royal favour, although Henry would never again entirely trust him.

His absence from Leinster with many of his troops was compounded by the loss of his best commander, Raymond *le Gros*. It followed the death of his constable (army commander), Robert de Quency, while on an expedition into Uí Failge. Raymond approached Strongbow requesting the vacant constableship and also permission to marry Strongbow's sister, Basilia. Neither proposal could be considered outrageous: Raymond was Strongbow's best commander and the preference of his troops, and marriage to Basilia would forge links between the Geraldines and Strongbow's own following. But surprisingly Strongbow turned down both requests, which suggests a degree of unease in the relationship between Strongbow and the Geraldines, perhaps reinforced by the appointment of Hervey de Montmorency as constable. Raymond's reaction was predictable and understandable: he withdrew from Strongbow's service and returned to Carew with his household troops.

The loss of military manpower and leadership seriously weakened the Anglo-Norman grip on Leinster. Ruardri Ua Conchobair's son led an expedition into Leinster which destroyed the newly built castle at Kilkenny, while the Dublin garrison suffered a defeat at Thurles while attempting to retrieve the situation. The threat to Strongbow's hold on Leinster was serious enough for him to plead with Raymond to return. Raymond agreed to do so in return for his appointment as constable, and Basilia as his wife – terms which, this time, were accepted with alacrity.

Ireland continued to be disrupted by war between Ruardri Ua Conchobair and the kings of Déise, Desmond and Thomond in Munster, in which Raymond *le Gros* became embroiled. Eventually, a peace of sorts was brokered by the leaders of the Irish church, formalised by the Treaty of Windsor in October 1175. Its terms required Ruardri Ua Conchobair to submit to King Henry II – though not on feudal but on Irish terms, by agreeing to pay annual tribute. In return, he was confirmed as High King for those parts of Ireland still ruled by Irish kings.

This policy had a short life, as the situation in Ireland was dramatically changed in 1176 by the death in Dublin, possibly of gangrene, of the forty-five-year-old Strongbow. In an act that revealed the continuing tension within the overlord's family, his sister Basilia communicated news of his death to her husband, Raymond, by means of a cryptic message: 'The large molar which has caused me so much pain has fallen out.'

Interlude in Leinster: 1176–1189

KING HENRY'S PLAN

Strongbow's death opened a new phase of Irish history that was to last for thirteen years. For the liberty, the consequence was the reversion of possession into the hands of the English crown, pending the outcome of identifying Strongbow's rightful heir and whether he was of full age (twenty-one). These questions presented no problem, since Strongbow and Aoife had two legitimate children. The elder was a boy, Gilbert Fitz Richard, whose name continued the de Clare family tradition of alternating the same two names to identify the eldest son: the father's forename became the son's surname, hence Fitz (son of) Richard. Their younger child was a girl, Isabel, named for Strongbow's mother, Isabel de Beaumont. However, since they had been born between 1170 and 1176, both were in their minority and consequently became royal wards, with the liberty continuing in the king's hands and to his profit.

This would come to an end when Gilbert reached his majority. Under the feudal system, he would then do homage and fealty to the king, who would bestow upon him *seizin* (formal possession) of his inheritance. He would also be required to pay the king a sum of money known as a *relief.* This was in effect akin to an inheritance tax, but more importantly, it would be an affirmation of Gilbert's status as the tenant – not the owner – of the liberty of Leinster. King Henry was determined to keep his hands firmly on Leinster.

Until such time as young Gilbert inherited, the liberty of Leinster would be administered to the king's benefit by men appointed by him. For this purpose, King Henry II split the liberty into three parts. The largest part he placed in the hands of Hugh de Lacy, with his base in Dublin. This was a sensible selection, in that de Lacy was constable of Dublin, *Custos* of the royal estates in Ireland and lord of Meath. The others were William Fitz Audelin, based at Wexford, and Richard le Poer,[1] who would operate from Waterford, which lay just outside the liberty. It is clear that de Lacy was particularly active in the role, building five castles (Forth, Knocktopher, Castledermot, Leighlin Bridge and Tullow) to help consolidate Anglo-Norman control.

But Strongbow's death had consequences for Ireland as a whole, as well as for the liberty of Leinster.[2] In 1177, at a meeting of the royal council held at Oxford, Henry II expounded his master plan for the whole of Ireland: this was part of his wider scheme for the division of his empire between his four sons after his death.

The eldest son, Henry, would be king of England, duke of Normandy and count of Anjou. His second son, Richard, would inherit his mother's title, that of the duchy of Aquitaine; while Geoffrey would become duke of Brittany by virtue of his marriage to Constance, the current duke's heir. His youngest son, John, was to be king of Ireland subject to papal approval, which Pope Urban III eventually gave in 1187. It was not Henry's intention to personally conquer the whole island and displace its native landowners with Anglo-Norman incomers, as had happened in England after 1066. Rather, he envisaged a culturally divided kingdom in which parts were settled and controlled by Anglo-Normans, while other parts continued under the control of the Irish kings. The only thing the Irish and Anglo-Norman rulers would have in common was that all would be tenants-in-chief of the king of England. Provided that this was understood and accepted, local arrangements would prevail, as they did in all other parts of his empire.[3]

But Henry qualified this vision by taking steps to ensure that a much greater part of Ireland was brought under Anglo-Norman control. In other words, he wanted John to come into a more balanced inheritance. He promoted a scheme in 1177 which focused on the southern half of Ireland, stipulating any land grants made on the understanding that they would benefit both the grantee and the crown. First of all, he enlarged Hugh de Lacy's lordship of Meath and doubled his military obligation from fifty to one hundred knights. He then granted the two kingdoms that made up the ancient province of Munster. The southern kingdom of Desmond (or Cork) he granted to two of Strongbow's stalwarts, Robert Fitz Stephen and Miles de Cogan, for the service of sixty knights. The northern kingdom of Thomond (or Limerick) proved to be more difficult – the reason being that the original grantees stepped away from the deal when they realised the crown would retain the city of Limerick. Further, the financial cost they would incur, along with the expenditure in time (and probably blood) required to conquer it, made it an unattractive deal. Their replacement was Philip de Briouze, also for the service of sixty knights.

Desmond was brought under Anglo-Norman control and settlement by the mid 1180s. In Thomond, the process was much more prolonged: in fact, it lasted until the early years of the thirteenth century. By that time it was in the hands of William de Burgh, brother of Hubert de Burgh, who was to dominate the government of England as justiciar until the early years of Henry III's reign.

But there was also an additional, somewhat maverick episode concerning the kingdom of Ulaid, which King Henry did not instigate.[4] It was engineered by John de Courcy, a man with family roots in a Somerset township that still bears his name, albeit in a corrupted form: Stogursey (Stoke Courcy). His ambition lay northwards when he eyed up the kingdom of Ulaid (roughly the modern counties of Down and Antrim). Henry did not give him a formal feudal grant but rather offhand, informal permission amounting to 'Go if you must, conquer if you can' – and that was exactly what de Courcy did, with a force of no more than twenty-two knights and 300 other troops. In securing the prize, he exemplified typical Norman characteristics: self-confidence, daring and tenacious courage in pursuit of an objective. But King Henry's attitude in this case was also typical: a slight 'nod and a wink' to his chosen knights to conquer lands and, if successful, an expectation that they would share the spoils with him. If the venture failed, he simply disassociated himself from it, for it lacked his formal approval. Monarchs do not do their own dirty work.[5]

PRINCE JOHN AS LORD OF IRELAND

It was in the hope of bringing greater order and stability to Ireland through the introduction of more effective and efficient government that in 1185, King Henry II set in motion proceedings to install his youngest son, John, now aged eighteen years of age, as king of Ireland.[6] The scheme was launched in dramatic fashion by the assembly of a large and lavishly equipped expedition to Ireland. Most conspicuous was its obvious military contingent of 300 knights and 3,000 other troops, doubtless intended to impress and overawe both the Irish and Anglo-Normans. But the multitude also included some of Henry's most able and trusted ministers, the sort of men experienced at creating an effective government structure.

This huge gathering of military and civil talent landed at Waterford on 25 April 1185 and remained in Ireland until December. The fact that Prince John chose to cross back to England in the winter – the most dangerous time of year for sailing – tells us that this carefully planned and orchestrated scheme had ended in complete failure. Why is not entirely certain, although I find two factors that to me seem clear enough. One was John's immaturity. He and his young companions were said to have been guilty of coltish, adolescent behaviour, so that he utterly failed to impress both the Irish kings and the gnarled survivors of the pioneering Norman days. Plainly, he was seen as unfit to do the job his father had chosen for him. The other factor was Hugh de Lacy. On his return home, John complained bitterly to his father that de Lacy regarded himself as the king of Ireland, an opinion shared by others; and in this there may have been some truth. Hugh de Lacy was an able and very experienced man, who had discharged the role of *Custos* very effectively and who I can imagine may not have wished to defer to a young whippersnapper like John. However, de Lacy's murder in the following year removed a potential source of future trouble.

Although denied the kingship of Ireland, John retained the title Lord of Ireland and the powers that went with it. In the course of the later 1180s he granted estates in Leinster and elsewhere in Ireland to several of his friends, most notably to Theobald Walter, whom he appointed as his hereditary court butler. This title Theobald's descendants adopted as their surname. John's grants involved two large estates in Leinster, centred on Tullow and Gowran, and also the castle at Arklow. Theobald was the brother of Hubert Walter, one of the most distinguished English civil servants of the medieval centuries. At the time of his death in 1205, Hubert was justiciar, chancellor and archbishop of Canterbury, the three greatest offices of state in England. Hubert's eminence explains why Theobald Walter was the only one of John's grantees allowed to retain his grants in Leinster. Coincidently, in 1185 another very significant event occurred: the death of Gilbert Fitz Richard, Strongbow's young son and heir. The fate of the liberty of Leinster now rested with two vulnerable women: Aoife and her daughter, Isabel.

On Strongbow's death, his widow, Aoife, became entitled to her *dower* – a portion of the deceased husband's estate assigned to widows to enable them to live in the manner to which they were accustomed. At this date, the size of the portion allotted to the dower was still not fixed, although custom was hardening in favour of one third. We know little of Aoife's life as a widow, except that it was spent in England, where she was known as the 'Irish countess'. Whether this was her wish, or whether she was deliberately kept away from Ireland by royal command, is not known. Nor did she remarry, as many widows were encouraged or even pressed to do by the king; especially those widows with a valuable dower. Again, we do not know whether this was Aoife's decision or that of the king. There is even uncertainty about the year of Aoife's death, though 1190 is thought to be most likely. What we do know is that she chose to be buried in the church of the Cistercian Abbey at Tintern, in Monmouthshire. The abbey was founded by the first member of the de Clare family to possess the estate of Netherwent. All things considered, I think it likely that a suspicious-minded king like Henry II would have wanted to keep Aoife within his easy reach. Aoife, however, was yesterday's woman.

Not so Isabel, who was now in her early teenage years and, as a consequence of her brother's death, heir to the liberty of Leinster. From the crown's point of view, it was vital that the decision of when and to whom Isabel was married was in no way compromised. She had become a pearl of great price. This is attested by King Henry II's retention of her wardship, neither arranging a marriage for her nor selling the wardship to a third party, which he is known to have done on many occasions. Wards were a lucrative commodity.

Isabel's last known address was the Tower of London, which among its many functions was a royal palace. In the Tower she would have been safely protected as well as being provided with her own small household of trustworthy women, under the watchful eye of Ranulf Glanville, Henry II's justiciar.[7] The choice of the Tower is significant, since it was the most abduction-proof of all royal residences. This was not a pointless precaution, as abductions and enforced marriages of desirable heiresses were not unknown. It was essential for a wealthy heiress to be kept under strict, close protection so that her marriage could be arranged by the lord of her estate.

After her brother's death, therefore, it was likely that Isabel de Clare endured a quasi-monastic existence for four years, during which time she would have grown to womanhood and perhaps been prepared for her role as a nobleman's wife. This existence came to an end in July 1189 when Isabel, now aged sixteen or seventeen, was married to William Marshal, a man more than twice her age and most certainly a modest landowner. Their marriage took place at the door of a London church, which may have been St Paul's Cathedral. To appreciate how this marriage came about and to understand why it did not disparage Isabel, we need to have knowledge of the career of William Marshal to this point.

WILLIAM MARSHAL'S LIFE AND CAREER TO 1189

Isabel's husband, William Marshal, was to become one of the most influential men in the history of both England and Ireland. It is therefore important that we trace his early career and understand why two kings, Henry II and Richard I, were prepared to hand over to him the most desirable heiress in the royal collection.[8]

The date of William's birth was almost certainly sometime in the year 1147, in the middle of the long civil war between King Stephen and Henry I's intended successor, his daughter, Mathilda. William Marshal was not only born during the war, he was a consequence of it. Both statements are signally appropriate, since throughout his adult life William Marshal was engaged, always enthusiastically and usually successfully, in combat.

At the outset, however, his position within his family was not propitious in that he was the second son of a second marriage. His father, John Marshal, was a middle-ranking landowner with an estate scattered over Berkshire, Oxfordshire and Wiltshire. His base was the Berkshire township of Hamstead, near Newbury, to which the word Marshal was appended in the thirteenth century (it is known today as Hamstead Marshall). It was there that John Marshal built his castle, the earthworks of which are still visible, but perhaps his best asset was the hereditary office of Master Marshal of the King's Court. Like the family of Theobald Walter in Ireland, whose royal office as butler became his surname, the men of William's family were customarily given the surname Marshal whether or not they held the position of Marshal. Butler and Marshal were, in fact, very early examples of a title converting to a surname.

John Marshal inherited his office in, or shortly after, 1129 from his father, Gilbert Giffard (as noted earlier, Giffard was a nickname meaning 'chubby cheeks'). Whether Giffard was the original holder of the post of Master Marshal of the King's Court, or whether he inherited it from his father, are questions that I cannot answer.[9]

Along with being in charge of the horses at the royal court, the Master Marshal was also responsible for the efficient functioning of a complex organisation – made more so by the almost constant movement of the king and the huge travelling entourage of administrators required to control and govern his kingdom. Regular movement between Westminster,

Winchester, the royal castles and hunting lodges in England and the king's domains in France must have been a logistical nightmare. Most of the work was done by the Marshal's deputies, but in his capacity as an officer of the court John Marshal would have access to important information and men of influence.

Without doubt, he was very much a man of his time. In an early fracas he had lost an eye, and his face had been badly disfigured when he was trapped in a burning church during a contretemps with a rival faction. Despite this, Marshal was apparently an attractive, engaging, strong personality, a fighter and a warrior and a dependable head of his family; but he was also an inordinately ambitious man, prepared to satisfy his aims by ruthless cunning, deception and force. In the early years of Stephen's reign he enjoyed success by securing command of the important royal castle at Marlborough and its associated borough, achieved no doubt by his ready acceptance of Stephen as king. But once civil war broke out in 1138 and royal authority became less effective, there was scope for unscrupulous men to engage in 'turf wars' with their neighbours with the aim of extending their influence or control. John Marshal was not shy of engaging in such activity, and avariciously acquired land in his native area of Wiltshire and Berkshire at the first sign of an opportunity to profit.

In the end, however, he came up against an equally strong man whose wealth was nearly three times greater than his: Walter, constable of Salisbury Castle and sheriff of Wiltshire. Despite these offices being vested in Walter, they were actually discharged by his eldest son, William, and very effectively too. When William died in 1143, his responsibilities were immediately assumed by Walter's other son, Patrick, a name uncommon in England at that time. It was Patrick who reached a finely crafted accommodation with John Marshal that was to their mutual advantage.

In 1141, John Marshal defected from King Stephen's party and transferred his support to Mathilda. In 1144 he persuaded Patrick to join him, which earned Patrick the title of earl of Salisbury from a grateful Mathilda. The two families then cemented their alliance in the time-honoured way: by marriage. John Marshal wished to marry Patrick's sister, Sybil. But there was an obstacle: Marshal already had a wife, Adelina, by whom he had two children. These problems were solved by family agreement, and almost certainly by the church courts granting an annulment on the grounds of consanguinity. At that date, canon law prohibited marriage with up to a sixth cousin, which cast a net so wide as to render a valid marriage difficult, if not impossible. A change was brought about in 1215, when the Church accepted the problem and changed the canon law, reducing the range to the third generation.

The problem was solved with the unfortunate Adelina being set aside (but not for long, as she promptly married a minor Oxfordshire land-owner). The two sons she had with John Marshal remained legitimate even though their parents' marriage had contravened the consanguinity rule. This legal convenience opened the way to the politically expedient marriage of John Marshal and Sybil de Salisbury, which took place in 1145. The couple were to have seven children, the first being John, named for his father. Their second son, named William, was probably born in 1147. Forty-five years later he was to marry an Irish princess, Isabel de Clare of Leinster.

However, having been given life during the civil war, William came very close to having it taken away during those same years. In 1152, for reasons that are unclear, John Marshal decided to build a castle at, or close to, Newbury. By this date the war was in stalemate, but John Marshal's act was seen as aggressive and angered King Stephen into action by sending a small army to demolish the offending structure. Marshal fended him off by pleading for time to demolish it himself, meanwhile offering to Stephen his five-year-old son, William, as a hostage in surety for his compliance. Marshal, however, had no intention of keeping his promise. Consequently Stephen put the castle under siege and young William was condemned to hang. Marshal seems have been unconcerned by the threat to his child's safety when he persisted in refusing to surrender his castle to King Stephen, stating that 'he still had the hammers and anvils to create more and better sons'. Could it be that Marshal truly believed his own words? After all, he was a ruthless man, and William was not his heir. Or was it that he was prepared to take a calculated risk, banking on Stephen's reluctance to harm a little boy? After all, service at the royal court would have given John Marshal time to assess Stephen's character, which is said to have been sensitive (although no doubt only up to a point; after all, he was in a war situation).

It would seem that young William was an energetic, inquisitive child, even perhaps something of an actor, for during the siege which ensued, as he was being taken to the gallows, he begged his guards to let him carry a lance. Then, as his father continued with his refusal to surrender, it was decided that young William would be thrown into the castle. On seeing the catapult the child was excited and, it is said, he jumped in, thinking it to be a swing, even enjoying what he thought to be a game as he was swung over towards the castle.[10] Again, Stephen's sensitivity blocked the threat to carry it out. At the third and last attempt it was decided to use the little boy as a human shield at the head of their assault; but in the end Stephen, who had a benevolent nature, could not bring himself to sanction such a barbaric act, particularly as William's childish antics during his captivity had amused and beguiled him. William, who it appears had been unaware of his impending fate, spent the rest of the siege with the king in the royal tent. It is said that he played a game of 'knights' with King Stephen, their pretend swords being flower or perhaps plantain stems; probably the latter, as the presence of flowers in or around the royal pavilion at that time seems like a curious notion, unless of course it was to keep it sweet-smelling.

Young William was eventually returned to his mother. The precise date is not known, but it was most likely after Stephen's death two years later. Nothing further is known about William's life until 1160 (although in 1156, when his father sold some land, his name appeared alongside that of his brothers in a charter). In 1160, when he was thirteen years old, he was sent to be trained as a knight in the household of William de Tancarville, the hereditary chamberlain of the dukes of Normandy. This was a prestigious situation for William, secured for him through his mother and his uncle Patrick de Salisbury's family connection with Tancarville, whose castle was at the mouth of the river Seine and whose estates extended southwards towards Caen. He also held property in the west of England. It was a coup for William to be admitted to such an important establishment.

Before considering what William's education involved, we need to be aware that the institution of knighthood was dynamic and evolving. Two changes in particular occurred during Marshal's career as a knight. One was the widespread development and adoption of heraldry: this had a very practical use, as a means of identifying men in battle and in tournaments. But over and above this, coats of arms underlined the superior status in society enjoyed by knights and knightly families.

Being of military origin, heraldic designs were presented in the shape of a shield. As these designs became increasingly complex and detailed, heraldry developed its own terminology – using the French language – and its own rules.[11] William Marshal's arms are one of the earliest known to us. His shield was divided in half vertically, one side painted gold and the other green. The observer sees the gold on the left, the green on the right, but, crucially, to the bearer, they are all reversed, as in a mirror. Superimposed was a heraldic beast, a lion rampant, in red. In the language of heraldry, his arms were *parti per pale, or, et vert, lion rampant gules*. This design would leave the viewer in no doubt as to the bearer. The same, or similar, designs were also employed on the waxed seals used to authenticate legal documents, increasing numbers of which were written in the twelfth century.

The other development served to make knights more self-conscious and more self-aware of how distinctive and distinguished they were, which in turn made them more self-assured. This was literature, which in the main was not read privately or individually, but aloud to listeners in a group – the subject, above all others, being the stories about King Arthur, Queen Guinevere and their knights. The impetus to this literature was Geoffrey of Monmouth's *History of the Kings of England*, written in Latin in the early 1130s. The quintessential personal qualities of knighthood portrayed (perhaps preached) in these tales were courage and loyalty, both demanding a high level of resolve in the face of adversity. This ideal required a knight to place his duty and his honour above personal advantage, or even his life.

Young William is said to have been tall, handsome and a good horseman; he was also noted for his healthy appetite, which earned him the nickname *gasteviande*. He was clearly seen as a good trencherman, as well as reputedly good at sleeping when not eating. He appears to have been popular with his group of trainee knights and it was into this male, military world that young William Marshal was introduced in order to begin his education, which would be arduous and demanding and which, like any other apprenticeship, could last up to seven years.[12] The primary aim was to produce a highly trained, heavily armed and armoured cavalryman. The horse was of prime importance in a knight's life. This being so, it is curious that the word knight derives from the Old English word *cniht*, meaning servant, rather than the French term *chevalier*. A knight would own three types of horse: a *sumpter* for carrying baggage, a *palfrey* for general riding, and most importantly, a *destrier* – a mettlesome, specially bred warhorse that would now more commonly be called a charger. Destriers were mainly of Arab stock. The ability to control and direct such an animal while also using both arms to fight was a prerequisite for success in battle.

The knight had two basic weapons, the tools of his trade. One was the sword, which had totemic significance. It was a finely crafted weapon, with a pointed blade about 39 inches (1 metre) in length and balanced at the hilt. When fully sharpened it was a fearsome weapon, capable of severing a head or limb with one blow. The knight's other weapon was a lance, comprising a wooden shaft (preferably of ash) about 10 feet (3 metres) to 12 feet (3.6 metres) long and tipped with steel. To be fully effective, it was best used in a coordinated cavalry charge.

The knight was also a fully protected warrior. His body, down to the knee, was covered with a *hauberk*, a coat made of around 30,000 inter-linked iron rings, underneath which was a padded jacket, an *aketon*. Leggings and gloves were also of chain mail, as was the coif that covered his head and chin. The head was further protected by a conical iron helmet with a downward-projecting nose piece. Finally, the knight had a kite-shaped shield made of toughened leather fixed to a wooden frame. Assuming he was right-handed, he would carry the shield on his left arm with a strap over his right shoulder.

Singly or in a group, knights were formidable warriors and capable of defeating opponents far greater in number. But, as the description of their equipment suggests, this ability did not come cheap, particularly when it is remembered that every knight had (or should have had) a small entou-rage of servants to make possible his ability to function efficiently.

Military proficiency was not all that was demanded of a young trainee knight, at least in the household of a man like William de Tancarville. In addition, he would be taught to be numerate and to read French and Latin. In these matters it seems that Marshal was a recalcitrant student, and throughout his life he remained only semi-literate and semi-numerate. But in one other aspect of his education, he was a star pupil: he was adept at acquiring the social skills and the chivalrous good manners to make him a congenial member of a sophisticated society. Perhaps most important of these for future success was discretion – knowing when to speak and when to remain silent, what to say and how to say it. Failure in this field could be as fatal, socially at least, as engagement in battle.

When a young man was deemed to have reached the required standard, he would be knighted. At this stage, the ceremony had not developed any degree of elaboration and essentially consisted of belting a sword onto the knight's body. He was also likely to be given a new long cloak, and may have been cuffed with a fist to remind him that this was the last such blow that he was to receive without retaliating. Once these simple acts were performed, the knight became a member of an international brotherhood, required to treat fellow members with due respect.

William Marshal 'graduated' in 1166. He was involved in a brief bout of warfare in defence of the border fortress of Neufchâtel – in which he performed well, as he also did in his first tournament – before, surprisingly, he was dismissed from William de Tancarville's military household, his *mesnie*. The reason for his departure is not clear, particularly as there is no evidence that he had given offence or failed in any way. Perhaps the most plausible explanation is that Tancarville had taken him for training as a favour to his kinswoman, William's mother, and now that his training was completed he had no further obligation to him. Alternatively, Tancarville is known to have maintained an excessively large *mesnie* and he may well have decided it was time to downsize.

Whatever the reason, William Marshal was now a poor knight, of which there were many in search of a nobleman's *mesnie* with vacancies. Returning to his family was not an option, since his father had died in the previous year. Luck, however, was on his side, as his uncle, Patrick, earl of Salisbury, was willing to take him into his household. It was from this starting point that William Marshal was to rise to fame and fortune.

His first military engagement in the service of Earl Patrick was nearly his last. It took place in the spring of 1168 in the county of Poitou, the most northerly part of the duchy of Aquitaine. Patrick was acting as escort and guardian to Henry II's queen, Eleanor, as she was heading towards the capital city of Poitiers. Their peaceful progress was shattered by Geoffrey and Guy de Lusignan, the leaders of a violent, ambitious and perennially troublesome family who were members of the baronage of the county of Poitou.[13] It is safe to assume that their objective was to capture Queen Eleanor and then use her as a pawn to secure the repossession of their estates, recently seized by King Henry.

But the Lusignans bungled their attack badly. In the skirmish that ensued, Earl Patrick – a man with a high ransom value – was killed, while Queen Eleanor managed to avoid capture and escaped to safety. The Lusignans did, however, capture William Marshal, who was fighting a rearguard action to allow Eleanor to escape. He was severely wounded when fighting with his back to a hedge, which he had hoped would protect him as he fought off his Lusignan assailants; however, a lance was thrust through the hedge and driven through his thigh. Badly wounded and bleeding heavily, he was taken prisoner and held in appalling pain and discomfort for many months, having to tend to his own wound as best he could with dirty rags as his inadequate dressings. The conditions in which he was held were primitive, as his captors were on the run and constantly moving from place to place. There is a story which may have been often told by William, a noted raconteur: at one castle where they were given shelter, the lord's kindly wife took pity on his woeful condition and sent him clean linen bandages concealed in a hollowed-out loaf of bread.

Some months later, when Eleanor learnt of Marshal's action in facilitating her escape, she took steps to ransom him and make him a member of her household. However, two years after joining the queen's household, Henry II took Marshal away from her service, transferring him to the *mesnie* of his eldest son, Henry, who had recently been crowned king as Henry's heir and thereafter was known as the Young King. Marshal, now twenty-three years old, was given the role of training fifteen-year-old Henry in the martial skills required of a knight. Young Henry was seen as something of a playboy, leading a feckless life with his young courtiers. King Henry's introduction of William Marshal into his court was the start of a deep friendship between him and young Henry that lasted until the Young King's premature death in 1183.

What held them together was a mutual passion for tournaments,[14] which grew rapidly in popularity during the twelfth century throughout the French-speaking world – although they were banned in England by the ever-suspicious Henry II, who feared that they might be a cover for seditious plotting. There is no evidence that any tournaments took place in Ireland. Later they were permitted in 1194 at five official venues in England by Richard I under royal license. Tournament events were far from being the one-to-one jousts in confined lists that became popular from the fourteenth century. Tournament circuits operated in northern France and Flanders, and the events were advertised well in advance, attracting a huge following from England, France and Scotland. Hundreds of knights participated in teams at any one time, proudly displaying their shields and their lord's banners. Together with a knight's pre-tournament arrival would be their servants in charge of transporting their accoutrements and horses. There would also be a miscellany of supporting trades: farriers, armourers and other 'hangers-on' such as merchants and 'entertainers', all taking an opportunity to ply their trade to their advantage. The clamour and adrenaline-fuelled anticipation must have made it a noisy, riotous, vibrantly colourful spectacle before the action started. The tournaments were far from being controlled affairs. Rather they were mock battles fought by teams of knights, ranging over wide expanses of open ground and, as in war, any knight who was captured owed his captor a ransom. However, in spite of this they were spectator sports, in which ladies often provided a prize for the champion.

Marshal soon became a star performer in this sport, claiming later in life to have made over 500 captures. His claim to have made a lot of money from ransoms may have been true but, as he was only semi-numerate, he had a royal kitchen clerk named Wigain calculate and keep a tally of his winnings for him. As previously mentioned, Marshal was also a noted raconteur; so he may have been guilty, like Shakespeare's character Falstaff, of exaggerating his success. On the other hand, his international reputation as a warrior was such that even in his sixties men declined to face him in single combat.

William Marshal's association with the Young King was broken once, and only briefly. The cause was a mischievous rumour circulated by several other members of Henry's *mesnie* that Marshal had had an affair with Henry's wife, Marguerite (sister of Philip II, the new French king). There was no proof of this, but even so, Marshal had to go into exile. It may well have been a story fabricated by fellow members of the *mesnie* to discredit him and secure his removal – after all, these knights would have been familiar with the story of the adultery of King Arthur's queen, Guinevere, with Sir Lancelot.

Marshal's exile lasted only a few months. He was recalled to young Henry's court in the summer of 1183 when it was apparent that the Young King was dying, of what we take to have been dysentery. A few years earlier, like many other young men, Henry had 'taken the Cross'; that is, he had made a vow to go on pilgrimage to the Holy Land. As a public display of this promise, he had had a cross sewn onto his cloak. As he lay dying, he begged Marshal to help him keep his vow by taking the cloak to Jerusalem. This William promised to do.

Keeping his promise to his dead lord proved to be a life-changing episode in William Marshal's career. It took him nearly three years to journey to Jerusalem and back. Few details are known of his expedition, but it is clear enough that what had been undertaken as a pilgrimage by proxy had a deep personal impact on William Marshal. Hitherto, his religious beliefs and convictions appear to have been entirely conventional. But while in Jerusalem he became deeply impressed by the Knights Templar, who combined the demands of monastic commitment with the rigours and dangers of military life. He is said to have vowed to end his life as a Templar and, to that end, he brought home with him a valuable piece of cloth with which to cover his corpse when he died.

On return from his mission to the Holy Land, a grateful King Henry II immediately rewarded Marshal with the grant of the estate of Cartmel in Lancashire and the wardship of Héloïse, the heir of William of Lancaster, lord of Kendal, who had died in 1184. Marshal was expected to exercise his right to marry the girl, thereby acquiring the lordship of Kendal and with it high rank in the baronage. But he did not do so. Instead, after three years he relinquished Héloïse to become the wife of a colleague, Gilbert

Fitz Reinfrid. He is also known to have declined the king's offer of the Norman heiress to Châteauroux. His hesitancy was due not, I believe, to an aversion to matrimony but to his aim of obtaining a greater prize.

King Henry also made Marshal a member of his military household, and thereafter until the king's death in 1189 Marshal was with him in France, engaged on military tasks but also, as occasion required, diplomatic ones. These were all-consuming, as Henry was in conflict with the unnatural alliance of his enemy, King Philip II of France, and his own son Richard, duke of Aquitaine.

The cause of Henry's estrangement from Richard was threefold. One aspect was Henry's refusal to acknowledge Richard as his successor. The underlying reason for this was his partiality for his youngest son, John, but it was also because Richard refused to relinquish the duchy of Aquitaine, where he had ruled successfully for ten years. Henry's refusal to decide on the succession fuelled Richard's fears of disinheritance – fears that found ready encouragement from Philip II, whose long-term aim was to dismember the Angevin empire and restore the allegiance of its parts to the French crown.

By the spring of 1189, it was clear that Henry II was losing the military struggle – and moreover, that he had not long to live. At the beginning of July, he was forced to flee from Le Mans to avoid capture. William Marshal commanded a rearguard force to give the king time to escape. It was during these days that Marshal and Richard came face to face: Marshal fully armed, Richard without armour so as to be able to ride faster. Both men knew that Marshal could have killed Richard, whose only defence was to point out that it would ill become a knight to kill a defenceless man. Marshal agreed, and instead killed Richard's horse, so ending his pursuit. He is reputed to have said: 'The Devil may kill you; I will not.'

A Promise Fulfilled

THE MARRIAGE OF WILLIAM MARSHAL AND ISABEL DE CLARE

King Henry II died on 6 June 1189 at his castle at Chinon in Touraine. Shortly before his death, he publicly promised William Marshal the wardship of Isabel de Clare and with it the control of her marriage – which may well have been the prize Marshal had his eye on. This makes sense of his earlier decision not to marry Héloïse of Lancaster following his return from the Holy Land in 1186. His willingness to forego the lesser in order to obtain the greater prize had paid off handsomely, demonstrating that he was capable of playing for high stakes.

Now William Marshal was about to join the upper ranks of noble society. Richard I, on becoming king, made a public statement making clear that although his father had promised Isabel to William it was he, Richard, who gave her. Was this Richard discharging his debt to Marshal for sparing his life, even though he did not openly admit it? But there was more to it than that: what Richard was doing was securing the transfer of Marshal's loyalty from his father to himself. It was to prove a loyalty well worth the price.

As well as favouring William Marshal, the new king also promoted his own brother, John, endowing him lavishly with grants of land and making him count of Mortain in Normandy. Like Marshal, John's standing in society was greatly enhanced; from now until he became king he was Count John, on a par with his nephew Arthur, the young count of Brittany. Should Richard not marry and produce an heir, the two males qualified to succeed him were now identified and on level terms.

William Marshal now moved quickly. As soon as he was armed with King Richard's instructions and a confidential message for his mother,

Queen Eleanor, he made for England, stopping off at Longueville to identify himself as its new lord. In England his first destination was Winchester,
to meet with the king's mother and deliver the message from Richard.
Queen Eleanor had recently been released from the captivity she had
endured since 1174, which was her husband Henry II's punishment for her
supporting their sons in rebellion against him. Having done his duty by
Eleanor, his benefactress in the early years of his career, William Marshal
headed to London with marriage in mind.

On his arrival to take Isabel into his possession with the intention of
marrying her, he was met by her guardian, a suspicious and reluctant justiciar, Ranulf de Glanville. However, when Marshal produced Richard's
instructions, Isabel was released into Marshal's keeping.

Isabel now knew the identity of her destiny. The marriage of William
Marshal and Isabel de Clare was facilitated by one of the most powerful
men in the City of London, Richard Fitz Reiner, who had been sheriff of
London since 1187 and for many years Henry II's financial agent. He not
only accommodated Marshal in his London mansion in Cheapside, near
St Paul's Cathedral, but also loaned him the money to pay for their
wedding. (Fitz Reiner did not live long enough to reap the rewards of his
astute investment in a rising man; he died in 1191.) It is not known at
which church Isabel and William married, but it may well have been St
Paul's Cathedral. Another of William's friends, Enguerrand d'Abernon,
loaned him the use of his manor house at Stoke d'Abernon in Surrey for
what would now be called a honeymoon. Enguerrand was a major tenant
of the senior branch of Isabel's paternal family, the de Clares, in Surrey
and Kent, and also of the crown, in Hampshire.

The marriage changed both parties' lives fundamentally. Isabel was at
most seventeen years old, and had latterly lived as a closely guarded royal
ward. Like most girls, especially those in the upper circles of society, she
would have grown up knowing that her destiny was marriage (or a nunnery)
and that her husband would be chosen for her by her father or guardian
for dynastic, political or social reasons. How reconciled young women were
to the passive role required of them is little known. One response they had
at their disposal was resistance to 'disparagement', or marriage to a man
of inferior status. Otherwise, a woman would know her fate. If it was
marriage, that would be accompanied by a dower, which would augment
her husband's estate and give her status within the marriage.

One other aspect of which Isabel would have been well aware was that
within marriage, her primary role was to produce children: most particularly,

a male heir. In this way, land and title would be preserved. Enough is known about many marriages to indicate that plenty of wives were intelligent, forceful and supportive partners; Isabel de Clare was one such person.[1]

Isabel is unlikely to have met William before his arrival to claim her. What she felt at being married to a battle-hardened and no doubt battle-scarred forty-three-year-old warrior is not known. She must have been amenable, for there is no hint that she felt disparaged despite being aware that he had only a small estate and lacked title. On the other hand, she would no doubt have heard of his military prowess and his standing at the courts of both King Henry II and King Richard I; and William Marshal is reputed to have been a big athletic man, brown-haired with an open, good-looking countenance, an amusing wit and, although of limited education, a natural courtier. Isabel may even have viewed marriage to such a man with excitement. We have no knowledge about her feelings regarding the union, but equally, there is no evidence that it was anything other than harmonious and happy. No evidence exists that William Marshal ever took a mistress or produced any illegitimate children, either before or after his marriage, as was so common amongst his like. The marriage was certainly fruitful, producing ten children, five sons and five daughters, all surviving to adulthood.

If marriage propelled young Isabel de Clare into womanhood, it instantly raised William Marshal into the upper ranks of the baronage. The estate he acquired was extensive in both senses of the word, in that it stretched from Leinster in Ireland, through Wales and England, into Normandy. The bulk of it was his wife's inheritance, though supplemented by him through royal benevolence.

In the far west of his estates was the liberty of Leinster, although it had to be prised out of the clutches of Prince John – a feat that required the firm hand of his brother, Richard I. Even so, it is doubtful that Marshal made any impact on Leinster during the first ten years of his legal possession. Throughout the reign of Richard I, Marshal's attentions were focused elsewhere: with the government of England during the king's absence on the Third Crusade, and then while Richard was a captive of the Holy Roman Emperor Henry VI. After King Richard's return in 1194, and until his death in 1199, Marshal was with him during the constant armed conflict against King Philip II of France, in Normandy.

More accessible and manageable than the liberty of Leinster was the Welsh lordship of Striguil (now Chepstow), variously known as Netherwent or Lower Gwent. It comprised a compact block of land on the north side of the estuary of the river Severn, between the rivers Wye and Usk, and was dominated by the castles at Striguil/Chepstow and Usk. It was at Striguil/Chepstow that Marshal developed a small port to assist his commercial activity and serve as a place from which to embark for Ireland. Also, in contrast to Leinster, Marshal's English possessions, although yielding a higher income, were scattered. They were the manors of Weston (Hertfordshire), Parndon and Chesterford (Essex), Long Crendon (Buckinghamshire) and Caversham (Oxfordshire), the last becoming his favourite residence.

Finally, in Normandy he had the lordship of Longueville, a few miles/ kilometres south of Dieppe, and Orbec, near Lisieux. In addition, Richard I granted him (for a monetary consideration, to fill his crusading war-chest) the shrievalty of Gloucester, which included its castle, and the Forest of Dean.

Almost immediately, he took steps to relieve himself of the distant lordship of Cartmel.[2] He did this by making it the foundation endowment of an Augustinian canonry, the first group of inhabitants being brought north from a similar establishment at Bradenstoke in Wiltshire, where his father was buried.

But there was more to come, for in 1194, his older brother, John Marshal, died without leaving any legitimate offspring. Consequently, William inherited the family estates in Berkshire, Wiltshire and neighbouring counties, along with the hereditary office of Master Marshal. Finally, the title had caught up with his name.

His final gain, and perhaps the one he most wished for, was that of the earldom of Pembroke; that is, the restoration of what King Henry II had confiscated in 1154 from Strongbow, William Marshal's father-in-law. The grant was made by King John in 1199, shortly after his coronation. It was a fitting reward for Marshal's assiduous cultivation of Prince John, his junior by twenty-one years, during the 1190s, when he was loyally serving his brother Richard I. Marshal had learnt well how to practise the courtier's skills, but what may have clinched his title was the part he played in securing the succession for John.

At this date, the rules governing succession to the throne were not yet fixed.[3] It was not clear who took precedence: the son of an older brother, or a younger brother of the deceased king? John was Richard's younger brother, but a good claim could be made for Arthur, the sixteen-year-old son of John's elder brother Geoffrey, duke of Brittany, who had died in 1186 of injuries sustained in a tournament. It is recorded that on learning of Richard's death, Marshal had an urgent conversation with Hubert Walter, archbishop of Canterbury (and also papal legate, appointed in 1195), who favoured Arthur. He was talked down by Marshal in favour of John, whom he thought adult and competent. But more significant, maybe, is that Marshal knew that on his deathbed Richard had designated John as his heir and had commanded his men to do homage to him. Marshal's sense of loyalty would not have allowed him to do otherwise. The archbishop is said to have told Marshal, prophetically, that it was the worst decision of his life.

Marshal's rapid change of circumstances meant that he had to move from being a member of someone else's household to creating his own.[4] The members we know most about, although not as much as we would like, were the members of his military household, his *mesnie*. We have the names of twenty-one, although not all were permanent members. What is clear, however, is that with only one exception they were from the south of England, with roots and property in eleven counties extending up the Thames valley and into the border with Wales. The two counties most frequently mentioned are Berkshire and Wiltshire, Marshal's native heath. It is also clear that those offered a place in his household were known to him, and were trusted by him. A number of them stand out. Perhaps the most notable was John de Earley (Earley is now a suburb of Reading, Berkshire). His father, William de Earley, was a royal chamberlain. John was given to Marshal as a ward (although not given his lands) by the king, on being orphaned as a boy of fourteen or fifteen years old. He joined Marshal's household as a squire and remained with him as a knight. Marshal had implicit trust in him, knowing that his loyalty to him was absolute. He was Marshal's *fidus Achates* and remained a member of his small circle of close, intimate friends until William's death. Another very able knight was a Wiltshire man, Geoffrey Fitz Robert, whose close ties with Marshal were strengthened by his marriage to Basilia, Strongbow's sister and widow of Raymond *le Gros*.

Two others were to play notable parts in the crisis of 1207–8. One was Stephen d'Évreux, a cousin of Marshal and also his adviser, who had a substantial estate in four English counties along the border with Wales. Stephen d'Évreux's relationship to Marshal is not entirely clear but probably stems from the Salisbury family connection. The other was Jordan de Sauqueville, who had land in Normandy at Sauqueville, near Dieppe, and also in Buckinghamshire and Sussex. He joined Marshal's household after 1195, and had presumably become known to William through serving in Normandy. Other prominent members were John Marshal, the illegitimate son of William's half-brother, John Marshal of Hamstead Marshal; and Walter de Purcell, who was later given as a hostage to King John in 1210.

Geoffrey Fitz Robert came to Ireland in the 1190s and was almost certainly Marshal's chief agent in developing the lordship of Leinster. A very similar role was played by Thomas Fitz Anthony, a younger man, who arrived in Leinster before 1200.

Marshal, like all men of his standing, also had his own civil household, which would consist of two parts. One comprised men in priest's orders, whose concern was spiritual welfare. They would have acted as his confessors and celebrated mass, along with advising on ecclesiastical and religious matters. The other group, greater in number, was made up of clerks in minor orders who were administrators and would be literate in French and Latin to deal with correspondence and legal documents. Their skills were essential, especially as Marshal's level of literacy appears to have been very low, unlike many great barons. The most important of these clerks was Master Michael of London. His title implies successful completion of the basic academic curriculum in Latin that the West had inherited from its Roman past, comprising the *trivium* (grammar, rhetoric, logic) followed by the *quadrivium* (arithmetic, geometry, astronomy, music). Michael was a loyal, first-rate man who remained in Marshal's service until the end. Another valued member of his staff is known to have been a Master Jocelin, who was in holy orders and was rector of one church in London and another in Gloucestershire. He lived in Marshal's house at Charing, in the City of London, and appears to have been his agent in London; he was most certainly his eyes and ears in the capital.

Marshal was now a great lord and lived accordingly, which meant that he and his household were to a considerable extent peripatetic, moving between his many estates. As he travelled from one location to another, his status would have been demonstrated by the size of his entourage. This has been estimated at between forty and fifty persons, together with a train of baggage wagons and sumpter horses.

MARSHAL'S CAREER IN IRELAND

There is no doubt that William Marshal had a considerable impact on the liberty of Leinster, although much of it can only be perceived in broad outline, not in detail. I will consider his accomplishments in Part III of this book, but here I should make clear that it was not a one-man show. The part played by his wife, Countess Isabel, is largely hidden from us, but the glimpses we have of her show her to have been an intelligent woman with a strong personality and an astute grasp of political advantage – particularly when shrewdly and firmly insisting on the development of her ancestral territory in Ireland. She was very aware of being the daughter of a king and of the fact that Leinster was particularly and peculiarly hers. William Marshal was styled lord of Leinster, but he was only so 'by right of his wife'. To his credit and advantage, Marshal was genuine in his acceptance of this – perhaps the more so since he was now earl of Pembroke in his own right. Mention should also be made of the excellent groundwork done by members of his household, most notably Geoffrey Fitz Robert, who appears to have been his chief agent and been busily active in Leinster in the 1190s.

The accomplishments of William and Isabel are all the more remarkable given the relatively short time they spent in the liberty, and also given that during much of that time they were hampered by their enemies – not least King John, from whom William had become disaffected. Their first visit, in 1200, was in fact a flying visit and might well have been their last, since their crossing from Pembroke was rough and prolonged by a violent storm that put them in fear for their lives. The journey was so perilous that Marshal vowed that if they came safely to land, he would found a monastery in thanksgiving. The result was a Cistercian abbey on the shores of Bannow Bay, of which substantial remains still exist in a most beautiful, tranquil area. Because it was an offshoot of Tintern Abbey in Monmouthshire, founded by Gilbert Fitz Gilbert de Clare in 1116, it was known as Tintern Parva; and also as Tintern *de voto* (Latin: of the vow). Short though their visit was, it was time enough for them to impress upon their Anglo-Norman subjects that their new and rightful lord and lady had arrived.

But why 1200? One possible reason is that with Richard I's death, Marshal was liberated from the war in Normandy and although this proved to be a brief respite, it did allow him time to look to his own affairs. Perhaps another factor was that he had become earl of Pembroke: in addition to the status and power and a certain income this gave him, he now had a convenient departure point for the short crossing to Ireland. In fact, it completed the chain of his possessions which ran from Leinster to Striguil to Longueville, with relatively short distances between them. But above all, it was an opportunity for them to see their inheritance, which neither of them had seen previously – instead, they had been obliged to rely upon second-hand knowledge. Seeing Leinster for themselves was an opportunity to assess it and determine how it could be developed to their ideas and satisfaction.

Their other period of residence was an extended visit from 1207 to 1213. It came about as a result of one of Marshal's rare political blunders, which sprang from King John's rapid loss of Normandy, Anjou and Maine to King Philip II of France in the years 1203 and 1205. The collapse of the Angevin empire, especially the loss of Normandy, had serious implications for those Anglo-Norman families in England who also had estates across the Channel. Most were horrified to lose a significant part of their patrimony. Marshal was among them and he may well have felt the loss of his valuable estates at Longueville and Orbec keenly, having only recently come into possession of them, and having expended so much of his time and energy in 1202 and 1203 fighting to stave off this disaster. However, in 1205 he believed he had found a solution. In the course of a diplomatic mission to Philip II, he petitioned the French king to allow him to retain his Normandy estates. Philip was willing to agree, on condition that in order to retain them Marshal should do homage to him. That may possibly have been acceptable to John, but Marshal went a step further by doing liege homage. This was a step too far, in that liege homage carried with it the stipulation that if King John should invade Normandy in an attempt to recover what he had lost and saw as his birthright, Marshal would be obliged to fight for the French king against him. William Marshal may have believed, or hoped, that it would not come to this. He also may have felt that the warm relationship he had enjoyed with John over many years would count in his favour. It was a serious miscalculation. John, who had an inordinately suspicious nature, saw Marshal's action (rightly) as an act of betrayal. Immediately, Marshal, that most astute courtier, lost royal favour, the worst thing that could befall a courtier.

By going to Leinster, Marshal and his countess put distance between themselves and King John. But their leaving England was not a straightforward matter, since crown tenants needed royal permission to leave the realm. This John gave, but only on condition that their eldest son and heir, William, then seventeen years old, was handed over to him as a hostage. It was John's standard means of control against those he mistrusted. Moreover, it was a public statement of the loss of royal favour.

However, this self-imposed exile was a blessing, in that it gave them an opportunity to reassert lordship control over the liberty, which had diminished in the years after Strongbow's death. Their main stumbling block was Meiler Fitz Henry, whom John had appointed justiciar of Ireland in 1200 with a brief to impose greater royal control over the Anglo-Norman baronage there. Marshal's prime concern was to regain the overlordship of

Offaly, with its important castle on the rock of Dunamase, which Fitz Henry refused to concede. Marshal brought his grievance to the notice of the king. Before doing so, however, he took the precaution of securing the support of the other Anglo-Norman landowners, who also felt threatened by Fitz Henry's powers.

John's response was to summon both parties to appear before him at the royal court. Marshal, well aware that refusal would be construed as rebellion, complied in September 1207, accompanied by a number of his household knights. Once in his grasp, John attempted to induce Marshal's knights to leave his service by offering them grants of land and lucrative offices. Eight of them, including Marshal's nephew, John Marshal, took the bait. This sort of desertion was an unforgiveable breach of the feudal code of honour, and rightly earned the contempt and disdain of those who remained loyal.

Marshal, however, had not left Leinster without taking steps to safeguard his position. In a dramatic piece of theatre enacted in Kilkenny Castle, he presented a heavily pregnant Countess Isabel to an assembly of his tenants, appealing to them to protect and keep her safe during his absence, as it was she who was the true lord of Leinster. Theatrically impressive though it was, it was not fiction. He also appointed John d'Earley, Jordan de Sauqueville, Geoffrey Fitz Robert and seven other members of his *mesnie* to govern in his absence.

This was a wise move, since with Marshal at court, John released Fitz Henry to return to Ireland with *carte blanche* to take Leinster, while ordering Earley, Sauqueville and Fitz Robert to return to England or forfeit their estates. It was now that Countess Isabel and the knights of her husband's *mesnie* had to decide whether to fight or capitulate. They chose the former and forged an alliance with another major Anglo-Norman magnate, Hugh de Lacy, created earl of Ulster in 1205.

Complete success justified their stance. Fitz Henry invaded Leinster and burnt the infant town of New Ross. But he then suffered a catastrophic defeat and was captured by the combined forces of de Lacy and Marshal's knights. He had no option but to surrender Offaly and its castle at Dunamase, and all his other properties in Leinster. He was also obliged to give hostages. Among those that took King John's offer and came back with Meiler Fitz Henry to Ireland was a Wexford knight, Philip de Prendergast: he had accompanied Marshal to England and then deserted his lord. He was taken prisoner when Fitz Henry was defeated. His betrayal was the most heinous in feudal terms, in that he had not only allowed himself to be suborned by King John but had actively taken up arms against his lord. It is said that Marshal accepted his submission, but with no more than icy formality. Prendergast's son remained Marshal's hostage in England until 1215. William's nephew John Marshal, another captive, was more readily forgiven: perhaps because he had not been in arms, or perhaps because blood is thicker than water. The other traitors were given the 'the kiss of peace' by William Marshal, which showed he was prepared to draw a line under their treachery but not to restore his benevolence. In contrast, Countess Isabel was all for exacting savage revenge, but her husband was more circumspect, knowing that harsh treatment might provoke an unfavourable reaction.

Meanwhile, back in England, John taunted Marshal, telling him that news had reached him from Ireland informing him of the decisive defeat of his men by Fitz Henry, with many of his knights having been killed. Marshal received the news with equanimity. Sense told him the king was lying – it was unlikely he could have received a message, because the predictably treacherous weather conditions at that time of year meant that ships rarely crossed to and from Ireland during the winter months. When sailings resumed William learned that all was well in Leinster, and John learnt the truth. His response was to confirm Marshal's right to Offaly and to sack Fitz Henry, sending over to Ireland John de Grey, bishop of Norwich, as the new justiciar of Ireland. Fitz Henry disappeared into obscurity, dying in 1220. His departure marked the end of the Strongbow era: he was the last of the 'old Leinster hands'.

King John was not the man to accept defeat at the hands of one of his own subjects: his reaction was always to hammer them into submission. With this intention he mounted an expedition to Ireland with a force of 700 knights and several hundred other troops, landing at Waterford on 20 June 1210.[5] Walter de Lacy, lord of Meath, immediately submitted and was deprived of his lands for five years. His brother, Hugh de Lacy, earl of Ulster, made a show of armed resistance but then fled to Scotland, together with another baron, William de Briouze, lord of Brecon, who was already on the run from John and in fear for his life. John had two grudges against him.

Ten years earlier, John and Briouze had been close associates; Briouze was in fact in high favour as the man who had captured the boy, Arthur of Brittany, who in the opinion of many had a better right to the throne of England than had John. By 1210, however, Briouze was a traitor on the run. The main reason for his fall from favour was money, for which John had an insatiable greed. Foolishly, Briouze had offered the king large sums of money for royal grants of land and official offices. John demanded payment, but Briouze's debt to him was mountainous and well beyond his capacity to pay. In desperation, he rebelled, but when this failed he fled to Ireland with his family, where he had some property and was briefly afforded hospitality by Marshal and the de Lacy brothers, Hugh de Lacy being his son-in-law.

John's arrival in Ireland prompted Briouze and Hugh de Lacy to flee, leaving behind Briouze's wife, Matilda, and their son, both of whom fell into the hands of the king. They were taken to England and incarcerated in a cell at Windsor Castle, where they were left to die of starvation. This act of exceptional barbarity had a singular cause. On an earlier occasion, John had demanded that de Briouze hand over their son as a hostage. Matilda angrily refused, telling the royal officers who had come on this errand that she would never entrust her son to a man who had murdered his own nephew – a fact she must have learnt from her husband, one of the few people with certain knowledge of what had happened to Arthur. It was John's willingness to transgress the behavioural norms of society that helped fuel the intense hatred many members of the baronial community felt towards him.

In contrast, Marshal came through this dangerous time relatively unscathed, a feat he managed in large part through his skills as a courtier. He began by crossing to Pembroke in order to join the royal army before it embarked for Ireland; it was a public gesture of submission.

Then, when John challenged William about his failure to place Briouze in custody on his arrival in Ireland, Marshal put forward two excuses, both of them almost certainly false. He swore that he had been unaware of John's quarrel with Briouze; and he claimed he was a tenant of Briouze in Ireland and therefore, had to honour a vassal's obligation to offer hospitality to his lord. Whether John believed either story is to be doubted, but he seemed to be satisfied with Marshal's act of abasement.

As a result, his punishment was light, handing over to the king the castle at Dunamase and a number of hostages including John de Earley, Jordan de Sauqueville and Geoffrey Fitz Robert, his most trusted and faithful knights. Their retention lasted for only one year, although during that time Geoffrey Fitz Robert died in Hereford Castle. John also issued a new charter for the liberty, which reduced its privileges by transferring to the crown the right to hold episcopal estates when a bishopric was vacant: again, money for King John.

Marshal made further progress towards regaining royal favour by participating in the king's campaign in 1211 against the dynamic and dominant king in north Wales, Llewelyn ap Iorworth. He followed this by persuading the barons of Leinster to renew their oaths of loyalty to John after the exposure of a plot to depose and murder him.

The following year, John recalled Marshal from Ireland. The tensions and mistrust were already rising that would eventually culminate in John putting his seal to Magna Carta in 1215. This made it imperative for John to put aside any remaining doubts about the loyalty of William Marshal and have him in close support.

WILLIAM MARSHAL IN ENGLAND

Marshal remained in England for the final six years of his life: these were indeed very eventful years. The demanding part he was required to play in the political and constitutional crisis of these years banished any hope of returning to Ireland, although his household recognised that should matters become hostile or threatening, Leinster might prove to be a bolthole.[6]

The root of the crisis lay in the relations between King John and the leading members of the English baronage, for the majority of whom he had become immensely tyrannical and threatening to the extent that his most extreme opponents, Eustace de Vesci and Robert Fitz Walter, were determined to depose and murder him. The problem was that John's temperament verged on the paranoid. He regarded the baronage, which he needed to play skilfully, as so congenitally hostile that he felt the need to have them in the grip of his power. His main method of coercion was financial: he contrived to ensnare them by manipulating the rules governing feudal matters, so that he got them so deeply in debt to him it was beyond their capacity to repay. On top of this, men remembered the fate that had befallen young Arthur of Brittany and Matilda de Briouze and her son.

But John had another serious problem, this too of his own making. Since 1207, England had been under a papal interdict, which suspended all church services: in effect, the clergy were brought out on strike by Pope Innocent III. Two years later, matters became worse: the pope excommunicated John, turning him into a social outcast. The cause of the stand-off was the decision to find a replacement as archbishop of Canterbury after Hubert Walter's death in 1205. The king's choice was John de Grey, bishop of Norwich and justiciar of Ireland, but the pope rejected him. After two

years of stalemate, Innocent III finally settled the matter in 1207 by consecrating Stephen Langton, an Englishman and also a distinguished biblical
scholar in Paris, whom he had made a cardinal in 1206. John flatly refused
to accept the appointment or to allow Langton into England. In the hope
of forcing John to accept Stephen Langton, the pope went so far as to give
papal blessing to a proposal by King Philip II of France that he invade
England, depose John and place his own son, Louis, on the English throne,
subject, of course, to his tutelage.

On his return from Ireland, Marshal, in conjunction with other senior
members of John's government, persuaded the king that the only way to
remove the threat to his crown was to make peace with the pope. John
finally agreed to this, and to accept Stephen Langton as archbishop; he
also agreed to reimburse the English church for revenues lost since 1207.
But then John went a step further: he handed over his kingdoms to the
pope, then received them back as a papal vassal, agreeing to pay tribute of
10,000 marks – 7,000 from England and 3,000 from Ireland, the latter an
indication of the extent of English control. John had executed a brilliant
diplomatic coup. At a stroke, the pope had been changed from enemy into
feudal lord, which meant he was obliged to support his vassal in a dispute.[7]
Therefore, Philip II's scheme was superfluous, and his chagrin was made
complete when the English fleet destroyed his naval preparations for an
invasion.

But the problem of the discontented baronage still remained and in
1214 worsened. Baronial opposition grew in strength, coordination and
more importantly, in formulating a clear-headed programme aimed at placing restraint on the king's exercise of regal power. Once the rebels had
secured control of London, King John had to negotiate. This process
reached its conclusion on 15 June 1215 when, in a meadow by the side of
the river Thames at Runnymede, John's seal was appended to a charter
containing sixty-three clauses covering a wide range of matters of concern
to all legally free English men and women. As early as 1225, this document
was being referred to as Magna Carta, the name by which it has been
known ever since. William Marshal, who had been with the king throughout the entire crisis, played a leading part in bringing it to a conclusion.
He was a member of the king's negotiating team who went from Windsor
to London for discussions with the rebel leadership. The final document
was authenticated not by signatures, but by a formal statement of names
of the most prominent witnesses. The clergy were always placed first –
thirteen bishops headed by the archbishop of Canterbury, Stephen

Langton – but heading the list of laymen was William Marshal, earl of Pembroke, an unequivocal pointer to his importance.

King John had no intention of abiding by the restrictions placed upon him by Magna Carta. He agreed to it simply to extricate himself from a political cul-de-sac. Once free, he went on the offensive. His first move was to write to Pope Innocent III, giving him his version of events. Innocent's reply was gratifying: the rebel barons were condemned as contumacious vassals and the charter was declared null and void. Having secured papal confirmation of the validity of his position, John, with his army of mercenaries, set about ravaging the estates of his enemies. His progress was such that the rebels were driven to reactivate the arrangement with Philip II of France, with the result that a French army, commanded by Prince Louis, landed on the south coast in May 1216 and rapidly gained control of large parts of southern and eastern England. Marshal, however, was not involved, having been sent by John to defend the border with Wales.

What the outcome of this civil war with foreign involvement might have been is a matter of pointless speculation, as the context was radically and dramatically transformed on the night of 18/19 October by the death of King John. He died from dysentery at the bishop of Lincoln's castle at Newark-on-Trent. As he lay dying, John begged William Marshal's forgiveness for the wrongs he had done to him and asked him to take care of his nine-year-old son, Henry. Marshal's loyalty would permit nothing but assent. As soon as John's body had been embalmed, Marshal took it for burial in Worcester Cathedral, according to John's wish. They then went on to Gloucester, where John's son was crowned Henry III by the papal legate, Guala Bicchieri, using a lady's gold circlet in lieu of the crown, which was out of reach in the Tower of London. Young Henry, not Louis, was the legitimate king of England, and with papal approval. William Marshal had successfully discharged his first major task.

The nine-year-old Henry III could reign, but he could not rule until he came of age. Meanwhile, his rule of government had to be entrusted to a proxy. With very little discussion, the barons chose Marshal, his only rival being Ranulf, earl of Chester, one of the greatest magnates in England, who would have been preferred by some. Marshal was now nearly seventy years old and this, together with his steadfast commitment to the Angevin dynasty and his long years at the centre of affairs of state, made his selection self-evident. He was therefore designated *rector regis et regni* (regent of the king and the kingdom). In order that Marshal was free to concentrate on the affairs of the country, the day-to-day care and tutelage of the king was taken over by Peter des Roches, bishop of Winchester. As will become clear later, des Roches' influence on the young Henry was to have disruptive consequences.

The first task of the interim government was to establish its uncontested authority over the realm. This was no easy task, as the combined forces of the French invaders and the English rebels outnumbered those under Marshal's command, despite John's death having brought a number of rebels over to the royalist side. Among the rebels was Marshal's eldest son, William II, now in his mid-twenties. Later actions after his father's death reveal that he had a strong commitment to the baronial programme of reform, and this may be why he took the opposite side to that of his father. At the same time we are entitled to speculate that prior to John's death, with the father in one camp it was a sensible precaution to have a son in the other camp, so ensuring the family survival whatever the outcome.

In the spring of 1217, thanks to a blunder by Prince Louis, Marshal gained a priceless advantage. Contrary to basic military wisdom, Louis decided to divide his army, sending half to continue besieging Dover Castle while the rest advanced north, aiming to take the important town and castle of Lincoln. When Marshal's scouts brought this news to him, he calculated that a pitched battle, which all medieval commanders sought to avoid, was worth the risk. He quickly headed for Lincoln, where his rapid advance caught Louis's force (which was made up of French and English rebels) unawares as they laid siege to the castle. A confused street battle ensued on 27 May, taking place in an area confined within the city walls between the castle and the cathedral.[8] For once, we have reliable numbers of participants: there were around 400 knights with Marshal; about 600 rebels. However, a large number of troops of lower calibre would also have been engaged. The rebel commander, Thomas, count of La Perche, was killed, making a last stand at the west front of the cathedral. Once the rebels broke, Marshal's forces routed and pursued them as they fled down what is still and very accurately called Steep Hill, its precipitous descent allowing no time for the rebels to regroup. At the end of the day they had left their commander dead and many more of their number to be taken prisoner; Marshal held at least 380 very ransom worthy rebel knights. The account of the battle records the extent to which William Marshal was in his element: so eager was he to plunge into the mêlée, he forgot to put on his helmet and had to be reminded by his squire. Without doubt, this seventy-year-old warrior thoroughly enjoyed his last taste of combat. He was back where he started in what seemed like a tournament mêlée.

On learning of the disaster at Lincoln, Prince Louis abandoned the siege at Dover Castle and hurried north to secure control of London. There followed three months of negotiation between Marshal and Prince Louis, the latter probably playing for time in the hope of getting reinforcements from France. And indeed, another attempt was made in late August, ending in disaster on the 24th when a French naval convoy was intercepted and destroyed off Sandwich by the English fleet. This time, Marshal was restrained from taking part. Instead, William had a ringside seat on the cliffs overlooking the Channel, accompanied by the young King Henry III. This second defeat convinced Louis that his cause was lost and he rapidly negotiated repatriation terms for the French prisoners. England was now free of King John and King Philip of France. It was William Marshal's second triumph.

It now remained to bring those still in rebellion back into the fold and begin the restoration of normal peacetime government. Although bearing the title of rector, Marshal was now essentially a figurehead who gave validity to the work of experienced administrators – notably Peter des Roches, bishop of Winchester, and Hubert de Burgh, whom John had appointed justiciar of England in 1215 and who was to hold the post until 1232. Above them stood the papal legate. Between January 1216 and September 1218 the post was held by Guala Bicchieri, cardinal-priest of S. Martino. He was replaced by the papal chamberlain Pandulf, who became bishop of Norwich but was retained as papal legate until 1226. They played a major part in restoring stability to the kingdom not only as the pope's ambassadors, but also his representatives as the feudal overlord of England and Ireland. Nevertheless, Marshal could not be away long from the centres of government at London and Westminster. Going to Ireland was out of the question for him and therefore, frustratingly for historians and the reader, we have no information on how Leinster was being governed or indeed who was exercising the role.

In 1219, the end of Marshal's career and life came quickly. In January, for the first time in his life, he became seriously ill; he was suffering constant pain, and it was apparent that his death was not far off. As spring approached he retired to his favourite home, Caversham Manor, where he struggled to carry on but soon became too ill to continue in office and resigned as rector.

As the end approached, Marshal laid down how his estate was to be divided. Most significant was that Countess Isabel should receive back all that she had brought to the marriage, particularly Leinster. Only after her death was it to pass to their eldest son, William II. Marshal's debt of gratitude to his wife could not have been more clearly stated. To his second son, Richard, he gave the manor of Longueville in Normandy, which required Richard to transfer his allegiance from King Henry III of England to King Philip of France. In this is a clear indication that in the minds of many men of the time, England and France were simply parts of the Frankish and Francophone world: living in Normandy was no different to living in England. Marshal's third son, Gilbert, was expected to join the church and achieve a high ecclesiastical office. This was a standard part of family planning, designed to ensure a baronial role in government of the church as well as of the state. To his fourth son, Walter, he gave the estate based upon Goodrich Castle in Herefordshire, a property given to him by King John in 1204. But to his youngest son, Ancel, he proposed to give nothing, believing he should have to make his own way in the world, as his father had done to him as a younger son. This was too harsh for Marshal's *fidus Achates*, John de Earley, who shamed his master into providing Ancel with land in Ireland capable of yielding an annual income of £140.

Then William Marshal prepared for his impending death by having John de Earley fetch from Striguil the two lengths of silk he had brought back from Jerusalem in 1186, which were to cover his body prior to burial. He also ordered eighty-five fur-lined scarlet robes to be given to his retainers. With everything in place, he embraced Countess Isabel for the last time and then he was inducted into the Order of the Temple by Aimery St Maur, the Master of the Order in England. He had always been a knight; now he was also a monk. He passed away around midday on Tuesday 14 May 1219 and was buried in the round church of the Order's new preceptory in London. The ceremony was conducted by the archbishop of Canterbury, Stephen Langton, who described Marshal as 'the greatest knight to be found in all the world'.

Since his burial on 19 or 20 May 1219, William Marshal has not been left entirely in peace.[9] When the Temple church was extended late in Henry III's reign, his tomb effigy was moved away from the spot where he lay. Then in the 1840s the floor of the church was lifted to reveal a row of coffins in front of where the high altar had stood. One of them held the skeleton of a man six feet tall, which is believed to be that of William Marshal. The final indignity was inflicted by a German bomb on 10 May 1941 (very close to the 722th anniversary of his burial). The bomb damaged the church extensively, including Marshal's effigy. Happily, the 800th anniversary in 2019 passed without incident.

Countess Isabel's widowhood was brief, but not entirely trouble-free. Her husband's wishes were flouted by the regency government of Henry III when she was given only Leinster as her dower. Apart from this, we know little of her life thereafter; only that she died a year after her husband, sometime in 1220 – of what, and where, we have no knowledge. However, we do know that she chose to be buried alongside her mother, Aoife, and her de Clare ancestors in Tintern Abbey, Monmouthshire, though it is believed that her heart was taken to Ireland for burial in St Mary's Church, New Ross, Co. Wexford, which she and her husband had founded. If so, a vital part of her had come back to Ireland.

6

Sons of William Marshal

THE MEDIEVAL WORLD

Before looking at the individual careers of the Marshal sons, we need to recognise that the world in which they lived and operated was significantly changed from that which their father experienced when he obtained the liberty of Leinster and earl marshalship, and in two fundamental ways. In place of two kings with strong personalities and masterful temperaments, England (and the Anglo-Norman controlled parts of Ireland) now had a monarch who came to the throne at the age of nine. Consequently, the government was in the hands of a regency until he came of age and could assume personal control. Then he had to learn the art and skills of kingship. It has to be said that Henry III was not an apt pupil, in particular in developing the ability and confidence needed to dominate. There is no doubt that he wished to rule, but to do so untrammelled by controlling forces – particularly the barons, with whom he was not naturally at ease. In consequence, to find congenial support he gravitated to favourites, many of them from Poitou; notably his greedy half-brothers, the sons of Hugh de Lusignan, count of La Marche, and his father's widow, Isabel of Angoulême. After his marriage in 1236 to Eleanor of Provence, his favourites also included some individuals who followed her from her homeland, the county of Savoy. It might be said that Henry III was easily led by favourites, especially foreign favourites – and they invariably aroused jealousy and suspicion, all the more so since they were often enriched by his lavish and lucrative gifts of lands and offices.[1]

The Irish situation too was marred by Henry's eastward foreign policy ambitions. These were to regain control of the lost provinces of the Angevin empire across the Channel. In the end, by the treaty of Paris, signed in

1259 with the French king, Louis IX (St Louis), he came to terms with the loss and formally relinquished his claims to Normandy, Anjou, Maine and Poitou. He also sought to secure the title of Holy Roman Emperor for his brother, Richard, earl of Cornwall; and to gratify the papacy he agreed to finance the conquest of the kingdom of Sicily, which would be given to his younger son, Edmund.

With his attention directed eastward, Henry largely ignored looking westward towards Ireland. Anglo-Norman control was being expanded by ambitious men like Richard de Burgh in Connacht and Hugh de Lacy in Ulster (see the Afterword). A government did exist in Dublin, but it did not have the benefit of a permanent royal presence – had that been the case it might have brought about a united Ireland, albeit under English control. The fragmented nature of the Irish political structure then presented Henry III with an ideal opportunity, had he wished to exert control over the power and avarice of the Anglo-Norman barons. But instead of seizing the chance to exercise kingship, he dissipated his time and energy in chasing the unrealistic and obsessive ambition of regaining his lost French territories. This was never going to be realised in the face of a wealthy, powerful and fully experienced French monarchy; nor did he have any support from his barons. It was a lost cause.

The other fundamental difference was that after 1215, English society and politics operated within the framework created by Magna Carta; this was also true of Ireland, where the terms of Magna Carta applied after 1217. After 1215, and particularly after the definitive version of Magna Carta was uttered in 1225, all members of society were aware of what rights it had granted to them. The barons retained the collective awareness they had developed during the crisis and were committed to the concept that they, together with the bishops, were the natural advisers to the king, who they believed was obligated to consult them on all matters of national importance. Henry III never developed a comfortable relationship with his barons, partly because he lacked political nous, but fundamentally because at heart he wished to be able to exercise royal power without external restraint. There was an ongoing tension between king and barons that exploded into full-scale constitutional crisis and civil war in the 1260s. As leading members of the baronage, the brothers William and Richard Marshal were involved in two short but serious political crises – both starting in England, but the more serious of the two spreading to Leinster. Throughout, their actions make it clear that their attitude was very pro-Magna Carta.

WILLIAM AND ISABEL'S FIVE SONS

When William Marshal died in 1219, the liberty of Leinster he had inherited and then developed appeared to have a cloudless future: dynastic succession assured by the five sons born to him and Isabel, all of whom grew to manhood. But the fates were unkind; although each of the sons married, none produced a legitimate heir. In consequence the liberty fell back into the hands of the crown. Its future will be revealed after the lives of the five men have been examined.

William Marshal II, Earl of Pembroke and Earl Marshal, 1219–1231

William, the eldest and named for his father, was probably born in 1190, and was thirty years of age when he acquired control of the liberty of Leinster in 1220 on the death of his mother. He was now earl of Pembroke, lord of Leinster in Ireland and lord of Striguil in Wales, and earl marshal of England; he also held most of the Marshal manors in England. The spread of his estate and the wealth it generated placed him in the topmost rank of the English baronage. Sadly his marriage to Alice, daughter of his father's close friend Baldwin of Bethune, lasted only a year owing to her early death. His standing was loudly proclaimed, however, when he married as his second wife Eleanor, sister of Henry III; and later by the marriage of his sister Isabel to the king's younger brother Richard, earl of Cornwall.

Throughout the eleven years he was earl of Pembroke, he was engaged in public life, the more so since he was earl marshal of England and therefore an important official at the royal court. He spent four of the eleven years in Ireland, two of them as justiciar of Ireland, the king's deputy, between 1224 and 1226. There is good evidence that he was active in pushing on with the developments his parents had initiated in Leinster, one of which was the completion of St Mary's church, New Ross; and he was energetic in his support of the church, founding in Kilkenny the first Dominican friary in Ireland.[2] As will be explained later, he was also the 'secular arm' called upon to assist and protect the papal legate sent to impose tighter control and regulation on the abbeys of the Cistercian Order in Ireland.

But his role as earl marshal also took him to France in 1230 with Henry III's expedition to Nantes in Brittany, with whose duke the king had an alliance.[3] Henry's aim was to conduct a sweep through Poitou in an attempt at persuading the Poitevin nobles to return their allegiance to the English crown. However, the mission was aborted because of an outbreak of disease. King Henry and his brother Richard, earl of Cornwall, hastily scampered back to England with part of the army, leaving William Marshal II in command of those who remained. William's return with the remaining army was not long delayed, and he was able to attend his sister Isabel's marriage to Richard, earl of Cornwall, in 1231.

Alas, a few weeks after the wedding festivities he was dead. He was forty-one years old. There was no evidence of foul play, nor knowledge of any previous particular health problem. One obvious speculation is the possibility that he contracted the same unknown disease that abruptly ended the Poitevin expedition.

We are indebted to William Marshal II for his decision to commission a memoir of his father.[4] This must have been an act of filial piety, but equally it is evidence that William Marshal I was widely seen as a remarkable man. The result was a poem of 19,214 lines, written in French by a man named John, a native of Touraine, between 1224 and 1226. It carries a wealth of detail about William's life and is considered to be a particularly reliable source about his later years, for which the poet could also call upon the reminiscences of John de Earley and other men who had been in close contact with William Marshal I.

Richard Marshal, Earl of Pembroke and Earl Marshal, 1232–1234

William Marshal II's failure to produce an heir meant that his successor was his brother Richard, born in 1191. About Richard's right to succeed there was no dispute, only an obstacle. This was because previously, for over ten years, he had been a subject of the king of France. This was a necessary condition if he was to retain in accordance with his father's will the lordships of Longueville and Orbec. His commitment to France was enhanced by his marriage to a Breton heiress, Gervaise de Dinan, with whom came the lordship of Dinan and the title of Viscount Rohan. In order to succeed to the title and estates in England, Wales and Ireland, Richard would need to relinquish his Norman property and his allegiance to the French king, and then swear allegiance to Henry III. In the end this is what happened, although his entitlement was withheld for a year owing to the misgivings of a number of people, one of whom was King Henry III.

Richard's tenure of the Marshal inheritance was brief, cut short by his murder in 1234. The root of this tragedy lay in the first constitutional crisis of Henry III's reign. It began with a change of government in England.[5] In 1232, Hubert de Burgh, who had been justiciar of England since 1215, was summarily dismissed by the king and placed under arrest. No tears were shed: by this date, de Burgh's use of power to aggrandise himself and his family had made him widely unpopular, and he had lost the king's confidence by his lukewarm attitude to the royal expedition to Poitou.

But to secure his downfall required the intervention of an agent. This was Peter des Roches, bishop of Winchester since 1205 and the king's official guardian until he attained his majority.[6] Des Roches then spent the next five years abroad on crusade. On his return he readily persuaded the disgruntled and gullible Henry that de Burgh's administration had been grossly inefficient and that he had just the man to put things right: his nephew, Peter des Rivaux. In fact, this change of regime did little more than change the crew of the gravy train. But they overstepped the mark by treading heavily on the toes of Richard Marshal. Using their influence with the king, they secured the confiscation of a Wiltshire manor from Gilbert Basset and its transfer to one of his adherents, Peter de Maulay, the man suspected of carrying out the murder of Arthur of Brittany. The Basset family's roots were in Longueville; consequently they had a long association with the Marshal family and indeed, many members of the Basset family had been in service with the Marshals. It was therefore natural that Gilbert Basset should turn to Richard Marshal for support. This Richard Marshal readily gave, for King Henry's action was a blatant abuse of royal power. In effect, Henry was declaring himself to be above the law. This was his natural inclination, which was fully encouraged by Peter des Roches. Both men, in fact, looked back to King John's reign as 'the good old days'. The upshot was a minor constitutional crisis akin to that which led to Magna Carta in 1215. This rapidly got out of hand, escalating into a small-scale civil war. Henry renounced his feudal obligation to Richard Marshal, who found a willing ally in Llywelyn ap Iorworth, king of Gwynedd (North Wales), and together they ravaged the Welsh border and burnt the town of Shrewsbury. But before matters became even more serious, a group of bishops negotiated a truce in order to allow peace talks to take place.

This respite allowed Richard Marshal to cross to Leinster, where his castles were being seized by the justiciar of Ireland, Maurice Fitz Gerald, in alliance with Richard de Burgh – both of whom wished to downgrade Marshal's influence in Ireland.[7] In this they had royal encouragement, Henry making it clear to his officials in Ireland that he too wished them to tighten their grip on Marshal, who in his eyes was a traitor. A conference was arranged between Marshal and his opponents to meet on the Curragh of Kildare. Richard Marshal believed its purpose was to negotiate the return of his property, but his enemies had darker intentions and talk soon gave way to combat. Marshal was outnumbered, as he had only a small retinue of his household knights with him and many of his Irish feudal tenants refused to fight for him. Although severely wounded, he managed to escape southwards to Kilkenny Castle, and after lingering a few days he died there on 16 April 1234. However, there were suspicious uncertainties about his death, particularly in relation to the doctor sent to treat his wounds. There was a rumour that he was in fact recovering, and it was the doctor who brought about his death. The murder of an earl caused consternation throughout the baronage in both Ireland and England and had serious repercussions for the king and his government. Peter des Roches and Peter des Rivaux were removed from office and fled the country. Henry III was sufficiently shaken and concerned that he would be seriously compromised by having declared Marshal to be a traitor, that he felt it wise to seek sanctuary for a time in Westminster Abbey. There were, and still are, lingering doubts about the circumstances of Richard Marshal's death.

Short though his time in Ireland was, Richard Marshal made two significant contributions to Leinster. The first was the foundation of a Franciscan friary in Kilkenny, the first in Ireland.[8] The fact that both major orders of mendicants came early to Kilkenny is perhaps a pointer to the growth and importance of the town. It may also be a sign that Richard did not intend to be outdone by his older brother, William.

His other contribution was the deforestation of the forests of Old Ross and Taghmon,[9] which formed an almost continuous block of land between Carrick on the river Slaney and the river Barrow, a short distance downstream from New Ross. The full significance of this act can be understood only in the context of the development of royal forests from the days of King William I, who introduced them into England.

In this context the meaning of the word 'forest' was essentially legal, but not botanical.[10] A 'forest' was a defined area that would include woodland, but also moorland or heathland and farming communities. All who lived in a forest were subject to a special 'forest law', infractions of which carried harsh penalties, both corporal and financial. Behind the jolly tales of Robin Hood and his band of merry men in Sherwood Forest lay a grim and often tragic reality. The sole purpose of forests and forest law was to safeguard and preserve the royal monopoly of hunting red, fallow and roe deer, along with wild boar, known collectively as *venison*, and their natural habitat, known as *vert*.

The extent of royal forests in England increased considerably in the reign of Henry II, to a point where about a third of the whole country lay within their bounds. Twenty of England's thirty-nine counties had royal forests, while the entire county of Essex was subject to forest law. Not surprisingly, the subject of royal forests were of great concern to the barons who formulated Magna Carta, since all of them had land within or near forests and many of them had been punished for infractions of forest law. In the 1215 version of Magna Carta, four chapters were devoted to the subject; but when a revised version was issued in 1217, these chapters were omitted and replaced by a separate document of seventeen chapters known as the 'Charter of the Forest'. This had three main thrusts: all forests created since the accession of Henry II in 1154 were to be deforested; the number of officers administering the forests was to be reduced; and all forms of physical punishment were prohibited.

When the forests of Old Ross and Taghmon were created is not known, but it is safe to assume it was in Strongbow's time. As the successor to King Diarmait, the quasi-regal status of his liberty would have given him the right, which he would have exercised to underline his authority. Richard Marshal's decision to deforest most likely stemmed from the issue in 1225 of what proved to be the final and definitive version of Magna Carta. It was not a free gift, however: those who stood to benefit were required to pay him, collectively, the hefty sum of 600 marks (£400). Observance of Magna Carta's precepts could be profitable as well as virtuous.

Gilbert Marshal, Earl of Pembroke and Earl Marshal, 1234–1241

Although Richard married, he and his wife also failed to produce children, and therefore on Richard's death in 1234 the Marshal inheritance descended to his brother Gilbert (b. 1194), the third son of William I and Isabel de Clare. Early in his life it was decided that Gilbert would have a career in the church. Such decisions were common enough in baronial families. A clever young man with good connections might hope to rise to high office in the church, thereby securing a good income and political influence. Why Gilbert was chosen is not known, though it is fair to assume that as the third son, it would be unlikely that he would succeed to the Marshal inheritance. Also, he probably had the scholarly aptitude that was by now required of a cleric. He is known to have taken minor orders, but not to have proceeded to the priesthood. After 1225, he acquired a number of benefices, presumably ones that did not carry the obligation of 'cure of souls'; and in 1229 he paid a visit to the Holy Land, which suggests his commitment to a clerical career had some depth. But in 1234 he also went to Ireland with his brother Richard. This may have been out of sibling loyalty, although it is fair to say that all of the five Marshal brothers did seem to have had a genuine commitment to Magna Carta, what it stood for and the principles it enshrined.

It was Richard's murder that caused Gilbert to abandon his ecclesiastical career and accept a destiny in the secular world. His transition to layman was marked in two very public ways: he was knighted by the king, and at Berwick-upon-Tweed he married Margaret, a sister of Alexander II, King of Scots, a lady at one time considered as a possible bride for King Henry III. Curiously, Gilbert's first official duty as earl marshal was to supervise the coronation of the lady Henry did marry in 1236: Eleanor of Provence. That same year, Gilbert publicly 'took the cross'; that is, he vowed to fight for Christendom, a vow he renewed in 1239. Such vows were quite common among the baronial classes, but were more often broken than kept; however, they were seen as evidence of good intent.

Gilbert was embroiled in the second crisis of the 1230s, this too arising from Henry III's ill-considered actions.[11] The central figure was Eleanor, Henry's sister, but more particularly William Marshal II's widow and therefore Gilbert's sister-in-law. The other main character was Simon de Montfort, who in the 1260s was to lead a rebellion against Henry that provoked a major civil war. Montfort had arrived from France in 1231 to claim the earldom of Leicester, formerly held by his ancestor, who had died in 1190. He rapidly became a royal favourite, so that the king readily granted his wish to marry his widowed sister Eleanor. But Henry then blundered by arranging for their marriage to be held in secret. The reason for this was that following the death of her first husband, William Marshal II, Eleanor had taken a vow of chastity – a serious act, made more so by being undertaken in the presence of the archbishop of Canterbury. Consequently, her second marriage was seen as sacrilegious. Again, Henry III had made improper use of royal power, which caused deep disquiet in baronial circles that included the king's brother Richard, earl of Cornwall.

Gilbert Marshal, like his own brother Richard, met a violent end. His death was as a participant in a tournament held in Hertfordshire in 1241, against the express wishes of King Henry. Gilbert died as a result of injuries sustained when he was unhorsed and one of his feet caught in the stirrup; his panic-stricken animal dragged him a considerable distance along the ground before being brought to a halt. Mortally injured, Gilbert was taken to Hertford Priory, where he died. His body was later taken for burial in the church of the New Temple in London, where he was laid to rest with his father and his oldest brother, William. Gilbert's marriage to Margaret, sister of the Scottish king, did not provide him with an heir. He is known to have fathered a daughter by a mistress, but being illegitimate the girl could not be involved in the succession, which passed to his brother, Walter.

Walter Marshal, Earl of Pembroke and Earl Marshal, 1241–1245

About the fourth and fifth Marshal sons little is known. Walter, who was born in 1196, succeeded Gilbert to all the Marshal lands and titles as of right in 1241 – although because he too had been at the unauthorised tournament where Gilbert met with fatal injuries, Henry III punished his disobedience by delaying his succession for a year. The consequence of this was that Walter was in possession of the Marshal inheritance for only four years, 1242–5. He died suddenly at Goodrich Castle (the lordship being a gift to William Marshal I from King John in 1204, and bequeathed to Walter in his father's will) on 24 November 1245. The cause of his death is not known. He was buried at Tintern Abbey, his mother's resting place. Although Walter had married Margaret de Quincy, countess of Lincoln, there were no children of the marriage.

Ancel (or Anselm) Marshal, Master Marshal, 1245

The Marshal family inheritance now rested with the youngest brother, Ancel, born c. 1202. His succession lasted for a far shorter time than any of his elder brothers: barely a month. In fact, his sudden death at Chepstow on 23 December 1245 gave too little time for the formalities to take place that would have made him earl of Pembroke and lord of Leinster, and although he inherited the title of master marshal upon his brother Walter's death, there was not enough time for him to become earl marshal. Ancel had also married, his wife being Maud de Bohun, the daughter of Humphrey de Bohun, earl of Hereford; but sadly, their marriage too failed to produce children. Ancel was buried at Tintern Abbey alongside his family.

A FAILURE OF SUCCESSION

The liberty of Leinster lasted intact for only another twenty-six years after the death of William Marshal I in 1219, coming to an end with Ancel's death in 1245. During those years, the lordship of the liberty had changed hands five times in an unbroken sequence to the five Marshal sons, as a consequence of consistent reproductive failure to provide an heir. Although all five brothers married (one more than once), none of the marriages produced children. For this unremitting failure, there is no satisfactory explanation. Male infertility cannot entirely be ruled out, except in the case of Gilbert, who, ironically given his early clerical career, is believed to have fathered a daughter by an unknown mistress whom he named Isabel, for his mother. Female infertility is not a full explanation either, given that some of the brothers' widows bore children to their subsequent husbands. Contemporaries, of course, lacked our medical knowledge, although those in Leinster did have their own convincing explanation: it was a curse laid on the family by Ailbe O Maelmuídhe, bishop of Ferns (1186–1223), following William Marshal I's refusal to return property he had seized from the episcopal estate in 1208.

BREAKUP OF THE LIBERTY OF LEINSTER

With Ancel's death, the liberty of Leinster as created by King Henry II came to an end as an entity. As it had been a tenancy-in-chief, possession automatically reverted to the crown pending an inquest that would determine who was the rightful heir. About this there could be little dispute: none of William Marshal's sons had produced a legitimate child, male or female. Consequently, the heirs to the Marshal inheritance were his five daughters, each of whom would be entitled to an equal share.[12]

The essential preliminary was a series of inquests to determine the annual value of the liberty. Because of the size and complexity of the liberty, and there being five heirs, this process took two years to complete. The result was announced on 3 May 1247 in the King's Court, then staying at the royal manor of Woodstock in Oxfordshire, now famous as the site of Blenheim Palace. The annual value of the liberty was declared to be £1,716 7s 8½d, and each share to be £343 5s 6½d. The arithmetic was simple; what was not, was assigning properties that would yield precisely these sums. Consequently, while attempts were made to create compact blocks of land, this could not be entirely achieved.

The issue was even further complicated by the fact that by the time the inheritance was completed, four of the heirs were dead. The only daughter still living was the eldest, Matilda, and she died the following year. So, in the end, the true heirs to the Marshal estate were William and Isabel's grandchildren, by their daughters. In three of the five cases the issue was clear-cut; but in two others there was no male heir, only daughters. As a result, the number of participants in the inheritance rose from five to thirteen.

To go into detail about each case would be an exercise in genealogy and therefore I have reduced information to the barest minimum. The five sisters are listed in order of seniority:

Matilda: 1st m. Hugh Bigod, 3rd earl of Norfolk
 2nd m. William de Warenne, earl of Surrey
 Heir: her son Roger, 5th earl of Norfolk
Joan: m. Warin de Montchesni
 Heir: her daughter Joan m. William de Valence, half-brother of
 King Henry III, created earl of Norfolk in 1264
Isabel: 1st m. Gilbert de Clare, earl of Gloucester and Hertford
 2nd m. Richard, earl of Cornwall, brother of King Henry III
 Heir: her son Richard, earl of Gloucester and Hertford
Sibyl: m. William de Ferrers, earl of Derby
 Heirs: seven daughters, all married
Eva: m. William de Briouze, grandson of Matilda de Briouze, who
 was murdered by King John
 Heirs: three daughters, all married

The fact that ten of the heirs were daughters, all of whom married and united their shares of the estate with their husband's estates, meant the early fragmentation of the estate built up by William Marshal I.

Two further questions remained to be answered. One concerned who would acquire the role and title of earl marshal, and the answer was straightforward: by seniority, it had to go to the heir of Matilda, the eldest of William Marshal's daughters, who died the year following her inheritance. The recipient was her son Roger Bigod, 5th earl of Norfolk, who died without heirs in 1306. King Edward I then bestowed both titles, earl of Norfolk and earl marshal, on his younger son, Thomas of Brotherton. From that point on the two titles have descended together, the only change being that in 1397 the Norfolk title was elevated from earl to duke. Today the titles are held by Edward FitzAlan-Howard, 18th duke of Norfolk, earl of Arundel and earl marshal. He is the premier duke and earl of England. Unless there is a break in tradition, he, or his successor, will be responsible for arranging the coronation of the next British monarch, just as his predecessor, Gilbert Marshal, did for that of Queen Eleanor in 1236.

The other question related to the feudal service of one hundred knights owed to the crown by the lordship of the liberty of Leinster. In practical terms, this amounted to deciding who would be responsible for paying the 'royal service' of £2 (40 shillings) on every knight's fee. The allocation was as follows: Kildare was to be responsible for two fifths, that is, £66 13s 4d; Carlow, Kilkenny and Wexford were each to be responsible for one fifth, that is, £44 8s 10½d. This gave a total sum of £200. With the administration completed, the liberty of Leinster ceased to exist.

Carlow Castle. The one remaining side of the thirteenth-century quadrilateral castle built on the motte of its predecessor, lowered to provide a larger building platform. (Clare H. Lomas)

Inistioge Bridge, Co. Kilkenny. At this point, the River Nore (which flows from left to right) reaches its tidal limit. The bridge was built in 1763 as a replacement for one destroyed by floods. (Clare H. Lomas)

Thomastown, Co. Kilkenny. Thomas Fitz Anthony would readily recognise the basic features of the borough he founded: rectangular market place; parish church at the far end; road layout; the original burgage width appears to have been retained by several present-day shops. (Clare H. Lomas)

Grennan Castle, Co. Kilkenny. This castle, which retains the original Irish name for the area, was built by Thomas Fitz Anthony on the opposite side of the River Nore to Thomastown as a residence and as a statement of lordship. (Clare H. Lomas)

St Canice's Cathedral, Kilkenny. The lancet windows attest to its thirteenth-century construction. The ninth-century round tower, however, is proof that the site had long been of ecclesiastical importance. (Clare H. Lomas)

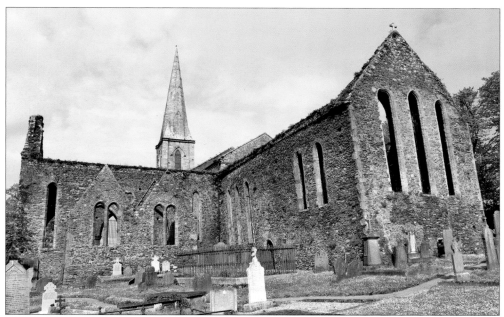

St Mary's Church, New Ross. The ruined remains of the choir and transepts of this once splendid parish church founded by William and Isabel Marshal. The spire is that of the early nineteenth-century church which replaced the original thirteenth-century nave. (Clare H. Lomas)

Tintern Abbey. The substantial ruins of the Cistercian abbey on the shores of Bannow Bay, Co. Wexford, founded by William Marshal to redeem his vow made during a stormy crossing from Wales, hence sometimes known as Tintern *de Voto*. Its original complement of monks was drawn from his wife's family foundation at Tintern Abbey, Monmouthshire, hence Tintern *Parva*. (Clare H. Lomas)

St Mullin's Motte, Co. Carlow. This well-manicured motte, originally surmounted by a wooden stockade or tower, would have been a dramatic statement of lordship, as well as dominating the gorge of the River Barrow. (Clare H. Lomas)

The Long Man. This effigy of Sir Thomas de Cantwell in the ruins of Kilfane Church(Co. Kilkenny) splendidly – and accurately – illustrates the Norman knights who conquered and settled in Leinster in the years after 1169. (George Munday/Alamy)

The Marriage of Aoife and Strongbow. Daniel Maclise's 1854 painting of the wedding of Aoife and Strongbow is an attempt not so much to accurately portray the event, but to highlight the symbolism of the occasion. (The Picture Art Collection/Alamy)

'Arrogant Trespass: The Normans Landing at Bannow', panel 3 of the Ros Tapestry, New Ross, Co. Wexford, Ireland. (Reproduced by kind permission of New Ross Needlecraft Limited / Grace Hall Photography)

Jerpoint Abbey. One of the fifteen Cistercian houses founded prior to the Norman invasion that were severely disciplined by the Cistercian 'visitor' Stephen de Lexington in 1228. (Clare H. Lomas)

Jerpoint Abbey Cloister. The cloister arcade showing added decorative carvings of an ecclesiastic and a knight. They would almost certainly be painted in bright colours, showing how far the monks had drifted from the original severely austere Cistercian style. (Clare H. Lomas)

PART III: IMPACT

The third part of this book attempts to assess how Anglo-Norman and Cambro-Norman settlement in Ireland changed social practices and economic institutions in Leinster. In effect, this means the extent to which the changes the settlers brought with them from England and Wales were imposed upon Ireland to produce something new and alien, or to modify what was there already. The picture that emerges is reminiscent of a jigsaw puzzle with most of the pieces missing. Largely this is due to the lack of records, either because none were written down, or because what was recorded has been lost.

It is also important to remember that on the eve of the invasion, neither Irish nor English society was static – therefore, had there been no alien intrusion, society in Leinster from 1170 to 1245 would still have changed through natural evolution. This said, there is little doubt that, to use Billy Colfer's striking phrase, 'an arrogant trespass' did skew the liberty's development.

Imposition of a Feudal Structure

FEUDALISM

It will already be apparent that the world with which we are concerned was a feudal world. It is therefore right to establish how the 'feudal system', as it is frequently called, functioned, and how it was brought to Ireland from England 'ready-made'. It will then be possible to see how it was bolted on to a very different Irish society. But before this can be done, we need a number of preliminary points clarified.

First, the word *feudalism* did not enter the English language until the late seventeenth century, at a time when what it described had already disappeared or been abolished. It then became a pejorative adjective: to be feudal was to be backward, crude and unenlightened. This misinterpretation of feudalism hinders a proper understanding of the intricacies of the basic structure of medieval society throughout most of Western Europe. Our understanding of it is undoubtedly hampered by its esoteric terminology, most of which is in Old French or Late Latin. While it would be readily intelligible to the people of the time, to us it is archaic and without obvious meaning: put simply, its terms need to be translated or explained. In a nutshell, feudalism was a clearly delineated social structure that met the needs and sat well with the conditions of its time. It had a code of conduct that laid stress on courage, loyalty, trust and honour, concepts which men and women were brought up to respect and accept as right. These were the essential ingredients in feudal society; to live by these rules was an aspiration well founded; to betray this code of conduct not only brought opprobrium to the perpetrator's name but also disgrace to his family.

Closely allied with feudalism was another foreign concept: chivalry.[1] The link between the two is clear: the root is the French word *cheval* (horse), from which comes *chevalier* (horseman, but more particularly, knight). Chivalry cannot easily be defined, but it can be seen gradually pervading feudal society, guiding it from crude barbarity towards greater order, restraint and sophistication.

The definition of chivalry may be elusive, but its formative, behavioural influences on the knightly upper crust of medieval society are more readily pinpointed. Wealth was certainly one aspect, particularly as a means of acquiring the rich quality goods emanating from the near and far east. The church contributed by gradually securing a degree of male restraint in dealings with non-combatants, particularly women, children and churchmen. It also preached strict rules governing personal and family relationships, although these may have been more readily absorbed through popular literature, which gave emphasis to order in sexual matters and in fighting only for righteous causes.

The evolving chivalric society developed its own outward symbols: fashion and opulence in dress; heraldry to proclaim status and lineage; and exclusive societies. The orders of chivalry were founded in all European kingdoms from the fourteenth century, the earliest being the Order of the Garter, founded *c.* 1350 in England by King Edward III and still in existence today. Finally, it is worth noting that William Marshal, who features so prominently in this book, was looked upon as an exemplar of chivalric knighthood.

The feudal structure imposed on Ireland in the twelfth and thirteenth centuries was essentially that which was imposed upon England in the years after 1066.[2] The use of the strong word 'imposed' is valid, since it accurately describes what happened. This was primarily down to one man, William II, duke of Normandy, who invaded England in 1066 and was crowned King William I. As William's claim to England was by right of conquest, it became his property; he was the sole owner. However, those who came with him to fight in his battles did so in the expectation of reward. The recompense they duly received from the king was in the form of land, not as owners but as his tenants. They were known as tenants-in-chief, and as such they owed him rent, which took the form of an obligation to supply specified numbers of fully armed and equipped knights: heavy cavalry. The numbers imposed upon the tenants-in-chief varied, and were individual and specific; in no way were they based upon a formula. Having received his grant of land, every tenant-in-chief was at liberty to grant parts of his acquired estate to members of the contingent of knights which he had raised and commanded. That process, known as subinfeudation, mirrored the arrangements of that between the tenant-in-chief and the king; they were in effect what we would recognise as sub-tenants. What was granted to them, however, was known as a knight's fee or fees, meaning the service of a specified number of knights.

The relationship between the king and his tenants-in-chief, and then between them and their sub-tenants, was far from being casual. It was in fact created in a formal, public, quasi-religious ceremony which had a psychological basis. It required the tenant, the *vassal*, to kneel before his *lord*, with his hands clasped together as in prayer. The lord then placed his hands around those of his vassal, and in this position the vassal swore *homage* and *fealty* to his lord. Homage meant that the vassal took possession of the land the lord had granted to him, for which he became the lord's *man*, that is, his follower and the performer of the service the lord imposed upon that land. Fealty was the oath of loyalty, even unto death, in return for which the lord granted him his support and protection. This feudal contract was binding and it was lifelong, broken only if either party proved to be grossly and wilfully delinquent in the performance of their obligations. However, it was possible for a vassal to renounce his fealty. This required a formal act, known as a *diffidatio* (from which the term 'defiance' is derived); this was an act not lightly undertaken. All these acts of service, loyalty and trust, being at the heart of the feudal system, were essential for it to operate smoothly. Unfortunately, it often fell short of expectations. Not surprisingly, as in all human institutions and organisations, levels of performance were often at variance – sometimes grievously so – with what was expected or demanded.

MILITARY SERVICE

The purpose of the feudal contracts William I made with his tenants-in-chief was fundamentally and unambiguously military, to ensure the existence of a large fighting force of trained knights. The total number of knights imposed by William I upon his tenants-in-chief has never been accurately calculated, although it is known to have been at least 4,000. It quickly proved not to be the complete answer, but a basis for the development of a more flexible system for raising an army. This came about in large measure through the answer to a number of contingent questions, perhaps the most urgent being: what should happen if a feudal tenant was unable to meet his military obligation? From early days, kings were prepared to accept, and in fact came to prefer, a money composition known as *scutage* in lieu of service, since this could pay for the hire of more effective mercenary troops, of which there was no shortage. Indeed, knights from all parts of Europe hired themselves out as mercenary warriors.

But what should happen to the military service obligation when a tenant died? Here too, from the outset both parties accepted that the tenancy should be inherited on unchanged terms by the dead tenant's rightful heir, who had to be formally identified. They were then given possession (*seizin*) once they had sworn homage and fealty to their lord and paid an agreed sum of money (*relief*). The latter was in financial terms an inheritance tax, but perhaps more importantly, it reaffirmed the heir's status as a tenant.

However, if the heir or heirs, having been correctly identified, proved to be under age – that is, under the age of twenty-one – they became a ward of the lord, who retained possession of and profits from the land until the ward came of age and could assume the tenancy. If the heir was a male, during his minority his lord would find him a suitable wife, that is, suitable from the lord's point of view. But from time to time tenants died leaving only a daughter, or daughters. Then the estate was distributed accordingly. An only daughter inherited the entire estate; if there was more than one daughter, the estate was divided equally between them; and if married, each would convey her portion to her husband, who would assume responsibility for her fraction of the military service owed by her deceased father's estate. If a daughter was under age, she too would become the ward of her lord, who would enjoy the benefits and profits of her estate during her minority and who could marry her to whom he saw fit.

The death of a male tenant might leave a grieving widow, who did not expect to have her living standards lowered. The solution was the dower, a portion of her dead husband's estate assigned to the widow for life, which came to be fixed at one third. The grieving widow might now be a rich widow, and thereby an attractive proposition to unmarried men seeking to enhance their fortune. Kings frequently tried to force widows into remarriage with men of their choosing. Not all widows, however, relished a second round of matrimony. In such cases, money usually talked: the king being prepared, for a consideration, to allow a woman her widowhood or even to allow her own choice of second husband, subject of course to his approval.

The freedom feudal tenants enjoyed had two further consequences. One was the concept of *liege lordship*. This came into play when a man became the feudal tenant of more than one lord, a practice which rapidly became widespread and accepted. But with it came the obvious problem of divided loyalties. In such cases, loyalty to the liege lord overrode other loyalties, but not absolutely. For all men holding land by knight's service there was an ultimate liege lord, the king. This was an inviolable principle firmly laid down by William I in 1086.[3] The same freedom also allowed the creation of small sub-tenancies that carried the obligation of a fraction of a knight's fee, a problem to which the payment of scutage was a neat solution.

The feudal system in England had achieved a superficial stability by the time of Henry I's death in 1135; thereafter, very little subinfeudation by tenants-in-chief occurred. What was missing was a system of accepted or agreed rules governing such matters as the amount of money the king could charge for scutage or for reliefs; or his power to force disparagement (marriage with a person of inferior social status). As anyone reading Magna Carta will readily perceive, it was King John's outrageous excesses in these matters that had provoked the revolt of a large section of his tenants-in-chief, the barons.[4] The outcome was the start of what developed into a complex set of rules governing the feudal relations between lords and vassals.

The feudal system was never static. In the hundred years between the birth of William Marshal I in 1147 and the breakup of the liberty of Leinster in 1247, its personnel changed in style and balance. This was particularly true of the knights, the basic constituents of the feudal system. By 1247, it was clear that their number had contracted substantially. One contributing factor to the fall-off may have been the long period of inflation that afflicted Western Europe in the last quarter of the twelfth century and the first quarter of its successor, which drove up the costs of increasingly sophisticated armour and weapons to a point where some men or families were unable bear the financial burden. But financial pressure may not be the whole story, and perhaps not even the most important part of it. Significant change was taking place in the function of a knight, which edged away from an essentially military role to one of a more civil nature. The thirteenth century saw important developments in local government at county level, responsibility for the discharge of which the crown placed upon the knights.[5] Consequently, these pressures rendered knighthood less attractive, with the result that men who could afford to become knights often chose not to do so. From the 1240s, the shortage of knights became of such concern to the royal government that from time to time they went to the extent of identifying reluctant potential knights and either imposing a fine upon them for non-compliance, or threatening to do so. This heavy-handed process was called 'distraint of knighthood'.

However, the most significant aspect of the decline in appeal and falling numbers was that it made knighthood more socially exclusive, which as a consequence made it increasingly the preserve of the aristocracy. Knighthood was gradually ceasing to be a purely military caste; instead, it was becoming a high-status social condition.

Above the ranks of mere knights stood the aristocracy. At the apex were the earls. Before 1066, earls wielded real power as provincial governors. After the accession of King Henry II in 1154, they were gradually emasculated as regards power. Their titles were little more than that: they drew only small sums from the counties of their titles and their social kudos stemmed from the smallness of their number, which was only twenty by 1220 – but also from the fact that the right of bestowal rested exclusively with the king. If an earl was influential, it was through his wealth and personality, not his title. Nevertheless, then as now, the lure of a title was magnetic.

Below the earls were the barons, of whom there were fewer than one hundred. Unlike the earls, the title of baron did not become a subject of royal appointment until the late fourteenth century, although it gained distinction in the late thirteenth century when barons received a personal summons to meetings of Parliament, then in its early stages of development. During the period covered by this book, barons were recognised as such because they held land as tenants-in-chief and possessed very large estates, big enough to accommodate large numbers of feudal tenants. In brief, the baronage comprised the wealthiest landholders in the kingdom.

Below the knights was a fringe of uncertain depth: these were men who were classed as *gentle*, in that they derived sufficient income from the land to live without having to labour. Records show their existence under a variety of titles, the precise meanings of which are not readily intelligible to us. Two are worth noting, since they are frequently found living or working in association with barons or knights. One was the *esquires*, of whom there were a large number. Some of these men were the subjects of 'destraint of knighthood', while others displayed knightly qualities and a matching lifestyle. In warfare they are frequently described as *men at arms*, who were found fighting alongside the knights in battle, were similarly armoured and wielded the same weapons. So often, however, they remain unrecorded, but it is reasonable to assume that any force of knights would be bolstered by a large number of men at arms serving for lower wages.

FEUDALISM IN THE LIBERTY OF LEINSTER

The framework of the feudal structure imposed on Leinster, as it had been in England, was the tenancies-in-chief. They were largely the work of Strongbow in the brief period of four years, between 1172 and 1176, when he had a free hand in the liberty.[6] As with King William I in England a hundred years earlier, he worked within the pre-existing land divisions – but there was a fundamental difference between the two operations. William I created his tenancies-in-chief by making grants of the estates which had belonged to dispossessed Englishmen. Since these were in many cases scattered over several counties, compact blocks of territory rarely resulted. In Ireland, by contrast, Strongbow's creations were based upon twenty-eight petty kingdoms that were relabelled *cantreds*, deriving from the Welsh word *cantrefs* (meaning one hundred farms or hamlets), which were the sub-divisions of Welsh kingdoms. The cantred names that appear in the records are corruptions of the names of petty kingdoms; for example, the kingdom of Uí Fáeláin became Offelan, and that of Uí Buide became Oboy.

The names of Strongbow's seventeen tenants-in-chief are known to us. Four were from the group that have been called the Geraldines: Maurice Fitz Gerald, Meiler Fitz Henry, Raymond *le Gros* and Miles Fitz David. A further four were Flemings from Pembrokeshire: Thomas de Fleming, Gilbert Boisrohard, Philip de Prendergast and Maurice de Prendergast. Almost half of Strongbow's tenants-in-chief were, therefore, Cambro-Normans from South Wales, hence the adoption of the Welsh *cantref*.

The others, however, were men Strongbow recruited in England, all of whom were of Anglo-Norman ancestry. Two were the commanding officers in his army: Robert de Quency, his constable, who was from Long Buckby in Northamptonshire, and John de Clahull, his marshal, who probably came from Clayhill in Somerset. The provenance of Adam de Hereford and that of Robert de Bermingham is self-evident, while Walter de Riddlesford's origins lay in Lincolnshire or Yorkshire.[7] The origin of Robert de St Michael's name may indicate his family was from either Mont-Saint-Michel in Normandy, or St Michael's Mount in Cornwall. The origins of two others, however, are unsolved mysteries: Robert Fitz Richard and Robert de Bigarz. Finally, there was Hervey de Montmorency, Strongbow's uncle and closest adviser. Some of these men, notably Maurice Fitz Gerald, were the progenitors of durable dynasties. Others, such as Robert de Quency and Robert de Bigarz, disappeared without trace very quickly;

while Walter de Riddlesford's dynasty in Leinster was of a moderately short duration.

The distribution of these foundation tenancies-in-chief was uneven. Much of Kildare, which then included parts of the present counties of Offaly and Laois, together with Carlow and central and southern Wexford, were carved up into feudal tenancies. Not so Kilkenny, then Ossory, which in 1176 was largely free of feudal tenants, except for half of Aghaboe in the north and Iverk in the south. This gap was to a large extent filled by John, as lord of Ireland, and then by William Marshal I.[8] Most of John's grants were, thanks to the pressure put upon him by his brother, Richard I, cancelled after William Marshal succeeded to the lordship of Leinster. However, there were three substantial exceptions, Gowran and Tullow with Arklow, in Wicklow, which John had bestowed on his court butler, Theobald Walter. Much of what Marshal recovered, he then granted to his own closest supporters: Geoffrey Fitz Robert, Thomas Fitz Anthony, John de Earley, Jordan de Sauqueville, and his standard-bearer, Maillard. Other grantees included some of his other knights, some with names that were to have longevity in Ireland: Avenal, Devereux, Fanyn, Grace and Rochford, who were enfeoffed with nineteen *baile* in the central cantreds of Galmoy, Odogh and Shillelogh. As in England, the total number of knight's fees created by the tenants-in-chief of the liberty is not known, but such evidence as we have, suggests that it may well have been close to 100, and which if so, was the service imposed on Strongbow by Henry II in 1171.

Most of these grants would have been accompanied by a charter, which in effect was a title deed. Charters were written in Latin, which was the language of law and religion, and which was concise and had a vocabulary with very precise meanings, understood by those who wrote charters and those able to read them. The precision of the language itself added validity. The issuing of charters became increasingly widespread in the twelfth century and thereafter it became the norm. One surviving Irish example is that drawn up for Strongbow to record his grant of half of the cantred of Aghaboe to Adam de Hereford.[9] It begins, as all charters did, with a greeting by Strongbow, using his given name and his title: Earl Richard Fitz Gilbert, to his friends and his men, French, English, Welsh and Irish, an order that we can regard as deliberate and therefore significant. The charter then goes on to set out what is covered by the grant: that it is not only for Adam de Hereford but also for his descendants; and that for this grant, Adam de Hereford owed the service of five knights. The document, written on parchment, concludes with two guarantees of authenticity. One is a list of thirteen witnesses headed by Raymond *le Gros*, by that time Strongbow's constable. The other authentic mark is his wax seal. This was attached to the document by a tape and shows a wax impression of Strongbow, mounted and brandishing an unsheathed sword and carrying a shield bearing the de Clare coat of arms. The use of seals and coats of arms grew rapidly in the twelfth century as symbols of wealth and status.

SUBINFEUDATION

The internal development of tenancies-in-chief was rarely recorded. However, what is available is the broad picture of the results of subin-feudation in 1245, thanks to the detailed surveys made of the liberty of Leinster in preparation for its division between the heirs of Ancel Marshal, who died in that year. They reveal the existence of 196 feudal tenancies, the number of which should be regarded as the minimum.[10] Of this total, seventy-seven were in Kildare, fifty-nine in Wexford, forty-five in Kilkenny and fifteen in Carlow. More significant is the fact that, of the 196, only sixty-seven, or 34 per cent, were single or multiple knight's fees. Of the rest, sixty-three were half fees, forty-seven were quarter fees and nineteen were fees of smaller fractions. This reinforces the notion that, by the mid thirteenth century, a knight's fee was essentially a status symbol with financial commitment – the latter being the obligation to pay scutage, the rate for which came to be fixed at 40 shillings (£2) per fee.

The question I cannot satisfactorily answer is, what was the size of a knight's fee? In part, this is because of uncertainty about the two units of land measurement then in use. The more basic was the acre, but this is bedevilled by the fact that there were two different acres: the statute acre and the Irish acre, which was 1.6 times larger than the statute acre. Added to this is the fact that the documents do not always specify which type of acre is meant. The other frequently mentioned unit is the *carucate*, deriving from the Latin *caruca*, which means plough. This unit of land measurement was introduced into Ireland from England, where it began primarily as a base unit for obligation and dues owed by tenants. By the thirteenth century, however, carucates were generally accepted as being 120 statute acres in extent.

But over and above these difficulties, a notional size for a knight's fee did not develop either in England or Ireland. The degree of the variation is illustrated by three examples from Wexford, highlighted by the Irish historian Billy Colfer: Glascarrig 27 carucates; Kilcowan 11 carucates and

Mulranken 8 carucates, that is, 3,240 acres (1,311 ha), 1,320 acres (534 ha) and 960 acres (388 ha). Colfer thought that the large size of Glascarrig was due to its proximity to, and threat from, the Irish-dominated area of Wicklow: the greater the danger, the larger the fee needed to be.[11] However, I am inclined to think that the explanation lies more in the relationship between the grantor and the grantee: in the case of Glascarrig, the recipient was Raymond *le Gros*, Strongbow's brother-in-law. A close personal relationship, it would seem, clearly warranted beneficial terms.

GOWRAN: AN EXAMPLE

A feudal structure in its mature form is well presented in a document relating to Gowran, drawn up in 1306.[12] Though the date is well beyond the break-up of the liberty, the evidence it contains is still valid, since the structures it records would have been established many decades earlier. The document, which is written in Latin, is an *extenta* (extent meaning survey). Such documents had to be produced on the death of a feudal tenant in order to verify the name, or names, of the heir or heirs, and what would be inherited; also, to determine what parts of the estate were to be assigned to the widow as her dower. The necessary data was obtained by means of a sworn inquest. This process involved assembling a body of men, who were put on oath to answer truthfully questions to which they were expected to know the answers.

The Gowran inquest was held on 14 May 1306, presumably at Gowran, and was conducted by the two bailiffs who managed the estate, H. Lagles and W. de Cerney. The names of the jurors were not recorded, but it is safe to assume that they were prominent tenants of the estate. The resulting extent was concerned with two distinct institutions: the barony of Gowran, comprising the feudal tenants who owed knight service; and the manor of Gowran, which was made up of several more diverse parts that had been retained by the lord of the manor under his immediate control, and from which he drew income. In feudal language, this is known as the *demesne*. The extent recorded two different elements: the manorial farm (also known as the demesne farm) and the borough, both of which will be discussed in detail below.

The constituents of the barony of Gowran were fifteen tenants holding land in fifteen different places by knight service. Eight of them were burdened with the service of one knight; the remainder had obligations ranging from two and a half knights, to half a knight. In total, these feudal tenants owed the lord of the barony the service of seventeen knights, or, in feudal terminology between them, they were possessed of seventeen knight's fees. In practical terms, however, they owed suit of court and a fixed sum for royal service, scutage. They were required to attend meetings of the barony court, where barony matters were discussed and decided; the latter obligated them to pay a charge of £2 per knight's fee when the crown levied scutage. One of these feudal tenants is of particular interest: Sir Thomas de Cantwell, who held Kilfane and Rathcoole by knight service and whose fully armed effigy still stands in the impressive ruins of Kilfane church. If this was his grave cover, and if it is an accurate representation of his height, Sir Thomas is rightly known as Cantwell *Fada* (Irish meaning long), for he would have been 7 ft 10 in. (2.4 m) in height. The carved grave cover is also interesting in that it introduces us to the importance of heraldry in the feudal world. Although the sculpture shows only the *dexter* half of the shield (the right-hand side as seen by its bearer), it is enough to confirm that it displays the de Cantwell arms. In the esoteric language of heraldry, they were: gules, four annulets or, canton ermine. Had the painted colours survived, we would have seen a red (gules) field or background on which were four small rings (annulets) painted gold (or). The small square upper right (canton) was ermine, the stylised representation of the winter fur of a stoat, in colour white with black markings. It is likely that the canton was added after the coat of arms was devised and covered a fifth annulet, and was intended to show the attachment of the de Cantwells to an important feudal family. The name Cantwell was recorded in the Domesday Book of 1086 as Kanewella,[13] but by 1180 it had become Kentewella and later Kentwell. The village of that name has all but disappeared, but in its place is a splendid Elizabethan manor, Kentwell Hall, with a moat and magnificent gardens. More relevant to the present study is that Kentwell is a mere seven miles (11 km) from Clare, the centre of a huge estate granted by King William I to Strongbow's great-grandfather. It is therefore conceivable that the first de Cantwell in Ireland came as a member of Strongbow's contingent that arrived in 1170.

But perhaps the most informative aspect of this section of the extent is the insight it gives into what feudal tenants did with the lands granted to them. It shows that each of them created between three and ten tenancies, ninety-one in all. In size, these tenancies ranged from as little as 12 acres (4 ha), to seven carucates (840 acres or 340 ha) and amounts to around 10,300 acres (4,168 ha) of land, in most cases recorded in carucates. All the tenants had Anglo-Norman names, and some were members of the more substantial families of the liberty of Leinster. All were members of a class of free tenants, widespread in both England and Ireland. These men were not only legally free, but also held their land in free tenure; that is to say, at a fixed rent and on a hereditary basis. It is more than likely that some of the men listed were descendants of ancestors lured from England or Wales by the bait of this most advantageous form of tenure.

Although a considerable part of the liberty was in the hands of tenants-in-chief and their sub-tenants, the lordship retained substantial parts under its immediate control as its demesne. Some of these demesne manors dated from the early years of Strongbow, but others came to form parts of the demesne as a result of *escheat*, the repossession of feudal tenements as the consequence of failure to produce an heir, or committing a misdemeanour.

The distribution of the seventeen known demesne manors was uneven. The greatest concentration was in southern Wexford, where there were seven. Old Ross, Taghmon and Ferns were almost certainly Strongbow creations, but Great Island, Carrick, Bannow and Rosslare came through escheat. There were also seven in Kilkenny: Callan, Danesfort, Castlecomer, Lochmeran, Aghaboe, Jerpoint, New Town and Ballycallan. They, however, were almost certainly developed by William Marshal as part of his colonisation of central Ossory. And there may have been others, although if so, their early disappearance from the records suggests that they may have been failed ventures. In Co. Carlow, the only demesne manor, Forth, came into the hands of the lordship as the result of the death without heirs of Raymond *le Gros*. In Kildare there were only four, of which Leys and Carbury resulted from the fall of Meiler Fitz Henry. The others were at Ballysax and Moone. In addition, there were nodal points of the liberty: Kilkenny, Kildare, Carlow, Wexford, Dunamase, Ferns and New Ross, the structure and importance of which is more fully explained below.

CASTLES

Feudal society was also characterised by the castle, which was a structure previously unknown in pre-Conquest England and which the Norman intruders brought with them from their homeland. Although a few castles were built in stone from the outset, the most notable of these being the Tower of London, others were constructed more easily and the costs were far cheaper. These are known to us as motte and bailey castles. The motte was a raised mound of earth with a flattened top, which was usually circular, and surrounded by a deep ditch. To the flattened top of the mound was added a peripheral wooden palisade and a wooden tower. The motte was not intended to be a dwelling place other than when the castle was besieged. Fronting the motte was the bailey, a roughly rectangular enclosure which was created like the motte, with an inner mound of earth topped by a wooden palisade and the whole enclosure surrounded by a ditch. Within this defined and protected space there were habitable living quarters erected together with ancillary buildings, domestic and otherwise.

These castles were built as a response to the early, threatening phase of the conquest. In Ireland, around 350 such castles are known to have been built, eighty-six of them in Leinster: Wexford has eighteen, Carlow eleven, Kildare twenty, Kilkenny twenty-two, and Offaly and Laois fifteen.[14] They were located in good farmland and below the 547 yards (500 metres) contour. These mottes varied in height from 16 feet to 32 feet (5 m to 10 m), the difference being a function of wealth and also the ability to command enough labour for construction. There is no evidence to suggest that they were sited as an overall defence plan, but were simply private constructions raised for personal reasons by the lords of the estates of which they were the centres. Between them and their like in England and France, there was one stark difference: with a few exceptions, the Irish castles did not have a bailey. To date, the reason for this anomaly is unexplained.

What purpose did these castles serve? Other than as emergency refuges in time of war, their main role appears to have been to advertise as statements of status, power and authority. Very few were built, or rebuilt later in stone, if for no other reason than the prohibitively high cost. The castle at Maynooth was upgraded by the tenant-in-chief, the only one to do so, in this case, the FitzGeralds. Otherwise, the stone castles at Kilkenny, Carlow, Dunamase, Ferns and Wexford were the later work of the lords of Leinster, in particular William Marshal. By then, the castles had an additional and important function as the nodal points of a system of local government. Marshal's role in rebuilding is not surprising, given the detailed knowledge of castle architecture he must have acquired during his pilgrimage to the Holy Land; and, following his return, in the service of King Richard I, who was the most skilful architect (and taker) of castles in Europe. The products of Marshal's enhanced knowledge can still be seen in the impressive developments he commissioned for his castles at Chepstow (Striguil) and Pembroke.[15]

As well as castles, the Irish countryside is dotted with what are called 'ring forts', which were in essence baileys without a motte. When any of them was built can only be pinpointed by archaeology, and as yet it is not certain what percentage of them pre- or post-date the arrival of the Anglo and Cambro-Normans. Many may be the constructions of the settlers, since until the fourteenth century at least in England, landowners of modest wealth lived in wooden buildings within an earthen enclosure. After that time, wealthier landowners rebuilt in stone for protection and comfort, but also to display their growing status and power.

A FEUDAL VIGNETTE

So far this chapter has done little more than describe the social system known as feudalism and how it worked; the men and women who lived by this code have appeared as names only. To redress this imbalance, it may be interesting to become better acquainted with one of Strongbow's knights, who went with him to Ireland seeking his fortune and also found a little fame through playing a crucial role in a later battle to retain Dublin.

Walter de Riddlesford arrived in Ireland in 1170 as a member of Strongbow's large body of troops.[16] We are not sure of his place of origin, but it was either Rothwell near Leeds in Yorkshire, or Barnetby-le-Wold between Grimsby and Scunthorpe in Lincolnshire – both estates in the hands of branches of the de Riddlesford family. When and why he enlisted in Strongbow's Irish venture is not known, although the likely reason is that he was a younger son of a knightly family who was required to make his own way in the world far from home. If so, he was probably in his early twenties, which would have made him contemporary with William Marshal.

He appears in Ireland as a fully trained knight, a member of the inner core of Strongbow's military household who played a prominent part in Strongbow's campaign to impose his authority on Leinster after the death of Diarmait Mac Murchada, in May 1171. And he certainly demonstrated his prowess during the Viking attempt to retake Dublin. Walter de Riddlesford, sword in hand, helped to turn the battle by killing John le Wode, a Viking of prodigious strength who had already slain seven knights with his battle-axe. De Riddlesford's action played a crucial part in the repulse of the Viking onslaught.

His contribution to Strongbow's victories earned him the territorial reward he had come to Ireland in the hope of obtaining: it comprised two

baronies, Kilkea in Kildare and Bray in Co. Dublin, both substantial properties that amply justified his decision to put down roots in Ireland. He
made his *caput* at Castledermot, where in 1181 he built a castle and a
borough with the aim of stimulating economic growth.

His new-found wealth and status secured him a suitable wife: Amabilia,
sister of a comrade-in-arms, Meiler Fitz Henry. The linking of colonial
families through marriage continued in the following generations: those
of Walter and Amabilia's children and grandchildren who married did so
within this restricted circle. Among those who became part of the de
Riddlesford nexus were Hugh de Lacy, earl of Ulster, and at a slightly lower
level, Richard de Cogan, brother of the more famous Miles de Cogan, and
Eustace de Rupe – both of whom were de Riddlesford tenants.

Every baronial family aspired to found a dynasty, an ambition successfully realised in Ireland by the Butlers and the FitzGeralds. The de
Riddlesfords, however, like the Marshals, were denied by fate. Although
Walter and Amabilia produced their desired son and heir, Walter II, he
and his wife, Amicia, did not. Consequently, when Walter II died *c.* 1239,
the estate passed through female heirs, eventually to be acquired by John
Fitz Thomas (d. 1316), 1st earl of Kildare.

The de Riddlesfords, however, did leave their mark in another way: the
Augustine nunnery they founded at Graney, a few kilometres east of
Castledermot. The nature and extent of the personal piety that prompted
them to establish it is hidden from us; but what can be said is that their
action proclaimed their wealth and social status. Moreover, as founders
and benefactors they could expect their souls to enjoy a special place in
the prayers of the nuns, who also could provide, should the need arise, safe
haven for an unmarried daughter or a widow unwilling to remarry.

Although only briefly on stage, Walter de Riddlesford is typical of the
men and women who came, conquered and then settled in Ireland.

Manors and Manorial Farms

MANORS

In the years after 1066, Norman England was a land of manors: everyone was part of one, either as its owner or one of its tenants.[1] The Norman impact, however, may have been more apparent than real. What we know of the social structures and organisation in late Anglo-Saxon England suggests a broad similarity with that in France. The changes wrought by the Norman incomers may, therefore, have been largely of language and terminology for the purposes of record, rather than a complete physical change.

It was this concept of the manor that was transferred to Ireland by the Anglo-Norman intruders. Manors are most accurately defined as lordships: the size was irrelevant to the definition, and manors could and did vary widely in size from a few to many thousands of acres. The pertinent fact was that the lord or lords of the manor – whether singular or plural, male or female – had legal possession of its soil and what lay beneath it (with the exception of precious metals), and all who lived within its bounds did so as the lord's tenants. There were several categories of these, some of which we have already encountered in the extent of the manor of Gowran.

In Ireland, at the bottom of the scale of tenants were two distinctly different groups. One was comprised of *betaghs*, normally of native Irish stock, who were unfree; that is, they were part of the stock of the manor and were not at liberty to leave it. Most lived in their own separate *betagh* communities and cultivated their land, for which they paid rent. However, *betaghs* shared bottom place with *cottagers* – these were people who had only the land on which their house stood. It was possible for a cottager's small garden plot, if assiduously worked, to produce much of what a family needed by way of food. But most of them looked to supplement their income by occasional, mainly seasonal work for cash wages paid by their employers in need of extra hands.

Above these two groups were two others who were socially and almost certainly economically advantaged. One we have already met at Gowran – the free tenants, who were not only legally free, but holding land heritably and for fixed rents. The other group, which is somewhat ambiguous, was the burgesses, holding what were known as burgages. The burgage tenure is seen as being specific to urban communities, and as such will be more fully explained below. To find it in rural situations looks out of place. An explanation for this apparently incongruous arrangement, which has found widespread acceptance, was put forward by Jocelyn Otway-Ruthven.[2] She suggested that these burgess communities were formed by immigrants from England and Wales who were tempted to cross the Irish Sea by promises of more advantageous terms of tenure than they could hope for at home. What is not known is whether the landlords who created these also harboured hopes that the settlements might develop into genuine urban communities.

There was another distinct type of tenant, the *firmarii* (in English, farmers). The word at that time meant a 'lessee', that is, someone who held land for a contracted number of years on an agreed annual rent. In the main, farmers were men who leased land that lords of the manor had retained in their own hands, but now found surplus to their current requirements.

Tenants, by implication, paid rent, though what form this took varied. In some cases rent was in the form of services, though the heavy farm labour services found in some parts of England were rarely found in Ireland. Otherwise, rents were in cash, or at least recorded as such; but service in lieu of cash was not unknown. Here it needs to be remembered that in the years covered by this book a cash economy operated, but only just.

Until 1334, there was only one type of coin circulating in England – the penny,[3] which was, or should have been, 92.5 per cent pure silver. This made it soft enough to suffer from rapid wear, and also made illegal 'clipping' easy and tempting. All this meant in turn that the exchange of old for new coins was a frequent necessity. On paper, a penny was signified by the letter d, which was short for *denarius*, a Roman silver coin. From the reign of King Henry II (1154–89) until British currency was decimalised in 1971, there were 240 pennies in the pound sterling – a word deriving from the

Old English *steorra* (meaning star). Although 'silver' coins now no longer contain silver, the notion of a pound of silver was maintained in the continuous use of the symbol £, the Latin capital L with an abbreviation mark, the first letter of the Latin word *libra*, meaning pound weight. Scales were used to weigh bags of coins, rather than counting them. During the years covered by this book, coins were struck at the rate of up to 750,000 a year in mints, not only at the Royal Mint in London but also under royal licence at mints in five other places: York, Canterbury, Durham, Bury St Edmunds and Winchester; and also at Dublin, Kilkenny, Limerick and Waterford in Ireland. Because pennies were so soft, they could easily be cut in half to create halfpennies and in quarters to create what became known as 'farthings', from the Old English word *feorthing*, meaning fourth part.

However, a single currency was not convenient for keeping accounts and consequently three other 'currencies' were devised to exist only on paper (or parchment) as currencies of account. One was the £ of 240 pennies. Another was the shilling, derived from the Old English word *scilling*, the value of which was 12 pennies. The third was the mark, which signified two thirds of a £ – that is, 13s 4d – and was very useful in being readily divisible by two: 13s 4d, 6s 8d, 3s 4d, 1s 8d, 9d, 4½d. One final complication must be mentioned: medieval accounts always record money in Roman numerals, which makes the arithmetic more challenging (or at least it does to the author of this book).

MANORIAL FARMS

Lords, tenants and rents had long existed in Ireland in native forms. What was novel in the manors created by the Anglo-Norman occupiers was the manorial farm. Manorial farms are also known as demesne farms, a word deriving from the Latin word *dominium*, meaning lordship. In a corrupted form, it is still found in the names of many Scottish farms known as 'the Mains'. A manorial farm was a purpose-formed agricultural unit whose function was to generate large profits: it was an avowedly commercial enterprise. Almost all manorial farms were 'mixed farms', engaged in both agrarian and pastoral aspects of agriculture. The agrarian focus was almost exclusively on four cereals: wheat, rye, barley and oats. The first two were sown in autumn, and were primarily intended for bread. The other two were spring sown: barley for brewing ale and oats for fodder. This was, of course, the ideal: men and women, particularly those at the lower end of the economic scale, made their bread and brewed their ale with whatever came to hand. Cereals were field crops; for the modest range of vegetables and fruit, gardens and orchards were created. Pastoral farming was principally concerned with cattle and sheep, the former producing milk for consumption and for milk products such as butter and cheese; in death, they provided hides. The commercial value of sheep was primarily as a source of wool. Also present on manorial farms were pigs, poultry, rabbits and doves, all of which produced items for sale.

The incoming Anglo-Norman lords also brought with them the three-course rotation system: wheat and/or rye; barley and/or oats; then the land was left fallow, to give a year's respite to allow it to regain fertility. This system required large open fields divided into areas known as furlongs or flatts, the size and shape of which were dictated by the lie of the land. These were then cultivated in long, narrow strips, a form made necessary by two constraints. One was to get the maximum draw from a plough team of eight strong but clumsy oxen before needing a rest and negotiating a cumbersome three (or more) point turn. The other was ploughing up and down a slope, which over time created ridges with furrows in between, assisting drainage.

Separate from the arable fields, and much smaller in area, was the meadow, the purpose of which was the production of hay – a winter fodder for essential animals, particularly the oxen who were vital to those working the land. Oxen were the tractors of medieval farming. As far as possible, sheep and cattle gained their sustenance from grazing on the open, unenclosed and uncultivated parts of the farm, known in England as the moor or the common, but the Irish documents of the time use the word 'mountain' to describe such land.

MANORIAL FARMS AS COMMERCIAL ENTERPRISES

The Anglo-Norman invaders came from a land with, to a land without, manorial farms. Neither in England nor in Ireland has the number of manorial farms been accurately determined. In the liberty there are known to have been at least twenty-three; there may have been more, but the total is unlikely to have been great, as creating a manorial farm was a major and costly operation.

In Strongbow's time, most lords did not engage in the direct management of their farms, but leased them to *firmarii* or lessees, frequently for the duration of three or more lives. This created a problem. At a time when lease contracts were not committed to paper, it was all too easy for subsequent generations to be unsure of what their predecessors had agreed, which in turn opened the way for fraud and dispute.

This was about to change. From *c.* 1180, the lords of the manor began to take their farms back in hand and to impose their own management structures, one element of which was a standard accounting system which has provided us with a wealth of detailed information about farming practices and the agricultural economy. An example of such a farm, at Ballysax, is analysed below.

The underlying reason for the shift away from leasing to personal exploitation of the land was inflation.[4] This was a Europe-wide phenomenon that began in the last two decades of the twelfth century, and continued for many years after 1200. Its effect was to shift the balance of economic advantage from the lord of the manor to the lessee. While the value of currency was stable a lord of the manor could put his farms into the hands of lessees, confident that the fixed rents they paid him would retain their value. But inflation blessed the lessee with increasing profits, while the lord of the manor's income remained fixed and therefore declining in real terms. This innovative, hands-on approach to estate management was already being adopted in England when the Anglo-Norman conquest and colonisation of Leinster began. It is likely, therefore, that the new feudal landowners were fully conversant with that system of land management, which they then began to introduce into their new estates.

In both England and Ireland, little evidence has survived of the creation of manorial farms. One rare exception is Kells in Ossory, which was founded by William Marshal's trusted subordinate, Geoffrey Fitz Robert.[5] Although the precise date is not known, it must have been before 1208, for he died that year; and it could possibly have been before 1200. In her detailed study of Kells, Miriam Clyne showed that Fitz Robert's enterprise had a dual purpose. Its focus was two islands, no longer existing, but which had been in the King's River. On one he built a motte and bailey castle for himself; on the other island, he gave land and erected a new house for the order of Augustinian canons. He also provided his new foundation with its initial congregation, which he brought to Ireland from a well-established house at Bodmin, Cornwall.

His castle was the *caput* of a large farm that straddled the river, the area of which extended to 2,320 acres (938 ha). Not all of this would be put under the plough; there would be a large area left to be used as rough grazing for cattle and sheep. He also founded close to his castle a community of burgesses, eventually numbering seventy-one. To the Augustinian canons he granted a further 736 acres (298 ha) of land, which was in two parts on either side of his farm. He also granted land elsewhere, which enabled them to create four outlying farms, which are known as granges.

BALLYSAX: AN EXAMPLE OF A MANORIAL FARM

Manorial accounts of the type mentioned above have survived in relatively large quantities in England, but regrettably not in Ireland. The Irish accounts that still exist, however, are in the same format as their English counterparts. They are in the form of parchment rolls, which are made up of narrow strips sewn together, head to toe, then rolled up. They are written in the standard hand of the time, in abbreviated Latin. Their existence is proof that in the thirteenth century, there was a growing army of clerks trained in calligraphy and with sufficient Latin to perform what was a fairly low-level role.

The inner face of the parchment roll carries the record of cash income and expenditure. The outer face, known as the *dorse*, is devoted to the recording of crops and livestock. The basic purpose of the account was to place on record what the farm manager was responsible for over the year, and to show whether he discharged his office honestly or fraudulently. However, whether the farm made a profit or a loss is not immediately evident, although it can be ascertained by diligently extracting the relevant data.

The example I have chosen for analysis is one of a group relating to the manor of Ballysax in Co. Kildare, which was one of the properties assigned to Matilda, eldest daughter of William Marshal, when the liberty of Leinster was broken up in 1247. Through her marriage to Hugh Bigod, 3rd earl of Norfolk, her inheritance and the title of earl marshal came into the hands of her husband's family. The account for the manor of Ballysax, which was prepared for publication by Mary C. Lyons,[6] begins conventionally with a statement of the name of the farm manager, the title of his office and the period covered by the account. The manager was David de Bonham, whose title was *prepositus* (reeve). The account ran from the feast of St Michael, 1284, to the same feast in the following year. Throughout England and Ireland, Michaelmas (29 September) traditionally marked the end and the beginning of the farming cycle. By that date, the year's harvest would be expected to be finished and the autumn ploughing and sowing under way for next year's crops. It was also the time when herds, flocks and draught animals were assessed with a view of the sale of surplus or weak stock and the purchase of replacements or additions.

The first item of 'income' de Bonham recorded was the total of arrears, amounting to £53 5s 9¾d. Income is recorded in inverted commas because it did not represent money that he had actually collected. Rather, it was a record of arrears, which almost certainly had accumulated over several years and for which de Bonham was now responsible.

Then came the income from two sorts of rents: £22 7s 3d *redditus assisae*, which were fixed rents from an unspecified number of freehold tenants in Ballysax; and secondly £25 9s 1¼d, *firma*, which was income from leases. One of these was for the manorial mill, to which all tenants of the manor owed 'suit'; that is, they were obliged to have their corn ground there. For this 'service' they paid a standard fraction of the resulting flour. This was retained by the miller, who sold it for his own profit, out of which he would have to find the rent for the mill. This clever arrangement meant that both miller and lord of the manor profited. The losers were the tenants, who were convinced that they were being cheated – and possibly were, hence the universal dislike of millers which Chaucer exploited in his *Canterbury Tales*. To add to the tenant's woes, the possession and use of hand querns was forbidden, as was having their corn ground at another mill. Conviction of either offence in the manor court would incur *amercement* (pecuniary punishment) and confiscation. The other lease rents were almost certainly for parts of the farm that were surplus to requirements. In all, the reeve was responsible for securing income from rents amounting to £47 16s 4¼d – and there is nothing in this account to suggest that he did not succeed. In many manorial accounts success was not achieved, which explains the accumulated arrears.

A much larger sum, £66 13s 10½d, was realised from the sale of farm produce, of which cereals were by far the most important. They were the product of the three-course rotation system applied to 240 acres (97 ha): 80 acres (32 ha) devoted to wheat; 80 acres (32 ha) to oats, with a further 80 acres (32 ha) lying fallow. Of these two cereals, wheat made the greater contribution: 143 crannocks, 5 bushels, sold at prices ranging from 3s 4d to 6s 8d per crannock. Far fewer oats were sent to market – only 47 crannocks, 5 bushels with a price range of 5s 7d to 6s 8d per crannock. The term *crannock* appears to have been universal in Irish accounts; the equivalent term in the English records is *quarter*. However, as both crannock and quarter contained eight bushels, they can be considered as equivalents. These quantities of cereals from Ballysax yielded an income from sales of £57 2s 9½d.

Sales of stock and the produce of stock only added £9 11s 1d to the total income, over half of this sum arising from the sale of 43 stones of wool.

By the late thirteenth century, the demand for wool from the manufacturing towns of Flanders had reached voracious proportions. Consequently, both English and Irish wool enjoyed the benefit of a buoyant market. Other sales included the sale of doves, the skins and meat of 95 rabbits, 38 stones of cheese and unspecified quantities of apples and eggs. Also sold were 30 sheep, 4 oxen and a horse, probably because they were no longer in prime condition and for them there was a ready second-hand market. Even in death, animals could add to the reeve's income: there was money to be made from demand for the hide of a dead horse, and also for the flesh of a dead ox.

The final items of cash income amounted to £2 16s 11d, all but £1 arising from the manor court, which tenants were required to attend, known as 'suit of court' and which controlled most aspects of their lives. Without knowing the scope of the court's competence, it is not possible to know whether the sum of money arose from amercements, which were imposed for infractions of manorial regulations; or, whether they were from fines, which were payments made to secure agreement. This may or may not have included entry fines, known as *gressums* – money paid by a man or woman to secure possession of a landholding. Probably not, since the sum of £1 paid by Geoffrey de la Hulle for permission to enter land at a place called Balifetheran was recorded as a separate item.

David de Bonham's total cash income, therefore, was £117 7s 1¾d, out of which he had to finance the operations of the farm. His expenditure was recorded under seven headings, but can be more conveniently and validly described under three.

His largest outlay was on the remuneration of the *famuli*, a Latin word meaning servants. On manorial farms in both England and Ireland the term described the specialists, hired annually and living within, or close by the haggard – a term used in Ireland, but not in England, where it was known as the farmyard or in the Latin of the documents, as the *curia* (court). There were ten such people at Ballysax: the reeve, the *messor* (harvest manager), farm ploughmen, two carters and two shepherds. Their pay consisted of annual cash sums and weekly food allowances. In addition, when needed, three more specialists were hired for shorter periods: a harrower (8 weeks), a lambing shepherd (16 weeks) and a dairy maid (26 weeks). The total wage bill for these farm servants was £11 18s 4½d.

The *famuli* could cope unaided with the routine tasks of the farm, but wheat and oats required additional labour at three stages: weeding and hoeing during growth; cutting, stooking and leading during the harvest; and threshing and winnowing after the harvest. For all of these tasks, men and women were hired at day wages. How many were employed for this work was not recorded, but as casual, seasonal hands they must have been members of the wider Ballysax community. In all, their pay added £7 14s 6½d to the reeve's wage bill, which came to £19 12s 11d in total.

His remaining expenditure, £5 5s 4½d, covered a variety of purchases and services. Perhaps the most important purchases were those of an ox and two horses, which were essential draught animals without which the manorial farm could not have functioned. Of the two, the price of an ox was twice that of a horse, a clear pointer to the role of the ox in ploughing. Horses, being weaker, were generally used for hauling carts or harrowing. The manorial farm at Ballysax generated enough income for the reeve to sell off the weaker or older animals in the second-hand market and to buy quality replacements. Added to this were the costs of any necessary repairs to ploughs and carts. All of these costs would have occurred annually, although the sums involved would vary. Also, there would be annual costs for the washing and shearing of the sheep and the carting of their wool to the manor of Old Ross, which appears to have been the hub of the earl of Norfolk's pastoral organisation. Finally, the upkeep of the manorial buildings was the reeve's responsibility. In this year's account he had to pay for the repair of the barn door and 22 yards (21 m) of the haggard wall, as well as the construction of a new dovecote.

The reeve's final item of expenditure was the cost of preparing the account. Because this involved writing and the use of Latin, David de Bonham called upon the services of a Brother Walter (clearly in holy orders), whose fee was the large sum of £1. Where he came from was not noted, but it was most likely to have been Kilrush, as its chapel was a cell (outpost) of the Augustinian priory of Cartmel in Lancashire, to which the church of Ballysax had been appropriated.

Total costs for the year came to £23 18s 2¼d, which is 3s ¼d more than the total of the sums recorded in the account. This error is perhaps not surprising, given that illiterate reeves had to keep their records of receipts and expenditure by means of notched sticks, added to which was the difficulty of doing arithmetic in Roman numerals.

The financial performance of the farm can be measured by subtracting the reeve's expenses from the income he achieved through sales of produce. The result was a profit of £42 15s 6½d, more than enough to back the decision to engage in direct management. But the reeve was also a rent collector, which raised his income to £117 7s 1¾d and his cash surplus to £84 11s 7¼d.

What did he do with the money when it was gathered in and the end-of-year accounts were finalised? Over half of the money received, £47 12s 4½d, was transferred to the earl of Norfolk's treasurer, based at Carlow Castle. His name was Thomas Wade, and he served in this capacity for most of the 1280s at an annual salary of £13 6s 8d. He was responsible for receiving cash surpluses from the earl's outlying manors[7] and for authorising certain types of expenditure. He was, however, subordinate and answerable to the earl's steward, Sir William Cadel, who held the post from 1282 until 1287. His annual salary was the princely sum of £100, far above what he could have commanded in England. He and his predecessor, Sir Philip de Bockland (or Buckland), were experienced administrators who had learnt their trade in royal service. This, together with their high salaries, testifies to the need felt by an absentee landlord to have a man on the spot who was both expert and trustworthy.

As well as the monies forwarded to the earl's treasurer, Thomas Wade, a small sum of cash (£2 3s 4¾d) together with a quantity of animal fodder (twenty-six bushels of oats), was given to Thomas de Clene. He held the office of bailiff, which had oversight of the reeves at Ballysax and three other manorial farms belonging to the earl of Norfolk. He was, in modern terms, middle management.

In 1284/5, the financial returns from Ballysax helped to swell the earl of Norfolk's coffers. Two years earlier, however, his greater need was for corn. As earl marshal, he was heavily engaged in King Edward I's second campaign to subjugate North Wales; and the army was in need of supplies. Consequently, in 1282 the reeve at Ballysax sent via Dublin to Rhuddlan in Wales 64 crannocks of wheat, 29 crannocks of oats, 8 oxen, 14 cows, 40 sheep, a boar and 28 hogs, plus 12 stones of cheese. The presence of cows in this list may help to explain the absence of a vaccary at Ballysax in the 1284 account. What is clear, however, is that in 1282 the manors at Old Ross and Ballysax largely provisioned the earl's contingent of troops with Irish food while they were operating in North Wales.

Returning to the analysis of the Ballysax manorial account: the outer face of the account was devoted to recording crops (wheat and oats) and livestock (oxen, horses, wethers, ewes, hogs, lambs, rabbits, hens and wool). Each was recorded using the same format, which began with a statement of the quantity or number on the farm the day the reeve took office, and ended with the number or quantity there on the day the account was made up. Between the figures was noted the quantity of crops harvested, the amount sold and the amount reserved for seed or otherwise consumed on the farm. With animals, the sandwiched figures were of sales and purchases, births and deaths, and in the case of lambs, wool, rabbits and hens, the number paid in tithes to Ballysax church.

This brief exposition of the 1284/5 account of Ballysax manorial farm throws up a number of significant points. Two highlight absence: one is that no barley was grown, although small amounts were grown in previous years. In this respect, Ballysax was at one with other Irish manorial farms, where barley features only marginally if at all. There is no obvious explanation for this, particularly as barley is the most suitable grain for brewing and distilling; and much of Ireland is suitable for its cultivation. The other absence is that of a vaccary. This is exceptional, since cattle were reared throughout Ireland for their meat, their milk and milk products and their hides. However, this may have been no more than an interlude, since, as already noted, in 1282 fourteen cows were sent from Ballysax to feed the earl of Norfolk's troops in North Wales.

Two further noteworthy features are 'then and now' contrasts. One is the low yield of cereals: from 80 acres (32 ha) only 986 bushels were harvested; and the yield of oats from a like acreage was worse, only 483 bushels. The pastoral element had an equally low productivity: the flock produced less than one lamb per ewe, a quarter of whom died of 'murrain'. I cannot identify this disease in modern medical terms, although liver fluke is a possibility, as is foot and mouth disease. One final point is that the sales of rabbit flesh and skins, and of doves, were not byproducts of pest control but of a rabbit warren and a dovecote respectively.

As regards the workforce, no details were recorded except for David de Bonham, the reeve, whose name points to links with a township of that name in Wiltshire, although his given name suggests a Welsh connection – if so, he was of immigrant stock, although whether it was he or his ancestors who migrated is not known. The *famuli* may have been descendants of immigrants, but it is more likely they were indigenous Irish men and women who, where necessary, would have been trained in imported skills and methods.

This single account is a snapshot of a year's activity on one farm. Only a sequence of accounts over many years can provide knowledge of changes in farming implements and methods and the progress, or regress, of the agricultural economy. Alas, it is Ireland's misfortune to be woefully short of such evidential records.[8]

9

Boroughs

A borough was as commercial in its purpose as the medieval manorial farm but differed in its ethos, in that it was founded upon marketing and manu-facture. However, they were alike in that they were both products of careful planning, as underlying both was a steady increase in population. More people meant increased demand, which is always a major stimulus to change.

The word 'borough' – like its equivalents in place names, 'burgh', 'brough', 'burton' and 'bury' – derives from the Old English word *burh*, meaning 'fortified place'. *Burhs* were constructed on the orders of King Alfred of Wessex (870–99) and his successors, to act as nodal points in defending their kingdom from the Danish onslaught and then in reimpos-ing English control over Danish-occupied areas.[1]

In the hundred or so years before the Normans conquered England, many *burhs* that had evolved from a primarily military function into civil-ian settlements, in response to the rising population and expanding economic and administrative importance. Similar developments also took place in those settlements that had not begun life as *burhs*. I have identified at least fifty places recorded in the Domesday Book as having borough status.[2]

By the time the Normans invaded England it was already becoming a country of boroughs, although as yet there was no clear concept of what a borough was, could be or should be; that was still to be formulated. What is clear in this matter is the contrast between England and Ireland, where the only recognisable boroughs were still those created by the Vikings.

The Norman Conquest is seen, rightly, as constituting a sharp break in the history of both England and Ireland. But in the matter of borough foundation, this was not the case in England: the uninterrupted growth of the population inspired an increasing number of urban settlements, the emergence of which led to a clear, legally defined concept of a borough. Between 1066 and 1300 in England, 151 boroughs were founded, 136 of them before 1250.[3] There was one difference, however: before the Conquest, borough foundation had been essentially a matter for the crown, whereas after 1066 it was more and more undertaken by the baronage, ecclesiastical as well as lay.

In Wales, the pattern was different. There were no boroughs created before 1066 and up to 1250, only twenty-five came into being: mainly in the south, including the future Marshal towns of Chepstow, Usk and Pembroke.[4] However, a greater number, thirty-five, were set up between 1250 and 1300, mostly in the north, and used as instruments in Edward I's ruthless drive to snuff out Welsh independence. Scotland was different again. There borough (or burgh) foundation did not start until the accession of that arch-Normaniser David I (1124–53), but by the end of the twelfth century there were thirty burghs in Scotland, two thirds of them founded by the crown.[5]

Borough foundation was not, of course, confined to Britain. The same stimuli produced a like response throughout Western Europe. In two areas, Germany and Spain, there was also the additional lure, or temptation, of conquering, colonising and Christianising heathen Slavs and Muslims.[6]

All boroughs shared common features. Every borough was a defined area of land, clearly demarcated from the surrounding countryside. Initially, demarcation took the form of a ditch and earthen bank, surmounted perhaps by a wooden stockade, with gateways to allow access and egress. This structure not only served to define and confirm the borough's boundaries, but also gave a measure of security. But above all it was the means by which trading activity, ultimately the borough's economic lifeblood, could be regulated and controlled. Subsequently, the wealthier boroughs replaced the earth and wood with stone walls. These not only performed the same functions, they also gave greater security and had the added benefit of being status symbols and testimony to confidence and success. However, to build in stone was very expensive, with construction in many places taking up to a hundred years to complete. Extraordinary measures were required to raise the necessary capital, the most important of which was the right to levy *murage*, a word derived from the French word *mur*, meaning wall. It was the privilege of levying a monetary charge on traffic in and out of the borough. Murage grants were obtainable only from the crown and were always for a specified duration.

Within the borough's defined boundary a street plan was laid out, the most basic being a spinal street across the length of the borough from which side streets could diverge. Along this street, or streets, building plots were laid out, normally narrow in width and resulting from the use of a surveyor's rod. Such is the durability of boundaries that in many boroughs the standard width is still clearly identifiable in present-day buildings. Plot lengths, however, were not standard, but were determined by the lie of the land and were rarely less than five times longer than the width. One result of this was that houses were built gable-end to the street so as to allow for a narrow passageway from the street to the rear area of the burgage plot. The houses of the burgage holders had, at this date, almost certainly wooden frames, perhaps resting on a stone foundation. The walls would be made of wattle and plaster and would be topped by a thatched roof. The back area of the property had a variety of uses, including a kitchen garden and a workshop for carrying on a trade. Every borough had a range of craft-based trades. Some catered for most of the needs of life, such as brewers, bakers, butchers, tailors, shoemakers and tanners. Others were concerned with fashioning useful or necessary items out of wood, iron and tin. Because membership of these trades was multiple, it was natural that they should form organisations – guilds – with aims such as price regulation, maintenance of standards of workmanship, apprenticeships and running insurance schemes to deal with such matters as the cost of burial and the support of widows.

Borough trading took place not only with the internal market of the borough, but also with the farming communities in its vicinity. For this interchange of goods a dedicated site was required: the marketplace. These took a number of different forms. Some marketplaces were created by widening a section of the borough's main street. Others were square or triangular areas at the junction of the roads in and out of the borough. Markets were weekly affairs, held on a day specified by the lord of the manor, and attendance was dictated by the practical problem for country dwellers of being able to get to market, sell their goods and then return home within the day.

Most of the largest and most prosperous boroughs acquired an additional trading facility: a fair. This required a royal licence and was limited to a number of specified days in the year. Fairs brought traders from a distance and their wares would be considered luxuries, such as foreign spices or fine materials such as silk. Fairs were also occasions for the buying and selling of stock, particularly horses, cattle and oxen. This aspect made it essential for the fair to be held on a site outside the borough boundary. Fairs were always a notable and eagerly awaited event in the yearly round of borough life.

One final point on the physical aspect of a borough was that it was assigned an area of land adjacent to its perimeter, the purpose of which was to allow the borough inhabitants to engage in agriculture as a supplement to their other activities. How important this became, or remained, would be a measure of the success of the borough's urban activities: the more the borough flourished as an urban entity, the less importance was placed on farming matters.

BOROUGH SOCIETY AND COMMERCIAL ACTIVITY

Within these physical boundaries lived a human community. The building plots they occupied were known as burgages, and their tenants styled burgesses. At the outset, they would likely have been mainly immigrants to the area. Luring them to the borough would be an urgent matter for the founder, since to have a flourishing community would require the presence of people with a diverse range of skills. This influx of immigrant settlers was very apparent in Irish boroughs; the best indicator of where they came from is their surnames.

What drew them to the borough was undoubtedly the attraction of burgage tenure, which gave four advantages: a low, fixed annual rent; the right of free disposal, covering inheritance, sale, division and sub-letting; commercial privileges within the borough, and in many cases extending throughout the territories of the owner; and its own court, to which all burgesses 'owed suit', that is, their presence was required at its meetings. It was in the court that changes of tenancy were registered, and it was the forum in which inter-burgess disputes were adjudicated according to borough custom and the judgement of peers.

Despite these advantages, all burgess communities had one bugbear: the lord's reeve, a word derived from the Old English word *gerefa*. The reeve was the man responsible for collecting all money owed to the lord and for presiding over the borough court. Reeves often had a bad press due to their widespread abuse of power. While some may have been honest and trustworthy, a reeve had considerable scope for corrupt practice. Many were unjust and self-serving, and saw the powers given to them by their office simply as a means of enriching themselves. The solution was for the burgesses to acquire the right of self-government. The degree to which they succeeded was determined by the lord's willingness to meet their wishes, which could be stimulated by a suitably large financial inducement. Consequently, the wealthier the borough, the greater the chances of attaining success. The aim of all burgess communities was to 'farm the borough' – that is, to pay to the lord an agreed annual sum, in return for which they would be licensed to manage all or most of their own affairs. Their ultimate prize was to achieve the status of a self-governing corporation, whose contact with the lord of the borough was reduced to little more than the payment of the annual fee.

The rights, obligations and privileges enjoyed by burgesses were set down in a legal document, a charter. This was uttered by the lord and witnessed by a significant number of his advisers and associates. The charter was a precious document, as it was the bedrock on which their corporate existence rested.

Where founders chose to locate their boroughs was a crucial decision, since the site chosen would be the underlying determinant of the borough's success, or lack thereof. Boroughs on the coast would need to develop port facilities, but also needed to be at the mouth of a navigable river, thereby giving easy access to a prosperous hinterland. For those inland, the most likely guarantee of success was a location where a major land route needed to cross a major river; better still if the river gave access to the sea. One further advantage was the presence of or proximity to a castle, a cathedral or a monastery, all of which had need of services and could also be centres of estate management and administration. Not surprisingly, the most successful boroughs were those founded by the crown.

The years of borough proliferation and expansion came to an end in the fourteenth century, largely due to a drastic fall in the size of the population, which by the end of the century was roughly half of what it had been in 1300. This drastic demographic change was due to mortality. It began in the second decade of the century with a series of disastrous harvests between 1315 and 1317, brought about by appalling weather. In Ireland, this was compounded by the devastation caused by a Scottish army led by Edward Bruce, the brother of the Scottish king, Robert I: he aimed at reducing Ireland's capacity to supply food and other commodities via Carlisle to English armies in Scotland.[7]

But the long-term damage was caused by the great pandemic of plague known as the Black Death, which swept over Europe between 1346 and 1351.[8] Although accurate figures are hard to come by, enough are available for us to be confident that the death toll was between a third and a half of the entire population. But the killer blow preventing population recovery was the recurrent outbreaks of plague, which continued until the seventeenth century. As always, those with the best advantages survived and prospered, but the casualty rate was high, with some boroughs shrinking to a non-urban condition while other boroughs disappeared entirely.

BOROUGHS IN THE LIBERTY OF LEINSTER

In addition to a paucity of records, the study of Irish boroughs is hampered by the question of definition: what must a settlement include to qualify as a borough? This problem is peculiar to Ireland. There is a simple answer: if a settlement has burgages and burgage tenure, then it is a borough. As already noted, however, this simplicity was questioned by Jocelyn Otway-Ruthven when arguing that many colonial farming settlements had burgages and burgage tenure, because their founders used them as bait to tempt farming tenants to come from England and Wales in the knowledge they would enjoy better terms than could be obtained back home. If this argument is correct, the number of boroughs in Ireland would be sharply reduced, an idea given support by Avril Thomas's detailed study of Irish walled towns.

The impact of Thomas's research is stark: she reduced the number of boroughs she was confident had been founded in the liberty of Leinster by 1245 from forty-two to twelve, with a further three for which she could not find any convincing proof. These lower totals I have accepted, believing that the evidence, although not absolutely conclusive, does support her figures 'beyond reasonable doubt'.[9]

The twelve boroughs that are considered certain are as follows (the figures accompanying them are their areas in hectares, as computed by Thomas):[10] Athey, 16 ha (40 acres); Callan, 10 ha (25 acres); Carlow, 13 ha (32 acres); Castledermot, 15 ha (37 acres); Gowran, 12–19 ha (30–47 acres); Inistioge, 4–7 ha (10–17 acres); Kildare, 9 ha (22 acres); Kilkenny (inc. Irishtown), 42 ha (104 acres); Naas, 13 ha (32 acres); New Ross, 39 ha (96 acres); Thomastown, 6.5 ha (16 acres); Wexford, 25 ha (62 acres).

NODAL BOROUGHS IN THE LIBERTY OF LEINSTER

These figures show Kilkenny and New Ross to have been by far the largest boroughs in Leinster. In this instance, size is an accurate indicator of importance. Moreover, they shared two features: both were founded in the early years of the thirteenth century by William Marshal, and both had suburbs known as Irishtown. In other respects, they differed quite sharply.

The development of Kilkenny began as early as 1172 with the erection of a motte and bailey castle.[11] As well as being sited to command the river crossing, it stood on ground previously occupied by a residence of the kings of Osraige. Strongbow's castle was surely deliberately intended to underline his claim to kingship. However, it had a brief life, as it was burnt down by his Irish opponents.

A fresh start on developing the site had to await William Marshal's inheritance as the lord of Leinster, although building was not begun by him personally but by his proxy, Geoffrey Fitz Robert, who was his most trusted agent and who appears to have been resident in Leinster from the mid 1190s. Although Fitz Robert originally restored the castle as a motte and bailey, he began its reconstruction in stone shortly after 1200.

It was at this time that the borough was established in the form of a spinal street, running up the hill from the castle to the boundary of Irishtown, a sector which covered an area of about 25 acres (10 ha) and which until 1640 was a separate borough. Within its walls stood the cathedral dedicated to St Canice (d. 600), which is on the site of the monastery he is reputed to have founded. Its pre-Norman religious importance is attested by the impressive ninth-century round tower which stands close by. When it became the centre of the diocese of Ossory is not entirely clear. It was already so designated at the Synod of Rath Bressail in 1111, and the present thirteenth-century building does contain fabric from that earlier period. Its role as the diocesan centre appears to be confirmed at the time of the death of Bishop Felix Ua Dubhlaine (O'Delaney) in or around 1202.

The physical layout of Kilkenny closely resembles that of Edinburgh, the capital of Scotland that was created by its reformist king David I (1124–53) in roughly the same decades. However, Edinburgh was designed with the royal castle built at the top of a hill and its borough, which consisted of a spinal street running downhill with adjacent side streets, became a different borough about two thirds of the way down (known as Canongate because its lordship was vested in another of King David's foundations, the Augustinian priory of Holyrood). Located at the bottom of the hill, this is now the royal Palace of Holyroodhouse, the British monarch's official residence in Scotland. Whereas in Kilkenny, William Marshal's capital of Leinster, he created and developed the borough structure in reverse. The arrangement differed from the Scottish capital in that the ecclesiastical development was at the top of the hill, with St Canice's cathedral standing prominently although surrounded by the different, separate borough of Irishtown. In Kilkenny as in Edinburgh the borough street pattern featured a spinal street and side streets off, running steeply downhill; but there the similarity ended, for in Kilkenny the spinal road ran down to the castle, situated at the bottom of the hill. The contrast between the two cities is interesting in the siting and importance of the religious and the secular *foci*. Was it a case of Norman priorities or expediency, I wonder?

About the foundation of the borough there is much greater certainty, thanks to the survival of the foundation charter issued by William Marshal in the first decade of the thirteenth century.[12] It begins, as do all such documents, with a statement of the donor's name and status, although interestingly on this occasion Marshal styles himself earl of Pembroke and pointedly adds that he makes the grant with the consent and counsel of his wife, Isabel. In doing so, he is drawing attention to the fact that his power to act is derived from his wife as the daughter of an earl, Strongbow; and, perhaps more importantly, emphasising that she was also the granddaughter of a king, Diarmait Mac Murchada. Clearly, through these pointed statements, Marshal is acknowledging that his power is derived, not inherited.

The rights and privileges contained in this charter fall into three categories. The first is the legal powers to be exercised by the borough court, which Marshal calls the *hundred* of the town. This word was introduced into Ireland from England, where its context was not urban. Rather hundreds (or *wapentakes*, 'weapon takes', in areas settled by the Danes) were sub-divisions of shires, the local government units, originally devised in the kingdom of Wessex but then imposed on other parts of the country as they came under their control. In England, all free men made up the community of the hundred, and consequently the use of the term by Marshal was a confirmation of the free status of the burgesses.

The charter lays down how the judicial system is to function in accordance with precise rules: amercements are fixed, one sum for serious crimes and another for petty offences. Precise regulations are enjoined for the process of distraint for debt, a vital matter in a commercial community. However, Marshal was most distinctive in his insistence that no death should be classed as *murdrum*. This law, introduced by King William I, made a community collectively responsible for the death of a Frenchman if his body was found within their boundaries, unless they could produce the killer. By the early thirteenth century this law had become moribund in England, although in Ireland it could still be seen as needed, given that the Norman influx was still a work in progress.

That the prime occupation of the borough was trade was made clear by the number of commercial privileges granted to the burgesses. One was the freedom to form a merchant guild, a self-regulating association of traders; and also other guilds, especially for craftsmen and others plying their particular trades within the burgh. Moreover, the merchant burgesses were exempt from all commercial charges within the liberty of Leinster, and also in William Marshal's lands in England and Wales. However, specific restrictions were imposed on 'foreign' traders wishing to sell bread or wine within the borough. One obligation from which the burgesses were not granted freedom was that of grinding their corn at the lord's mill, although the charge for this service was to be 'reasonable', which was a usefully ambiguous term.

The charter also granted the burgesses advantageous terms of tenure. Their annual rent for all burgages was at the fixed low rate of twelve pence. They were also granted the right of free disposal of their burgages – other than to a religious order, which would have made them subject to canon law, thereby precluding any chance of recovery. Allied to free disposal was freedom for themselves and their children to marry whomsoever they wished, a right which was also granted to their widows. The only restriction was that the right applied particularly to property held under this charter, and not to any other property they might hold from other lords.

The final part of the charter confirms actions already taken: that all burgages should be twenty feet (6 m) wide, and that they should be charged with an annual ground rent of twelve pence. It is therefore clear that the actual work of the foundation had been carried out earlier, probably by Geoffrey Fitz Robert.

What the charter did not include, however, was any scheme of self-government. However, this was granted at a later date, probably by William Marshal II, and was certainly in place by 1230.[13] It stipulated that the burgesses were to elect annually a council of twelve plus a chief officer, to be known as the sovereign. More significantly, they were granted the privilege of electing the reeve, whose responsibility was to watch over and safeguard the lord's interests. Verbatim versions of this charter were also granted to Old Ross and to Callan, suggesting a clear indication that William Marshal, Isabel and their advisers had devised a formula that could be applied throughout the liberty of Leinster.

While the success of New Ross was equal to that of Kilkenny, it was markedly different in its physical structure. There was no castle at New Ross,[14] although there was a motte and bailey structure erected by Strongbow at Old Ross, 5 miles (8 km) to the east. Nor did New Ross have a major ecclesiastical institution, the nearest being the cathedral at Ferns. New Ross was founded on what was virtually a 'green field' site, clearly and deliberately chosen with an eye to economic development. The site was a little over 2 miles (3.5 km) south of the confluence of two of Leinster's major rivers, the Barrow and the Nore, both of which were access routes to rich farmlands to the north and west. South of New Ross, the river Barrow flowed 15 miles (25 km) before reaching the open sea. Because of the increased volume of water due to its tidal nature, the river was navigable by seagoing vessels, particularly the cog, the typical merchant ship of the North Sea and the Atlantic Ocean.

New Ross rapidly became the port to which agricultural produce (notably wheat, wool and hides) could be brought south for transhipment for export, a trade which was balanced by imports. While not entirely in Ireland's favour, it was not hugely adverse, probably because the imports were of higher value. The bustling, go-ahead port equally served as the entrepôt for imported luxury goods, notably wine from south-west France, that trade being handled by the guild of vintners. The wine they imported into New Ross was a commodity that was not only for the Irish market, but was also re-exported to Scotland in considerable quantity. Other obvious imported luxuries would be cloth, silk and exotic spices from the Orient: the term 'spice' embraced more than pepper, nutmeg and cinnamon, and could include all manner of dried fruits too. The term 'spice cake' is sometimes still used to describe a fruit cake.

By the end of the thirteenth century, from a standing start, William Marshal's ambition for New Ross had been amply realised: it was a thriving borough and the largest and busiest port in Ireland. Thanks to information generated by a fiscal innovation introduced in 1275, we have more accurate data about one sector of the town's economy. In that year, the merchants of England – fearful of Edward I's (1272–1307) unbridled demands for money, and keen to protect themselves from the government's voracious and uncontrolled appetite for income – struck a bargain with the king. Both parties agreed to fix an export duty of half a mark (6s 8d) on every sack of wool (14 stones = 364 lb = 89 kg) and 300 woolfells (sheepskins with the fleece still attached), and a duty of one mark (13s 4d) on every *last* of hides (4,000 lb = 1,815 kg). Collection of these duties meant that customs officers were stationed at every port. The ports of most interest to us are New Ross and Waterford, and the customs records reveal that of these two, New Ross was the leading exporter of Irish wool – well ahead of Waterford, and far ahead of Wexford. But wool and hides were not the only primary products exported: corn (especially wheat) and fish also figure prominently, and to a lesser extent other animal skins. Export of manufactured goods does not appear to have taken place in large quantities, except for the much sought-after Irish mantles; these heavy woollen cloaks were much prized throughout Europe. It is clear that the fame of Irish mantles had spread far and wide, given the following quotation attributed to English poet Edmund Spenser (1552–1599): 'The mantle is a fit house for an outlaw, a meet bed for a rebel and an apt cloak for a thief.'

The tax yields from this same source emphatically show the measure of the commercial success enjoyed by New Ross in the years 1279–97, when the duties collected averaged £239 per year.[15] Their nearest rival was Waterford with an average of £214, while receipts at Dublin averaged only £77 and at Wexford, a paltry £1. Unfortunately, there is no similar information about other exported or imported commodities. Meanwhile, all these sea-borne goods were coming and going in ships that were tiny by today's standards: few carried more than thirty tons of cargo, and most were from ports on the west coast of England: Bridgewater, Bristol and Chester. But there were ships registered in New Ross, which accounts for the large community of mariners in the town.

In addition to the busy activity and clamour of a flourishing business at the port, twenty-three different trades or occupations were carried on in the borough, all controlled and protected by their respective guilds. They included a goldsmith, whose presence in this vibrantly diverse town was surely an indication that there was a considerable wealth in the borough; otherwise it is unlikely that he would have had the scope to profitably ply his trade. Further evidence of prosperity is the church of St Mary, which was regarded as one of the largest and finest parish churches in Ireland, the building of which must have incurred a hefty expense.

The number of trades present points to a wide variety of economic activity. Relatively few people would have been engaged in the export of primary products such as wool and hides, or the import of exotic goods such as wine and spices. However, luxury goods were also being made in New Ross, given the presence of a goldsmith and the guild of mantle-makers: both an indication of the production of desirable Irish goods that could be exported throughout the Norman world. The existence of such

THE BISHOP'S GATE.

A medieval gateway: *The Bishop's Gate* at New Ross is a rare illustration of a medieval town wall and gate, fragments of which still exist. It led from the original marketplace to the Fair Green and the suburb of Irish Town. Source: P.H. Hore, *History of the Town and County of Wexford*, Vol. 1 (London, 1900) luxury goods reflected the wealth of the borough, and those involved in the import and export of such goods were the aristocracy of the borough community, in that their economic activity was the most lucrative. The majority of the town's inhabitants, though, are likely to have been employed in the wide range of occupations related to the general needs of the borough's population and its economic catchment area.

All this points to a population of considerable size. A rough calculation can be made using evidence in the survey made prior to the breakup of the liberty in 1247. The income from burgage rents was a little over £25 per year. As the standard rent was 12d, the number of burgages must have been a little over 500. Therefore, using the most conservative multiplier of 4.5 persons per household, a population of 2,250 emerges. However, that should be regarded as the minimum; in reality, the figure may have been much higher.

The marketplace, which was one of the two commercial *foci* of the town, was located next to the churchyard, and was formed by a widening of the street that led directly up the hill from the bridge over the river to one of the gates in the town wall, beyond which was the significantly named Fair Green. Subsequently, parts of the market were built over, possibly after the market was re-sited close to the present tholsel (now town hall). This gate was one of six that allowed entry and exit through the borough wall, the building of which began in 1265. The decision to build in stone was apparently a response to a brief but disruptive bout of warfare between two feudal lords, Walter de Burgh and the FitzGerald clan, although it would also be unwise to discount an element of civic vanity in walling in stone. When completed, the wall was 2,543 yards (2,325 m) long, including 820 yards (750 m) fronting the river. It seems likely the construction was self-financed, since the earliest murage (money for wall repair) grant was not made until 1374.

One interesting byproduct of its construction was a poem by a man much taken with the town of New Ross, who extolled it as the 'finest of its size . . . in any country'.[16] For us, the added significance lies in the poem's language, Old French, which presumably was the language spoken by the inhabitants of New Ross at that time, or at least by the town's leading members. This in turn points to them, like their feudal counterparts, being drawn from the French-speaking classes of England and Wales.

Two further feats of civil engineering bear witness to the economic ambitions held for New Ross by the lords of Leinster. Their dates of construction are not known, but the fact that they would have taken several, perhaps many, years to complete make possible a belief that both were begun during the Marshal years.

One was the quayside, the second of the town's two commercial *foci*. At just over 711 yards (650 m) in length, it was one of the longest in Ireland. The method of construction was probably standard, as archaeologists have revealed elsewhere in Ireland and at Newcastle-upon-Tyne in England.[17] It began with the construction, in wood or stone, of a line of 'boxes' along the high-water mark of the river to exclude the water. These 'boxes' were then filled with rubble and general rubbish and given a paved surface. Once the work was completed, ships could be kept afloat throughout the tidal phases, thereby allowing for uninterrupted loading and unloading.

The other civil engineering feat was the construction of a bridge across the river Barrow. It was of unknown length, but certainly more than 219 yards (200 m). A bridge was desirable not only for commercial purposes, but also to guarantee uninterrupted communication between New Ross and Kilkenny. The bridge crossed the river a few yards or metres north of its present successor, its position being in line with the road up from the river to the original marketplace. However, it was destroyed by floods sometime in the last quarter of the thirteenth century. The length of time required to build a replacement, and the subsequent repairs, made necessary a reserve method of crossing the river; this was supplied by a ferry.

William Marshal also sought to help the economic development of the liberty by commissioning the construction of a lighthouse (which still functions) at the tip of the Hook peninsula. His purpose was to provide a navigational aid for ships entering the estuary of the river Barrow with a view to proceeding up river to the port he was developing at New Ross. But the lighthouse was equally helpful to shipping entering the estuary, then turning westwards to enter Waterford Harbour. As both ports developed, conflict arose between them that was to last until the early sixteenth century. At the heart of the dispute was Waterford's claim to monopoly control of the navigation of the rivers Barrow, Nore and Suir, requiring all ships to berth at its quay and pay dues or discharge their cargoes. In pursuit of this policy Waterford had a clear advantage: it was a royal port, and consequently its burgesses had the king's ear. There is little doubt that the ambition of the merchants of Waterford was to make their borough the commercial hub of much of southern Ireland. However, a compromise was always likely. It was achieved in the mid 1220s, almost certainly by William Marshal II using his influence as justiciar of Ireland to negotiate an agreement with the crown that granted the right of free navigation of the rivers

Barrow and Nore to all ships belonging to the lord of the liberty of Leinster and his tenants.

This did not prove to be an acceptable solution. Waterford appears never to have become reconciled to the loss of its outright monopoly, while New Ross engaged in the illicit practice of charging dues from all ships from Waterford and elsewhere that came within its reach. As a result, the years between 1227 and 1518 are littered with complaints to the crown from the Waterford burgesses, and with crown injunctions reiterating their rights.[18] This long-running dispute reached a climax in 1518, when a gang of miscellaneous ruffians assembled in Waterford and proceeded upriver to wreak havoc in New Ross. The burgesses of New Ross bought them off with the gift of a silver gilt mace, which is still in the Waterford Museum.

The rivers flowing into New Ross were the town's lifeblood. The river Nore has all the appearance of being the intended spine of the liberty, a 16-mile (26 km) waterway linking its administrative head, Kilkenny, with its economic powerhouse, New Ross. The notion that this was preconceived is given some support by two smaller boroughs founded at intermediate points along the river's route: Inistioge, 7 miles (11 km) from New Ross, and Thomastown, 8 miles (13 km) from Kilkenny. They were not founded by William Marshal, at least not directly, but by one of his trusted lieutenants, Thomas Fitz Anthony. However, Fitz Anthony's initiatives may not have been entirely unilateral, but taken after consultation with Marshal.

Thomastown covered about 17 acres (7 ha) with a rectangular marketplace, which is still clearly defined, that terminated with a parish church (now deconsecrated) at one end, and a road turning sharply towards the river ferry and later bridge at the other end. A small castle was built in stone, one mile (1.6 km), out of Thomastown and known as Grenan, the Irish name for the district.

While Thomastown, which bears its founder's name, was in secular lordship, not so Inistioge. The lordship of the borough of Inistioge was vested in the Augustinian priory founded by Fitz Anthony on the site of a pre-conquest monastery. It too had a castle (a motte and bailey that was never upgraded); a square marketplace was situated between the castle and priory and, like Thomastown, it had a ferry and then later a bridge. In both places, the commerce of the river played a major role.

The river Nore also had a navigable tributary, the King's River, which gave access to Geoffrey Fitz Robert's religious and commercial enterprises at Kells and beyond that to one of Marshal's largest manors, Callan, which included a borough covering 25 acres (10 ha) with a marketplace, walls and a motte and bailey castle.

The other river flowing into New Ross was the river Barrow, the valley of which extended much further north into the heart of Kildare. On its middle reaches were situated two important boroughs: Leighlin, an ancient ecclesiastical site that was developed as the centre of one of the dioceses of the liberty of Leinster; and Carlow, sited in the angle formed by the Barrow and its tributary, the Burran. Unlike Leighlin and many other boroughs, Carlow was not based upon an important pre-conquest site. Although not particularly large, for it covered only 32 acres (13 ha), it rapidly became an important administrative centre, a fact underlined by the rebuilding of the castle in stone early in the thirteenth century.

Kildare, the most northerly part of the liberty, had the least Marshal presence, basically because so much of it had been granted out to feudal tenants by Strongbow. This is reflected in the fact that of its four confirmed boroughs, only one – Kildare itself – was in Marshal lordship. It was one of the smallest known boroughs, probably because it only had a modest economic potential. Its importance arose from its ecclesiastical institutions, the great double monastery founded by St Brigid (d. 523) and its later designation as a diocesan centre: ironically, Co. Kildare is now home to one of Ireland's most important and lucrative economic generators, the horse racing industry.

The other three boroughs were founded by leading feudal tenants of the liberty: Athy by the St Michael family; Naas by Maurice Fitz Gerald; and Castledermot by Walter de Riddlesford. All were about 37 acres (15 ha) in area, and in that respect resembled Gowran. Of this group, only Athy was on the river Barrow, which meant that it could be linked to New Ross by river transport. Its location was also due, as its name indicates, to being at a point where the river could be forded.

One Leinster borough, that of Wexford, stands out from the others on two counts: it was a sea port at the mouth of the river Slaney, and it had acquired burghal characteristics before the arrival of the Normans, being, together with Dublin, Waterford and Limerick, one of the trading settlements founded in the ninth century by the Norse. Although it was to expand, it failed to capitalise on the head start it enjoyed. In part this was due to the phenomenal success enjoyed by New Ross, but it also suffered from the gradual silting of the harbour bar.

Perhaps to this list five others may be added, though with varying degrees of confidence. The case of Rosbercon appears conclusive, given that it was one of the places granted the identical privileges given to Kilkenny.[19] Tullow also has a strong claim,[20] although its full status as a borough appears to post-date the breakup of the liberty in 1247. It was sited advantageously at a fording point on a major waterway, the river Slaney. Its topography was typically burghal: a long street with side lanes, running up from the ford to a square-shaped marketplace. There is evidence of burgages, although not until 1285, when the number was likely to have been 106; this seems to have doubled by 1303. There was a castle, all signs of which have disappeared; likewise the walls, although there is evidence that grants were made to levy murage in 1303, 1344 and 1357.

Similar sorts of evidence survive for Ferns and Leighlin, both of which gained importance from being diocesan centres. Ferns was also a Marshal manor, and was important enough for its castle to be rebuilt in stone. Leighlin, or rather New Leighlin, situated by the river, is known to have been granted a charter by its first Norman bishop between 1201 and 1217; the charter was reissued in 1297.[21] There was also a castle, built by Hugh de Lacy, and a bridge across the river, commissioned by John as lord of Ireland. The possibile existence of walls is indicated by the murage grants of 1295 and 1310.

The one instance where the evidence is too slight to support anything but a not-proven verdict is the New Town of Leix, which in 1247 is known to have had 127 burgages. Its span of life was brief, as it succumbed to the Irish recovery of the fourteenth and fifteenth centuries. Even its whereabouts are not known for certain, though they are likely to have been adjacent to the great castle at the top of the Rock of Dunamase.[22]

After this, speculation takes over, and it would be wrong to see failures of fortune as failures of ambition. Clonmines, founded by William Marshal, might have burgeoned had it not been for the progressive silting of Bannow Bay. Likewise, the grant of a weekly market to Templeshanbo by the bishop of Ferns may have carried hopes of growth and prosperity. At the same time, there is much validity in Jocelyn Otway-Ruthven's theory of the use (perhaps misuse) of burgage tenure for rural purposes.

Local Government

INTRODUCTION OF THE SHIRE SYSTEM

Anyone living in Britain is familiar with the words 'shire' and 'county'. They are synonymous, describing the same institution, the difference being linguistic: 'shire' derives from the Old English *scir*, while 'county' is from the French *comté*. That these two words are still in common use is a consequence of the Norman conquest of England. The creation of counties in Ireland stemmed from the imposition of control of the country by the English government, and it reflected the long and chequered history of that process.

By the opening years of the eleventh century, the kingdom of England, which had emerged during the previous hundred years, had developed a system of local government based upon large territorial divisions known as shires (*scir*).[1] Some were echoes of small kingdoms of the early days of English settlement, while others were based upon administrative units created by the Danes. Many, however, were artificial, in that they bore little or no relation to any previous structure.

Shires were sub-divided into smaller units. For the most part these were known as hundreds, but in the six shires that had a high density of Danish settlement, the term used was wapentake (literally 'weapon take'). Every shire was in the charge of a royal officer, the sheriff – a word compounded from two Old English words, *scir* and *gerefa* (reeve).

By 1066, thirty-one counties or shires covered most of England. But not all of it: the large areas of the far north that eventually became Lancashire, Westmorland, Cumberland, Northumberland and Durham were not shired until later, when they were finally incorporated into the English state. One consequence of their pre-conquest shiring was that only one of them ever had the term 'shire' attached to it: the others have always been counties.

The utility and potential of this system of local government was readily accepted, retained and developed by the new Norman regime, in effect 'Normanising' it. Therefore it was natural that they should impose it on the other parts of Britain as they were brought under their control. The ways by which this happened were prolonged and developed piecemeal, inevitably awaiting the establishment of full crown control. In Wales,[2] the shire system was not finalised until the reign of Henry VIII (1509–47). In Scotland, creating shires was begun by the avidly Normanising King David I (1124–53),[3] but it could not be finalised until the late fifteenth century when the Scottish crown acquired Orkney and Shetland, the outer parts of the Norwegian kingdom in 1472 and the lordship of the Isles in 1493.[4]

The range of administrative duties imposed by the Normans, in particular upon sheriffs, was wide and varied.[5] It included the collection of dues owed to the crown, supervision of the managers of the royal estates and presidency of the county court, to which all free men owed suit, reviewing and discharging a wide range of royal instructions and delivering proof that they had been carried out. The sheriff also had command of the militia of the county, what the documents called the *posse comitatus* (Latin: power of the county); hence the sheriff's posse, with which all lovers of Hollywood 'westerns' are familiar. The seat of the sheriff's operations was a royal castle, of which he was the constable. It was there that he had his offices dealing with finance, records and correspondence. It was also there that the meetings of the county court were held, and where suspects he had apprehended were held in custody pending their trial before the itinerant royal justices. These duties required him to have a clerical staff, but also one with enough strength of arm to deal with rough characters and violent situations.

The year in which Strongbow launched his conquest of Leinster, 1170, was also the year King Henry II instituted an overhaul of the shire system in England. On his return from spending several years in his French domains, he was greeted by vociferous complaints about the corruption, venality and brutality of his sheriffs. His solution was to remove the office from the hands of the local magnates and replace them with what we might call civil servants: men who were accountable and could be dismissed at will without fear of political consequences. He also made their conduct subject to investigation by royal justices. This reform by no means eradicated the problem of abuse of power, but it did go some way towards containing it.

This, then, was the local government structure that the Anglo-Normans brought to Ireland, but not immediately. Initially, local government, such as it was, was based upon the twenty-seven cantreds into which the liberty of Leinster was divided. In each of these, there was a chief sergeant with a supporting staff: he was the chief agent of the lord of the liberty.

By the end of the thirteenth century, there were thirteen operational shires in Ireland: four in what had been the liberty, and nine created by the crown at Connacht, Cork, Dublin, Kerry, Limerick, Louth, Roscommon, Tipperary and Waterford. They were not, as in England, divided into hundreds or wapentakes. Instead, the pre-existing cantreds were retained as sub-divisions.[6]

Nor was the *frankpledge* system introduced in Ireland. This was a social control arrangement that operated in much, though not all, of England. It required all males over the age of sixteen to be in a *tithing*, a group of ten whose members were mutually responsible for their good behaviour, and particularly for producing in court any member accused of a crime. Failure to do so entailed collective punishment.

By 1200, English shires had acquired an additional royal officer, the *coroner*, who was concerned with 'pleas of the crown' – that is, offences that fell under the jurisdiction of the king's justices. Most particularly, he was required to investigate instances of sudden or violent death. It is not clear to me whether this office had appeared in the four counties of the liberty before 1247.

The decision to replace the cantreds with English-style counties was taken by William Marshal I. No details of the creation process have survived, though it seems it began early, since there is a reference to the county of Wexford as early as 1204. Next to have a change of designation was Kildare, in 1214. Kilkenny did not appear until 1224, by which date the lordships had passed to William Marshal II; and there is no mention of Carlow until 1247. This string of dates may well be an accident of record survival, but is not sufficient to rule out the possibility that all four counties were created simultaneously as a carefully considered restructuring of local government. On the other hand, it may reflect a more piecemeal process. Whatever the explanation, the counties survived the breakup of the liberty of Leinster, and the evidence for the portion awarded to the earl of Norfolk is sufficient to prove the existence of a functioning shire system.

The decline of power in the fourteenth and fifteenth centuries, however, stalled the process of county formation. By the early sixteenth century there were only ten functioning counties, although some others existed on paper. Ulster and Connacht, however, were as yet untouched. The process resumed as the English crown tightened its grip on Ireland. A start was made in 1556 under Mary I (d. 1558) with the formation of Offaly and Laois, carved out of Kilkenny and Kildare and known until the establishment of the Irish Free State as, respectively, King's County and Queen's County. The formation process was brought to a conclusion fairly rapidly between 1571 and 1586 with the creation of fifteen new counties.[7]

Church Reform

REVIVAL OF THE WESTERN CHURCH

This chapter is concerned with the Western Church, which between 1050 and 1200 developed into a forceful and dynamic authority system in Western Europe. At times it stood against lay rulers, yet it always sought cooperation with them in regulating European society and its codes of behaviour. Moreover, in the course of the first half of the second millennium, the church at all levels became a landowner on a massive scale and thereby a major economic force. Ireland felt the impact of these developments, sometimes directly from Europe and sometimes through England.

The starting point has to be the early eleventh century, when the condition of the church was dire, at least in the opinion of its high-minded leaders.[1] For them, the church was beset with a range of evils that prevented it performing what it conceived to be its divinely ordained mission. One was particularly urgent: clerical celibacy, or rather the lack of it, especially among the parochial clergy. Engagement in sexual activity, reformers believed, rendered a priest spiritually unclean and so vitiated his celebration of the mass. But, in addition, sexual activity would and did lead to the creation of a hereditary priesthood.

This and other specific issues were all aspects of the broader problem of lay control of the church. At the top level of the church, archbishops, bishops and many abbots were appointed by kings, who saw them as essential members of the state apparatus. At the base, parish churches were regarded as property belonging to the owner of the land on which they stood.

The starkly contrasting reformist view was that the church should be an autonomous, self-regulating institution working in conjunction with, but not subordinate to, lay authority so as to produce and regulate a harmonious Christian society. Clearly, the poet Coleridge may have had this in mind when he remarked that the church and state were 'two poles of the same magnet'. The more radical reformers went further, arguing that as human beings had two natures, spiritual and temporal, and the former was eternal while the latter was only temporary, spiritual authority should outrank temporal. Their conclusion was that in the last resort, those holding spiritual authority had the right to admonish and to correct their temporal counterparts.

In order to bring about the urgently needed change, one institution had a pivotal role: the papacy, the accepted head of the Western Church. But in this there was embedded a major problem: by the mid eleventh century the papacy had become mired in the sordid politics of the province of Rome. Papal elections had become the battleground of contending noble families.

Rescuing the papal office from the thraldom of local politics was accomplished in a fifteen-year period in the middle decades of the eleventh century, by three men. The first was the Holy Roman Emperor, Henry III (1039–56), whose authority extended over what are now Germany, Austria, Switzerland, Eastern France and parts of Italy. Henry began by intervening in the papal election of 1046, when he imposed a man of reformist views. Unfortunately, neither he nor his successor lived long enough to achieve anything. Not so Henry's third choice, Bruno, bishop of Toul in Lorraine, who took the name Leo IX (1049–54).

Pope Leo IX was a man of dynamic energy and total commitment, who galvanised the reform movement throughout much of continental Europe. His instrument for success was the synod, a conference of clergy where he promulgated his reform programme. He held an annual synod in Rome during Lent and then toured Italy, France and parts of Germany giving the same message to provincial synods.

The continued progress of reform might have stalled but for his successor but two, Gerard, bishop of Florence, who took the papal name Nicholas II (1059–61). He was fortunate to be elected, given the vigorous attempt by the Roman nobility to recover lost ground. It was this that prompted him to issue what would become known as the Election Decree, the core of which was the prescription that possession of the papal office was valid only if the man had been elected by the College of Cardinals. At this date the College numbered fifty-two: the seven bishops of the province of Rome, the twenty-seven priests of the city's parish churches and eighteen deacons.

The papal armoury lacked one essential weapon: a comprehensive, codified and therefore authoritative body of canon (church) law. What then existed, scattered around Europe, were collections of canons and decretals (papal judgements), none comprehensive or entirely congruent. The solution was produced in Bologna by a monk named Gratian, who compiled an acceptable synthesis that became known as the *Decretum*. Over the following hundred years, further volumes were added as canon law expanded and became more detailed and precise. The end product was the *Corpus Juris Canonici* (Body of Canon Law).

In the 180 years after the death of Nicholas II, twenty-three men were elected pope. All were reformers and all were able and competent, with some being of outstanding calibre. Under their direction, the Western Church evolved into the papal monarchy, a supranational authority ruling over a pyramid of territorial divisions and personnel. At the top were provinces, each under the rule of an archbishop. Provinces were divided into dioceses, each governed by a bishop. Every archbishop and bishop had a cathedral (Latin *cathedra*, or teacher's chair) staffed by a chapter, which was a corporation of clergy with the canonical right to elect their archbishop or bishop. Dioceses were divided into archdeaconries. Both bishops and archdeacons presided over courts that dealt with people and matters subject to canon law. The base of the pyramid comprised thousands of parishes.

The evolution of the papal monarchy, as it became known, was not a smooth process. Clashes between kings and popes were frequent and bitter, perhaps the most notable being that which culminated in the murder of Archbishop Thomas Becket in Canterbury Cathedral on 29 December 1170. Kings, however, were not fundamentally opposed to church reform. What concerned them was their loss of control over the appointments to the episcopate. Kings had traditionally appointed bishops as the means of paying or rewarding the senior members of their government, and for enhancing their royal authority. Such men were able and well educated, which meant they had a command of Latin, the language of law and government as well as religion. Moreover, every bishopric was endowed with estates, which made bishops in effect feudal barons in addition to being ecclesiastics. For the popes, these considerations were of little importance; bishops were to be churchmen, first and last.

Almost inevitably, this clash of views had to end in compromise: both parties had points of view with genuine validity. In the end, kings conceded the right of cathedral chapters to elect their own bishops. But in return the church conceded to kings the right to hold episcopal estates during periods of vacancy; to inform chapters of their preferred candidate; and to require the chosen man to swear fealty prior to his consecration.

The above structure constituted the *secular* church (Latin *saeculum*, the world), since its concern was with the affairs of the world of the laity. But within its framework were other clergy, the *regulars* (Latin *regula*, rule). They were so called because as well as observing the basic rules of clerical life, particularly celibacy, they belonged to communities that required obedience to additional rules specific to themselves. Between 1100 and 1300, this branch of the church expanded in both size and diversity.

In the year 1100, this sector comprised a relatively small number of en-closed monasteries that observed the rule devised by an Italian, St Benedict of Nursia (*c.* 480–*c.* 547), which required its adherents to retreat from the world and devote a celibate life to prayer, study and essential manual labour. These monasteries were free-standing institutions, not linked in any formal way, although subject to the bishops of the dioceses in which they were located. It was an arrangement that failed to guarantee conform-ity and uniformity. Concerns over these problems led to the founding of new orders of monks in the tenth century, notably those based on Cluny in Burgundy and Gorze in Lorraine.

But it was the Cistercian Order, founded in 1098 by Robert de Molesme, that had a revolutionary impact. At the foundation house at Cîteaux (Latin *Cistercia*) in Burgundy, a new style of monasticism was developed with an emphasis on austerity and simplicity: everything that was not essential was discarded. It was a puritanical lifestyle, proclaimed by the monastic habit of undyed wool; hence they were known as the White Monks. Their daily round was confined to worship and study, manual labour being transferred to *conversi* (lay brethren). To prevent slackening of performance, a strict system of control and inspection was imposed. Every new Cistercian house was founded as a colony from an existing one, and this 'mother–daughter' relationship remained permanent, with the mother house having the right to inspect its daughters annually. The Cistercian Order, therefore, was in effect a number of chains, all leading back to Cîteaux, whose abbot was in overall command. Finally, unlike Benedictine houses, Cistercian monas-teries were free of local episcopal control; instead they were under direct papal supervision.

The Cistercian order enjoyed spectacular success. By 1250, a total of 651 houses had been founded in those areas of Europe that acknowledged the headship of the pope. This rapid growth can only have stemmed from the popular appeal of the Order's aims and performance, particularly to the great landowners who donated the lands on which the Cistercian houses were founded. More particularly, two individuals stand out as having had a major influence. One was a Burgundian aristocrat, St Bernard (1090–1153), the abbot of Clairvaux, one of the four 'daughter' houses of Cîteaux. He was one of the most dynamic and charismatic personalities of the twelfth century. A measure of his impact is that of the 651 foundations by 1250, 339 (52 per cent) can be traced along the chain from Clairvaux. The other man was very different: Stephen Harding (d. 1134), an Englishman from Dorset, who composed the Order's constitution, the *Carta Caritatis* (Charter of Love) in 1119.

The appeal of an austere, self-denying but highly structured way of life was not exclusive to the Cistercians. Several other very similar congregations came into being around the same time, two of them of interest to us. One, founded by Vital of Mortain in 1112 at Savigny, between Le Mans and Tours, was so like Cîteaux that in 1147 the Savignacs merged with the Cistercians. The other, founded at Tiron by a monk from Poitiers named Bernard, continued as a separate congregation.

Equally influential, but in a very different way, were the Augustinian canons, whose rule was based upon precepts composed by the fourth-century theologian St Augustine of Hippo Regius (now Anaba, in Algeria), who died in 430. Between them and monks were two major differences: Augustinian canons were priests, which at this date few monks were; and unlike monks, canons were not confined to the cloister, but were permitted to work outside its walls. Although they too required endowments in the form of land, their income came increasingly from parish churches that were made over to them. Therefore, the canons were able to appropriate the dues owed because they could serve as parish priests themselves, or provide and pay for a vicar to carry out duties on their behalf. The papacy found in this arrangement an appealing solution to the problem of the married or non-celibate priest.

The more flexible rule of St Augustine proved useful for another kind of regular order that came into being in the twelfth century, the monastic knights. Four such orders were founded in the Iberian Peninsula and one in Germany: the Teutonic Knights. However, two military orders were supreme in that they enjoyed international appeal and support on a massive scale: they were the Order of the Temple of Jerusalem (the Templars) and the Order of the Hospital of St John of Jerusalem (the Hospitallers). Together, they substantially increased the defence capability of the kingdom of Jerusalem. But their existence posed a moral problem: how could a knight, who was trained to kill, be at the same time a monk who was committed to peace? It required the literary skills of St Bernard to square this circle in his book *In Praise of the Knighthood*. Both orders became immensely wealthy through the donations of money and land by Western Christians willing to support the good cause with their treasure, though not with their blood.

Finally, in the early thirteenth century, another very different style of regular came into being: the friars (Latin *frater*, brother).[2] In the end, the papacy permitted only four orders, fearing the consequences of unbridled proliferation. Papal concern was aroused by the lifestyle of the friars: mendicancy (Latin *mendicus*, beggar). Unlike all other regular orders, the friars refused to become owners of property and, like Jesus and his disciples, they opted to live without any visible means of support other than the generosity of those who approved of their work.

The largest and most successful of the orders were the Dominicans, founded by a Spaniard, Domenico Guzman (St Dominic) and the Franciscans, founded by an Italian, Francisco Bernadone (St Francis). In origin, at least, their motivation differed markedly. Dominic was concerned to create a well-educated body of men able to counter the beliefs of heretics, particularly the Cathars of southern France. From the start the Dominicans were a well-structured organisation with a well-thought-out constitution. Francis, on the other hand, was driven by an intense spiritual urge to live a life as close as possible to that which he believed Jesus had lived. It was only with the greatest reluctance that he succumbed to papal pressure and agreed to form an order with a constitution.

Two smaller orders, the Carmelites and the Austin (Augustinian) friars, came into existence slightly later. The origins of both are obscure and essentially organic, but they were organised and regularised as defined orders by the papacy in, respectively, 1229 and 1243. Papal concern at the proliferation of unregulated bands of wandering preachers, often with eccentric if not heretical beliefs, led to a decision in 1274 that no further orders of friars would be permitted and that some, such as the Crutched Friars and the Friars of the Sack, were forbidden to recruit and so were condemned to 'wither on the vine'.

Anyone viewing a map of any part of Western Europe that recorded the many and varied houses of the regular orders would readily perceive that no one then would be able to complete a day's journey without being in sight or sound of at least one of their establishments. These would certainly have been apparent to the bands of pilgrims as they made their way to shrines, such as those at Canterbury and Compostela.

One final point: eventually, the success of the church reform movement was proclaimed in stone, initially in the Romanesque style, which then gave way to the Gothic style of architecture after *c.* 1200 and the huge number of fine cathedrals, monasteries and parish churches in Western Christendom.

DIOCESES AND PARISHES IN THE LIBERTY OF LEINSTER

Around the year 1100, the church in Ireland, along with many other aspects of Irish society, was in a parlous condition, at least in the eyes of outside observers. This qualifying phrase is essential, since the observers were basing their judgements on reports, not personal observation or experience, and with prejudice, in that their yardstick was how the church was structured and functioned elsewhere in Western Christendom. On their arrival in England, Norman churchmen found much to dislike about the church in England and set about bringing it into line with Norman practice and up to Norman standards. However, in the end many were persuaded that all was not lost and there was much to admire and worth accepting in the pre-Conquest church in England.

In reformist eyes, however, the church in Ireland was not properly structured. It was dominated by a number of large and wealthy monasteries where liturgies differed from those in continental Benedictine houses. The root of the problem, as they saw it, was lay control. In Ireland, abbots were drawn from hereditary families while their estates were in the hands of hereditary managers. Therefore, both offices could be in the hands of laymen not in holy orders, and were part of the political fabric of the kingdoms in which they were located.

There were bishops, but not as reformers knew them. There were too many of them – over fifty – and they had no clearly defined territorial dioceses and no jurisdictional authority. All they were empowered to do was discharge the traditional episcopal functions of consecrating churches, ordaining priests and acting as confessors. To a visitor from England or Normandy, their status was very lowly.

To the reformers, these lamentable arrangements in Ireland were no longer to be tolerated, despite[3] the fact that their ranks contained a growing cohort of Irish churchmen who were well aware of developments in the European continent, and in England after 1066. In fact, four bishops of Dublin and one from Limerick and Waterford voluntarily submitted to examination by the archbishops of Canterbury and were consecrated by them; and, moreover, made professions of obedience to them.

All this was very welcome to Canterbury, whose first Norman archbishop, Lanfranc (1070–89), had become aware of an ancient tradition (although with dubious foundation) that the archbishops of Canterbury had papal approval to exercise supremacy over all churches in Britain and Ireland. The papacy too had a growing interest in Ireland, and perhaps of crucial importance, church reform had the active support of certain Irish kings, the most notable being Muirchertach O'Briain, king of Munster (1086–1119) and High King of Ireland.

Therefore, the breakthrough was made well before the Anglo-Norman invasion of Leinster in 1169, when at the synod held at Cashel in 1101 and, more particularly, in 1111 at Rath Bressail, in what is now Co. Tipperary, reform of the church was accepted. The necessary leadership came from two men: King Muirchertach and Gille Espuic (also known by the French name, Gilbert), who had been bishop of Limerick since 1107 and had been made papal legate by Pope Pascal II (1098–1118), a role he retained until his death in 1139.

Episcopal attendance at Rath Bressail was sufficiently comprehensive, together with the authoritative presence of the papal legate and the High King, to ensure the all-Ireland acceptance of the synod's decisions. These amounted to a fundamental restructuring of the Irish Church, which involved dividing the church into two provinces using the traditional line between *Leath Cuinn* (the north) and *Leath Mogha* (the south). The seat of the Northern Province was to be at Armagh, which was founded by St Patrick, while the Southern Province was to be based at Cashel, formerly the site of a royal residence that had been given to the church by King Muirchertach O'Briain in 1101.

Each province was to be ruled by an archbishop and was to be divided into twelve dioceses, each with a bishop. In adopting the number twelve the authors of the scheme may have had in mind Jesus's disciples. They may also have been aware of Pope Gregory I's (c. 540–604) injunction to his missioner, Augustine, who arrived in the kingdom of Kent in 597 briefed to begin the conversion of the pagan English to Christianity.[4] They would have learned this from Bede's account of the mission in which the pope advised Augustine to establish two ecclesiastical provinces, each with an archbishop, at the two former Roman capitals, London and York. This was in accord with Pope Gregory's vision of a Roman Empire revived as a Christian Roman Empire, but it took no account of the political structure of Anglo-Saxon England.

The Rath Bressail scheme was flawed in two respects. One was the failure to include Dublin as one of the dioceses. This was clearly deliberate, as Dublin had had a bishop since the mid eleventh century and was fast becoming the key player in Irish politics. The precise reason for this decision, is not clear, but one possible explanation is Armagh's fears of Dublin's ambition.

The second problem, which dragged on unresolved for nearly forty years, was the papal refusal to award *pallia* to the two archbishops. The *pallium*, although only a narrow strip of cloth, was a crucial element in archiepiscopal vestments in that its bestowal was a papal prerogative and, therefore, the essential sign of papal recognition. Without it, an archbishop was not rightfully installed in office. Why seven successive popes adamantly refused to relent is also not clear. But it is not hard to think that Canterbury may have been behind it, since the existence of two archbishops in Ireland might seriously compromise its claim to hegemony over the Irish church. Papal resolve even managed to stand firm against the pleading of its favourite Irish cleric, Máel Máedóc Ua Morgair (St Malachy), who visited Rome in 1139–40. On the other hand, there may have been serious doubts in Rome as to the viability of the Rath Bressail scheme.

Support for this possibility is to be found in the arrangements made by Pope Eugenius III (1145–53) for the legatine mission he sent to Ireland. It was led by John Paparo, cardinal priest of St Laurence in Damaso, who arrived in 1149 with full legatine authority to bring the matter to a conclusion. Significantly, Paparo brought with him not two, but four *pallia*, a clear indication that an alternative structure for the Irish church had already been planned. The formula for restructure emerged from a synod held in 1150 and 1151, some sessions being held at Kells in Meath, others at Mellifont Abbey in Co. Louth, and almost certainly having taken into account the realities of Irish life and conditions.

There were to be four provinces with archbishops at Armagh, Cashel, Dublin and Tuam, under whom were to be different numbers of bishops: Armagh ten, Cashel twelve, Dublin five and Tuam seven. In all, thirty-four dioceses, all with clearly defined boundaries and with bishops with authority under canon law over all ecclesiastical elements, except for those religious houses that came directly under papal jurisdiction.

This papally instituted structure was the one in place when the Anglo-Norman conquest of Leinster began and it was one with which the Anglo-Normans were familiar. It was completed in 1172 during King Henry II's visit to Ireland. At another synod held at Cashel, Henry laid down that henceforth the Irish church was to function in accordance with the rules and customs that governed the church in England. These included the requirement that archbishops and bishops should recognise that they were part of the polity of the king of England's realm by swearing fealty to him, as their English counterparts did. That the Irish bishops, all of whom were Irishmen, did so is a clear indication that they saw in Henry II a benevolent supporter of church reform.

What did the reformers hope to achieve now that a new structure gave them scope for action? Two matters in particular were of great concern. One was that the performance of the liturgy should not be full of irregularities. In effect, the clergy were to be required to adopt the forms of worship practised in England and in continental Europe. Their other great concern was the prevalence of what they saw as a casual attitude to marriage and sexual activity. What they wished to see was the latter confined within the bounds of marriage, an aspiration more readily accepted by men committed to celibacy than by the general run of mankind.

What Strongbow inherited was a very new church less than a quarter of a century old and with much still to be done before that framework was filled with its many interconnecting parts. Evidence as to when and how this work was done is sparse, but what we have tells us it was not completed until after 1200 – that is, it was not until after William Marshal assumed control that substantial progress was made. It was a slow revolution.

The land of the liberty of Leinster lay within the archdiocese of Dublin and encompassed four of its five subordinate dioceses: Ferns, Kildare, Kilkenny and Leighlin.⁵ Not included was the diocese of Glendalough, which was later absorbed into the diocese of Dublin with the agreement of Pope Innocent III (1198–1216). All four of its dioceses were carried over from the Rath Bressail scheme, and rightly so, since they were all important early ecclesiastical centres. At the time of Strongbow's accession all four were still held by Irish bishops, and it was not until 1223 that all of them were to acquire Anglo-Norman prelates. The changeover, which was all but inevitable, took place through natural wastage: the crown was clearly in no hurry to effect a rapid transformation.

The earliest dioceses to acquire Anglo-Norman bishops were Leighlin and Kilkenny, both in 1202. Nothing is known about events at Leighlin other than that it was a Cistercian monk, Herlewin, who was appointed to the diocese. We know much more about Kilkenny. The last Irish bishop, Felix Ua Dubhlaine (O'Delaney), was appointed in 1178 and remained in post until his death in 1202. His replacement was Hugh le Roux, the leader of the small group of Augustinian canons brought from Bodmin in Cornwall by Geoffrey Fitz Robert to be the foundation congregation of the canonry he founded at Kells.

The other two dioceses did not change hands for another twenty years. Little is known about Kildare except that Irish bishops continued to be appointed, the last being Cornelius Mac Gealine in 1206. When he died, however, his successor was an Anglo-Norman, Ralph of Bristol. We are better informed about events at Ferns, largely thanks to a long-running quarrel. The last Irish bishop, appointed in 1186, was Ailbe O Maelmuídhe. He was well regarded both in Ireland and in England, and at one point was considered for the archbishopric of Cashel. But the last years of his episcopate were marred by a bitter quarrel with William Marshal I, whom he accused of illegally taking possession of part of the episcopal estate. Both Marshal and his son and successor, William II, flatly refused to make restitution, which drove the frustrated bishop to excommunicate both of them and later to place a curse on the family. The bishop's death in 1223 opened the way for King Henry III to secure control of the diocese during the vacancy and then secure the appointment of John Fitz John, his treasurer of Ireland, as the new bishop. It was a classic example of an ecclesiastical benefice being used to reward service to the crown.

A bishop required a cathedral, and the Norman bishops who took over English dioceses were intent on having the best. Between 1066 and 1100, all the cathedrals in England were rebuilt or were in the process of rebuilding in order to exceed the grandeur, magnificence and size of the Anglo-Saxon churches they replaced. The motives of these builder bishops were mixed: the glory of God had undisputed primacy, however, episcopal vanity and competitiveness cannot be discounted; but, perhaps above all, these new cathedrals proclaimed the power and authority of the new ecclesiastical regime.

Their Anglo-Norman successors were driven by the same urges, with the result that all four of Leinster's cathedrals experienced a major reconstruction in the course of the thirteenth century, although not on quite the same scale as those in England. For this, there is a simple underlying reason: there were twice as many cathedrals and bishops in Ireland as there were in England, and consequently the wealth at their disposal to finance building programmes was more limited. Added to this was that by the time they began their work the Romanesque style had given way to Early English Gothic, which was more complex and therefore more expensive. The best surviving example of the latter style of architecture is the splendid cathedral dedicated to St Canice in Kilkenny, which was built between c. 1250 and 1285 by the successive bishops of Ossory, Hugh de Magilton and Geoffrey St Leger.

Cathedrals required chapters – these were corporations of clergy to maintain the fabric and sustain a complex and demanding liturgy, and also, when the occasion arose, to elect the bishop. Setting up a chapter was the responsibility of the bishop and in most cases this awaited the coming of an Anglo-Norman. In Leinster, as elsewhere in Ireland, the cathedral chapters were composed of secular clergy and were structured in the same form as their English equivalents.[6] The head of the chapter was the Dean and under him were three men with specific roles: precentor (liturgy), chancellor (administration) and treasurer (finance). They were known as canons, and their offices were endowed to provide them with an income. In addition, there were up to five more canons 'without portfolio', and they too had endowments known as prebends (Latin *prebenda*, forage or food allowance). These assigned endowments did not account for the entire income of the chapter: some sources of income were reserved for a common fund. Although the evidence for this form of cathedral chapter is sparse, there is sufficient extant to make it clear that this was the form in existence in all four cathedrals by the end of the thirteenth century.

Membership of the chapter also included an important official whose role had little to do with running the cathedral: the archdeacon. It was an office which had evolved during the twelfth century. English dioceses, on account of their size, had more than one archdeacon, whose jurisdictions in most cases covered a county. The smaller dioceses in Ireland meant that they needed only one archdeacon. His too was an endowed office, usually by its attachment to a wealthy parish church. The archdeacon's role grew with canon law. He had jurisdiction over the court dealing with the clergy of the diocese but also the laity in respect of matters that came within the purview of canon law.

Below the archdeacons came the rural deans. By the end of the thirteenth century all four dioceses had been divided into rural deaneries, with boundaries largely coinciding with those of cantreds. The rural deans were incumbents of one of the parishes of their deanery and were appointed by the bishop to act as a conduit of communication between the hierarchy of the diocese and its roots.

PARISHES

The base of the ecclesiastical structure was formed by parishes. They were the parts with which parishioners, then and now, are best acquainted and which most frequently impinge upon their lives. But, perversely, they are the parts about which we can be least certain. Even the number of medieval parishes in both Ireland and England has not been accurately recorded: in England the total is known to have exceeded 8,000, while in Ireland it is thought to be nearly 2,500. The latter number is based upon the evidence of the Civil Survey of 1650, which is believed to accurately reflect the medieval situation. Most resistant to research has been (and still is) how and when the parishes that functioned after *c.* 1200 evolved from arrangements that are known to have been different, but whose structure is only dimly perceived. Moreover, the struggle for discovery has been hindered, more so in Ireland than England, in two ways. One is the paucity of Irish records. The other is medieval churches, which, abundant in England as the result of continuous use, have been largely abandoned in Ireland, so that many are now alas crumbling, ivy-clad ruins. When archaeologically examined, they may yet yield valuable evidence.

Because of these uncertainties it would seem sensible to begin by establishing the nature of the parochial system in its final medieval form,[7] before attempting to suggest its origins. This approach has added relevance given the fact that the decades covered by this book were exactly those when the parochial system in England was still evolving into the form it was to retain, with relatively few changes, until the nineteenth century.

Parishes, as they existed in England by the middle of the thirteenth century, were areas of land with defined boundaries. They varied in size considerably, from thousands of acres to fewer than one hundred. Their size was not determined by the application of a formula, but was the product of singular conditions and the decisions of the individuals or institutions with control over the land and its inhabitants. Somewhere within the boundary of a parish stood its parish church. It was not, in some cases, the only church; but any others, chapels or private oratories, were subordinate to it.

Every parish and its church had a resident priest charged with *cura animarum* (Latin: cure, i.e. care of, souls). This duty comprised the baptism of infants, the churching of women after childbirth, marriages, burial of the dead and the celebration of mass, which was still evolving into an increasingly elaborate and theatrical ceremony at the heart of which was the challenging concept of transubstantiation. Baptism required a font and burial a graveyard, and the presence of these are considered to be vital indicators in Ireland of parochial status.

The resident priest was (or should have been) the *rector* (Latin: master). He was also known as the *parson* (Latin *persona ecclesiae*, the 'person' of the church). But it was increasingly the case that the rector was an absentee and that his duties were discharged by a resident deputy. Such a person had the title of *vicar* (Latin *vicarious*, deputy). Since it was known for rectors to default on paying their vicars, a more formal and certain arrangement was prescribed by the 4th Lateran Council summoned by Pope Innocent III in 1215. It laid down that a vicar should have a vicarage comprised of specific financial parts of the church's endowment over which he was to have direct control.

How, and by whom, was a rector appointed? In the late eleventh century most parishes, other than those under direct episcopal control, were in the hands of the owner of the land of the parish, who had the uncontested right of appointment. At that time parishes were effectively private institutions. Over the next one hundred years, church reformers succeeded in undermining this state of affairs. By the end of the twelfth century, the 'owners' of parishes had been reduced in status to 'patrons', with no more than the advowson, that is to say, the right to nominate the rector for the bishop's consideration. The nominee's appointment as rector would now be determined by the bishop's assessment of his 'sufficiency'.

Although some landowners clung on to their right as patron, many came to see this was an asset of little value. Consequently, they gifted the patronage to a religious institution (monastery, canonry, cathedral chapter, hospital or college) which, albeit with episcopal agreement, allowed the head of the institution to assume the role of rector and to appoint vicars as their resident workhorses. This arrangement, known as appropriation, enriched these institutions while debasing the status of the parish priests. Therefore, the only benefit to lay donors was spiritual, not material: prayers for their souls and the souls of their ancestors and descendants.

At the root of appropriation lay money – the money arising from sources that constituted the rector's income from a parish church. There were three such sources. One was the glebe (Latin *glaeba*, clod of earth), the land with which the church had been endowed, in most cases by its founder. There was no rule that a church must have a glebe, nor how large it should be. But if there was one, it enabled the rector to earn money by farming or, if he preferred, through leasing. Then he was entitled to the fees paid by his parishioners for his professional services, in addition to which he could expect to receive a small customary gift on certain feast days, particularly Christmas, Easter and Whitsun. Together these petty sums were known as altarage. But his most productive source of income was the tithe (Old English *teotha*, meaning tenth) of every man's income, in most cases in the form of agrarian or pastoral produce. In England, payment of tithes was made an enforceable legal obligation in the tenth century. And although the tithe was already known in Ireland, it was Henry II who, at the Synod of Cashel in 1172, brought Ireland fully into line with England.

The parish system that was operating in Leinster in 1247 when the liberty was broken up was essentially the same as that in England. It not only bound men and women tightly to the church by their spiritual needs, but also by material bonds.

Out of what did this system grow? The answer as regards both Ireland and England is barely perceptible.[8] In England, once the initial conversion phase was over, pastoral care appears to have been provided by large central churches, usually based on royal or episcopal estates, and in many parts of the country they were known as minsters. This word was a corruption of 'monastery', but monasteries they were not. Rather, they were corporations of priests who went out into the settlements of their district in order to preach the gospel and to celebrate mass.

These occasions would have originally taken place outdoors, but then small churches, which would initially be of wood, were built to accommodate the congregation. What changed this arrangement was the consequence of a radical change in the ownership of land that took place between the mid tenth and mid eleventh centuries, which resulted in the emergence of hundreds of small estates in the hands of men with the status of *thegn*. These were the distant precursors of the gentry. We believe that they either took control of an existing church, or built a new one and installed a resident priest to serve the inhabitants of the estate, thereby adding to it an ecclesiastical dimension: estate and parish became one.

Did Ireland follow a parallel course? It would appear that it did, though not to the same extent as in England. When the Anglo-Norman settlers arrived, Ireland had hundreds of small churches, many of considerable antiquity, which must have served as *foci* for the ministrations of priests based in large 'mother' churches. In other words, pastoral care in Ireland had functioned along very similar lines to those in England.

But, as far as can be seen, no church in Ireland was a parish church as described above. There could be various reasons why this had not happened before the Anglo-Norman intrusion. One reason may lie in the differences in the role and the status of the bishops in the two countries. For a parish system to exist and function smoothly, it needed to be within a defined diocese and under the rule of a bishop with authority underpinned by canon law. This condition did not exist in Ireland until the creation of the

diocesan structure in 1150. Therefore, the necessary conditions for a parochial system were still in their infancy when the Anglo-Norman settlers
arrived from a country where it was the established norm. It was they,
therefore, who created it, but within the framework of dioceses and the
validating authority of a bishop.

Parish creation was almost certainly a prolonged and stuttering process,
but by 1247 when the liberty of Leinster was broken up, it is likely that it
contained 438 parishes: Ferns 126, Kildare 92, Leighlin 84, Ossory 136.[9] In
creating them, the newcomers took the estates granted to them and, as had
happened in late Anglo-Saxon England, made their parishes coincident
with them. One result was their range in size, which is well demonstrated
by Billy Colfer's map of the parishes of Co. Wexford, which shows small
parishes in the south and east of the county and larger ones in the north
and west, so reflecting the varying density of settlement.

As well as having ready-made parish boundaries, the Anglo-Normans had
a plethora of churches from which to choose a parish church. A survey of
Co. Kilkenny revealed ninety-one churches that appear never to have attained
parochial status. The dedication of many of these churches is also known, and
almost all are dedicated to early Irish missionary saints. This indication of
antiquity is given further support by the proximity of a holy well or spring.
These are likely to have been pre-Christian ritual sites that the leaders of the
new religion thought it wise to adopt and to carry over into their own practices. This was an act of diplomacy deliberately commended by Pope Gregory
I to Augustine, the leader of his mission to the English kingdom of Kent.

Witnessing the creation of a parish is a rare event, but occasionally we
are given a glimpse of a particularly good example. In this instance, it
concerns a man, or rather his family, whom we have already met: Thomas
de Cantwell, who died in 1319 and whose nearly eight-foot-tall effigy stands
in the ruined church at Kilfane. Lay records tell us that the de Cantwells
were granted two estates by Theobald Walter – Kilfane and Rathcoole for
the service of two knights and a half knight, respectively – and how they
disposed of parts of both.[10] This information is supplemented by ecclesiastical records showing that each estate became a parish, Kilfane covering
3,486 acres (1411 ha) and Rathcoole 1,458 acres (590 ha).[11] It also records
that in both parishes they built a church (or perhaps adapted one) and a
castle. What the de Cantwells did at Kilfane and at Rathcoole would have
been replicated many times throughout the liberty.

Much of the parish system in place by 1247 arose from the desires of
the lesser feudal tenants with relatively modest budgets. However, there

was one outstanding exception: St Mary's, the parish church of New Ross, which was started, although perhaps not fully completed, by William Marshal I and his wife, Isabel. Although now part ruin, this once fine church, situated behind its nineteenth-century replacement, was once reckoned to be among the largest and most impressive parish churches in Ireland. That the Marshals intended it to be a splendid ornament to the new borough they were creating is underlined by the expense that must have been incurred by importing large quantities of honey-coloured oolitic limestone from a quarry at Dundry in the Mendip Hills of Somerset. It is reputed that Countess Isabel, who died in 1220, directed that on her death her body was to be buried alongside her mother in Tintern Abbey, Monmouthshire, which was a de Clare family foundation, but that her heart should rest in St Mary's Church, New Ross. If true, this says much about her loyalties and also about her wish to rest in Ireland in the fine, graceful, sumptuous surroundings of the church she and her husband had created.

REGULAR ORDERS: CANONS, MONKS AND NUNS

The introduction of the parish system into the liberty most likely came after, and as a consequence of, the Anglo-Norman settlement. But the same cannot be said of the influx of the new religious orders – most particularly of the Cistercian monks and the Augustinian canons, both of whom established a visible presence in Ireland before 1169. By the middle decades of the twelfth century, Ireland had become fertile ground for implanting fresh religious experiences and modes of expression. Consequently, it was receptive to the missionary work of a remarkable man, Máel Máedóc Ua Morgair (c. 1094–1248), canonised in 1190 as St Malachy.[12] The son of a teacher, St Malachy grew up and was educated in Armagh. He was ordained as a priest in 1119 and became an ardent reformer; but his deeper, lifelong desire was to live as a monk. This was realised in 1122, when he had the opportunity to enter the monastery at Lismore in Co. Waterford. He was there but a short time before he was summoned northwards by his mentor, Celsus, archbishop of Armagh, to be abbot of Bangor (Co. Down) and then as bishop of Connor. He was then, in 1127, persuaded to accept the nomination as archbishop of Armagh. St Malachy only accepted on condition that he would be allowed to return to his monastic life if he succeeded in removing the Clann Sinaich from the control of the church of Armagh, which it had exercised for over 200 years. His acceptance of the office

meant that his first crucial impact on the church was made when, as archbishop of Armagh between 1129 and 1137, he successfully fought off the
attempt by the Clann Sinaich to retain its hereditary grip on the church.
Alas, his longing to be a monk contained in his condition of appointment
to Armagh was yet to be some years away from fulfilment.

Throughout his life St Malachy continued yearning for a monastic existence, a yearning that was sharpened during his journey to and from Rome
in 1139 and 1140 in a failed attempt to secure the grant of *pallia* to the
recently created archbishops of Armagh and Cashel. In the course of his
adventurous journey he experienced Cistercian life at Clairvaux, where he
gained the deep affection of its abbot, St Bernard, an affection that was
reciprocated. St Malachy also visited the canonry of Arrouaise, near Arras,
which, under Cistercian influence, had developed a more rigorous version
of the Augustinian rule.

His experience was the impetus that fuelled his drive to bring radical
change to Irish monastic life. In 1142, he founded Ireland's first Cistercian
abbey, at Mellifont, Co. Louth. Two years later, he persuaded the nuns of
Clonfert, Co. Meath, to adopt the Arrouaisian rule, a change that spread
rapidly to other Augustinian houses.

The incoming Anglo-Normans were already familiar with Cistercian
monasticism and with Augustinian canonries, although not with the
Arrouaisian version of the rule, which never had as much impact in
England as it did in Ireland. Nevertheless, the work of St Malachy gave
them a solid foundation on which to build.

Between 1169 and 1207, seven Cistercian abbeys were founded in the
liberty, as well as one belonging to the congregation of Tiron.[13] This number
may not seem large, but it needs to be remembered that monasteries were
expected to have large numbers of monks and therefore required large
endowments of land. Consequently, founding monasteries was largely
confined to the topmost rank of society, whose members alone had sufficient disposable land.

The earliest Cistercian foundation in the liberty was Dunbrody. It was
initiated by Strongbow's uncle, Hervey de Montmorency, who in 1171
granted 3,600 acres (1,457 ha) of land in southern Co. Wexford to the
Savignac abbey of Buildwas in Shropshire. His generosity was spurned,
however, as the recipient house proved reluctant to create a 'daughter'
house on the land. Consequently, in 1182, negotiations took place that led
to the transfer of Hervey's gift to an Irish Savignac house, St Mary's,
Dublin, from which the founding community was drawn.

More than twenty years passed before two more Cistercian abbeys were founded, both by the new lord of Leinster, William Marshal, and his wife, Isabel. The earlier of the two, like Dunbrody, was located near the southern coast of Wexford, and known as Tintern *Parva* or Tintern *de voto*: Tintern because the 'mother' house was the abbey at Tintern in Monmouthshire; *de voto* because of Marshal's vow to found a monastery in thanks for the survival of himself and his wife when faced with the perils of a storm-tossed crossing from Pembroke to Bannow Bay in 1200. The choice of Tintern may well have been Isabel's, since it had been founded by her father's ancestor, William de Clare, in 1131, and was where many of her ancestors were laid to rest.

The second Marshal foundation would seem to have been in part inspired by a wish to maintain a family balance, in that the 'mother' house of the new venture was Stanley in Wiltshire, with which the Marshal family had a close association. But, as with Dunbrody, the founding process was not straightforward. In 1202 and 1204, abortive starts were made at Loughmerans and Annamult. Finally, in 1207, a permanent site was found in the wooded countryside above the western bank of the river Barrow, and the abbey named Duiske was created there (the name means 'black water'). The abbey church is still in use in the town which eventually grew up around it – Graiguenamanagh, Co. Kilkenny.

There were other foundations that were not new starts but were existing monasteries remoulded as Cistercian abbeys in the 1180s: they were at Abbeyleix, Co. Laois, Jerpoint, Co. Kilkenny and Monasterevin, Co. Kildare. Also, the sole house of the Order of Tiron was founded before 1190 at Glascarrig, Co. Wexford.

The Cistercian formula, which demanded a strict and non-negotiable rigidity, did not fit easily with the deep-rooted, traditional Irish monastic customs.[14] The result was an 'oil and water' situation that developed into a full-blown crisis in the 1220s: by then, it was clear that the Irish Cistercian abbeys were out of control. In modern speak, 'they were running wild', other than those founded from England by the Anglo-Normans. There was clearly a strong culture cleavage.

Drastic action was taken, or attempted, in 1227 in the form of a general *visitation* (an inspection), which was ordered by the abbot of Cîteaux and conducted by the abbot of the French house at Froidmont and his English counterpart from Buildwas. It achieved little, other than the reduction of the poorly endowed house at Kilkenny to the status of a cell of Duiske Abbey. The following year, a more robust action was taken. A visitor-general was appointed by the General Chapter (ruling body) of the Cistercian Order. He was Stephen of Lexington (now Laxton in Nottinghamshire), the abbot of Stanley, the 'mother' house of Duiske Abbey, who eventually rose to become abbot of Clairvaux in 1243. The Chapter armed him with *plenetudo potestatis* (Latin: fullness of power), which gave him complete authority over all the Cistercian houses in Ireland and full ecclesiastical power to do whatever he considered necessary to bring the Irish monks to obedience. It also licensed him to call on the secular powers to protect him and to suppress any monastic violence. Within the bounds of the liberty, this was provided by William Marshal II. Lexington's 'visitation', which lasted from May until September, had three results. One was the amalgamation of certain houses, notably Mellifont and Bective, but within the liberty the absorption of another small house with Dunbrody. More generally, Lexington revised the 'parentage' of the abbeys of Irish foundation, placing them under the authority of non-Irish houses: Clairvaux in France, Margam in Wales and both Furness and Buildwas in England.

Finally, he drew up a list of thirteen mandatory injunctions that were to be published and obeyed in all Irish Cistercian abbeys. The most pointed, which targeted the localism of the Irish monks, was a requirement that no man should be professed as a Cistercian monk who was not competent in French and Latin, respectively the vernacular and liturgical languages of the order.

Although Lexington's 'visitation' had some curative effect, the Cistercian congregation was never brought into full and happy obedience. It would seem that the gulf between the two monastic styles and traditions was too great. The fact that in 1274 the original 'parentages' of Irish houses was restored may be seen as a victory for localism and a defeat for central authority.

Augustinian canonries contrasted sharply with Cistercian abbeys in most respects.[15] They were far smaller communities and consequently required smaller endowments, particularly of land, since much of their income came from parishes they were allowed to appropriate. Because of this, the cost of founding an Augustinian house was much lower than the cost of founding a monastery, and therefore was well within the financial capacity of Strongbow's tenants-in-chief. In fact, they were responsible for all but two of the nine Augustinian canonries founded in the liberty between 1170 and 1247.

The two exceptions were the work of William Marshal I. At Kilrush, Co. Kildare, he did not found a canonry but granted it, together with the church at Ballysax and its chapel at Ballymadan, to the Augustinian house at Cartmel in Lancashire, which he had founded on the land given to him by King Henry II. Income from these properties was sufficient for the Cartmel canons to build and maintain a cell where two of their members could reside. Marshal's grant has been dated to 1201 or 1202. It seems certain that Marshal founded the canonry at Cartmel as a means of disposing of a property that was far distant from that part of England where his interests lay, and incidentally would earn him spiritual merit.

At Kilkenny, however, he did found an Augustinian canonry, dedicated to St John the Evangelist and with the obligation to care for the sick and destitute. Built on the west bank of the river Nore, it developed into a walled suburb of the borough. The foundation date is not known, but it appears to have been built and functioning by 1212.

Of the seven or eight Augustinian canonries founded by the tenants-in-chief of the liberty, the earliest was at Kells, Co. Kilkenny, and was founded by Geoffrey Fitz Robert in 1193. This was followed by four more in the first decade of the thirteenth century: Greatconnell, Naas and St Wolstan, all in Co. Kildare, by, respectively, Meiler Fitz Henry, Maurice Fitz Gerald and Adam de Hereford; and Inistioge, Co. Kilkenny, by Thomas Fitz Anthony. Later foundations were at Enniscorthy, Co. Wexford, by the Prendergast family, and at Wexford by the Roche family, both between 1216 and 1229. In addition, the canonry at Fertagh, Co. Kilkenny may date from before 1247.

Two smaller orders were also essentially Augustinian. The larger, the Fratres Crucifieri (Latin: cross-bearing brethren) founded seventeen houses in Ireland, three of them in the liberty.[16] When and where this order came from to Ireland, or indeed whether it was of Irish creation, is not known. Its name suggests that it was an order of friars, but this is misleading and incorrect. Rather, their houses were hospitals and their purpose was to care for the sick and destitute, the most vulnerable and least fortunate members of Irish society. What is clear is that they did not come from England, where they had no houses. However, there was in England a small mendicant order, the Crutched Friars (Friars of the Cross), whose members were identified by the cross sewn onto their habits. This order arrived in England from the Continent.

About two of the Leinster houses of the Fratres Crucifieri, there is no mystery. Both were founded in Co. Kildare, at Athy and Castledermot; both by wealthy tenants-in-chief, respectively Roger Pipard and Walter de Riddlesford; and both were in existence by 1216. The story of the third, at

New Ross, is more problematic. Traditionally it is attributed to William Marshal I and said to have been founded in 1195. The attribution to Marshal is probably correct, but I cannot accept the date, as it is earlier than the foundation date of New Ross. Whenever the house of this order was founded in New Ross, its life was short and its end violent. Its members were driven out of the borough by townsfolk incensed at the murder of one of their local inhabitants by a member of the Fratres. Clearly, this event had taken place before 1256, for after that date their premises were known to have been in the hands of the Franciscan friars.

The other order was even smaller, with only two houses in Ireland, one of which was at Kilkenny, the other at Carrick-on-Suir. Known as the Order of St Thomas of Acon (Acre in present-day Israel), its formation may have been the consequence of a vow made by Henry II to maintain a force of 200 knights to defend the Holy Land as an act of contrition for his hasty words that led to the murder of Archbishop Thomas Becket in Canterbury Cathedral in 1170.[17] If so, the loss of Acre, the last place in the kingdom of Jerusalem to be recaptured by Muslim armies, rendered his vow otiose. Instead, the order, which was based in London, served the same purposes as the Fratres Crucifieri. Its presence in the borough of Kilkenny is almost certainly attributable to William Marshal I.

The Augustinian rule – in all cases its Arrouaisian version – was adopted by the five nunneries founded in the liberty.[18] The origins of three of them pre-date the arrival of the Anglo-Normans. That at Kildare sprang from the famous double monastery founded by St Brigid in the sixth century. The other two, at Aghde, Co. Carlow and Kilculliheen, Co. Kilkenny, were created in 1151 by Diarmait Mac Murchada as dependant cells of the nunnery of St Mary de Hogges, which he had founded in Dublin five years earlier, in 1146. The convents founded by Anglo-Normans were both in Kildare and founded by tenants-in-chief: Graney was founded by Walter de Riddlesford, Timolin by Robert Fitz Richard.

The two main military orders of monks both rapidly established a prominent presence throughout Ireland. The earlier arrivals in the liberty were the Hospitallers, whose headquarters or priory at Kilmainham,[19] Dublin was on land given to them by Strongbow and confirmed by Henry II. By 1212, they had acquired six more properties, classified as preceptories, within the liberty, and a century later they had gained four more. These came to them as the result of the dissolution of the Order of the Temple in 1312 at the end of a five-year campaign by the King of France, Philip IV (1285–1314). The dissolution was conducted with Stalinist brutality and included burning at the stake sixty-three of its knights; it culminated with the weak and powerless pope, Clement V (1305–14), dissolving the order. The only mitigating feature of this sorry episode was that the properties of the Order of the Temple were transferred to the Order of the Hospital, although this process was prolonged and never fully completed.

The last orders of religious clergy to settle in the liberty were the friars, the mendicants. The earliest and largest of them, the Dominicans and the Franciscans, achieved formal status as religious orders only in the 1220s, and therefore it is not surprising that their presence in Ireland was still minimal in 1245.[20] The first to arrive were the Dominicans, who were established in Kilkenny in 1225 by William Marshal II. His brother and successor, Richard Marshal, followed suit by founding a Franciscan house, also in Kilkenny, during his brief period as lord of Leinster between 1231 and 1234. After the break-up of the liberty, both orders rapidly increased their presence, the Dominicans at Athy and Rosbercon and the Franciscans at Kildare, New Ross and Wexford. The only other Orders of friars permitted by the papacy after 1274, the Carmelites and the Austin (Augustinian) friars, did not appear until well after 1245.

Finally, at various times twelve houses, all dedicated to St Mary Magdalene, were set up to care for lepers, although we cannot be certain that all their inmates actually suffered from leprosy rather than other skin diseases.[21] All the houses were small and, because leprosy was thought to be contagious, were located outside towns. Their history is uncertain, in large part because leprosy had virtually died out in Europe by 1400.

OVERVIEW

A panoramic picture of the church in the liberty of Leinster as it changed under Anglo-Norman rule is revealed in the records of the ecclesiastical valuations made in the first decade of the fourteenth century. They were commissioned at the pope's command in preparation for the levy of a papal tax of one tenth on all clerical incomes. Although they post-date the break-up of the liberty by over fifty years, they almost certainly present an accurate description of the basic structure of the church, if not in detail. In using them, I have extracted only a minimal number of cash figures, and then only for comparative purposes, for the simple reason that medieval figures cannot meaningfully be multiplied to current levels. Furthermore, the figures in these documents are almost certainly under valuations designed to reduce tax liability. What follows is based primarily on the valuations of the diocese of Ossory, supplemented where appropriate with data from elsewhere.

The largest individual sum is that which the bishop of Ossory derived from his manors, which were not listed but are known from other sources to have been ten in number. The episcopal income they provided would have been made up of rents from land held in tenancy and from the profits of manorial farms – in other words, the estate he held from the crown. As these sources were temporal, they were referred to as 'temporalities'. Other income sources were ecclesiastical and were therefore known as 'spiritualities'. The bishop's total income from his temporalities was recorded as being just over £163. The fact that elsewhere the yield of the same manors was said to have been close to £260 supports the well-founded suspicion of undervaluation, which would certainly be of financial benefit to the bishop as it would reduce his tax liability. Such deceit would be hard to detect or prove. Even so, the bishop of Ossory enjoyed a greater income than that of his fellow diocesans at Kildare and Leighlin, whose temporalities earned, respectively, just over £72 and nearly £54.

Spiritualities were recorded in more detail, and reveal a total taxable income of almost £741. This sum was derived from 135 parishes grouped into nine deaneries, the names of which reflect their relationship to ancient cantreds. The size of these parishes was not recorded, but the wide variation in their valuations indicates considerable differences in acreage and, presumably, population. Two examples will serve to illustrate these disparities: Kilcowan, which extended to a mere 1,424 acres (576 ha), had a value of £1; in contrast, the valuation of Fiddown, covering almost 11,000 acres (4,452 ha), was £14, of which the rector was entitled to two thirds and the vicar one third. Whether individual or corporate, the rector always had the lion's share.

Eight of the nine deaneries appear to have been functioning normally. The exception was Aghaboe, where only Aghaboe itself was valued; the other fifteen parishes were recorded as *nulli* (Latin: none), or *pauci* (Latin: little). This may suggest the fact that Anglo-Norman and Cambro-Norman settlement in Aghaboe was thin and its hold tenuous; or that Aghaboe was already succumbing to an Irish revival.

What is distinctly evident is the distribution of advowsons, the right to nominate (for episcopal approval) a new rector. In seventy-five of the 135 parishes the advowson had passed into the hands of the heads of fourteen different ecclesiastical corporations. The list, however, was dominated by four of them, who had acquired over two thirds of the total: the canonries of Kells, Inistioge, St John's, Kilkenny and the Arrouaisian nunnery of Kilculliheen. All four lay within the diocese. Also within the diocese, the military orders had acquired three parishes; one by the Templars and two by the Hospitallers. The latter, however, had eleven parishes in Kildare diocese, close to their headquarters at Kilmainham.

Four institutions not in the diocese had thirteen of its parishes: these institutions were St Augustine's Abbey, Bristol, St Thomas's Abbey, Dublin and St Catherine's Abbey, Waterford. They had been founded as Augustinian houses, respectively in 1140, 1177 and St Catherine's Abbey before 1207. All were linked to the abbey of St Victor in Paris. The abbey, with its influential school, was founded in 1108 by one of the greatest intellects of his time, William of Champeaux. Our three abbeys were all reformed along Victorine lines in 1148, 1192 and 1210, and thereafter looked upon St Victor's as their 'mother' house. The abbey of St Thomas the Martyr had been founded by William Fitz Audelin on the orders of King Henry II, one of Henry's acts of contrition for the guilt he was required to assume after the murder of Archbishop Thomas Becket. There is a distinct possibility that St Thomas's foundation congregation may have been brought from St Augustine's, Bristol, which in 1542 was rededicated to the Holy and Undivided Trinity when it became the cathedral of the newly created diocese of Bristol. The fourth 'foreign' institution to acquire one of Ossory's parishes was the cathedral chapter of Exeter, another instance of the links between Leinster and the south-west of England.

All of the above institutions were following, albeit in their various ways, the Augustinian rule. Notable by their absence, however, were the monastic orders. At this stage only one parish, in Aghaboe, belonged to one monastic establishment, in this case the Cistercian house of Duiske.

It is likely that these advowson transfers to religious orders were from lay patrons and that most of them were made, as they were elsewhere, in the thirteenth century. However, the process was still ongoing after the valuations had been made: around 1318, the de Rupe family (who changed their name to de la Roche), lords of the manors of The Rower, 8865 acres (3588 ha) and Listerlin, 5645 acres (2284 ha), made over the advowsons of the two parish churches to the Cistercian abbey of Jerpoint. When the abbey was dissolved in 1540, its possessions included two parishes, The Rower and Blanchvillestown, but not Listerlin. Their two transfers reduced the number of lay patrons to twenty, five of whom were in Aghaboe Deanery and had incomes too small to be worth acquiring; the motive for appropriation was always financial.

In Ossory, almost one fifth of the parishes remained under the control of a small group of senior clergy based at the diocesan centre. The bishop had seven parishes at his disposal, the income from which he needed in order to provide an income and make provision for the appropriate status of those senior members of his household in holy orders. A greater number of parishes belonged to the cathedral chapter, and the dean, the chancellor and the precentor, together with the archdeacon, were all provided with rich parish livings. Surprisingly, there was no reference to the treasurer, as there was at Kildare, which is puzzling since this was one of the standard offices in all non-monastic chapters. It is possible that the treasurer was among the holders of the nine parish livings assigned to named members of the chapter. What is certain is that he would be the manager responsible for the chapter's common fund.

From this survey a picture emerges of a diocese dominated by a small group of senior clerics and a number of houses of the various religious orders, who between them had contrived arrangements that allowed them to syphon off a fair measure of the wealth generated in the parishes. In doing so, they reduced the capacity of the parochial clergy serving on the front line to provide the necessary pastoral care to those in need. Clearly, the system had as its primary purpose the regulation of the lives of both laity and clergy, and other considerations were reduced to a secondary role. How successfully the primary purpose was served can be gauged only through the records of an Archdeacon's Court. Evidence of pastoral care is, however, and is likely to remain, beyond our view.

Afterword

The liberty of Leinster, on which this book has focused, was the work of four generations over the span of almost eighty years. While the course of events is clear enough, as is the nature and workings of the foreign institutions implanted into Ireland, there remain questions that I cannot answer with confidence, if at all, although they need now to be addressed.

The story began when the deposed king of Leinster, Diarmait Mac Murchada, turned to England for help in regaining his kingdom. Mac Murchada was, it seems, a man of temperamental extremes, capable of acts of cruel barbarity yet giving active support to church reform and the introduction of new religious houses that proclaimed a purer form of Christianity. Was he typical of the Irish kings of his day; or was he an exception, rather akin to King John of England? It seems to me that his intentions and behaviour were much the same as the other Irish provincial kings: they fought for power, or to defend their territory. It is far from clear what Mac Murchada's ultimate aim was. Although he certainly wanted to be restored to his patrimony in Leinster, I am equally certain that he ardently wished to become the *Ard-Rí*, High King of Ireland, following in the footsteps of his grandfather, Diarmait Mac Máel na mBó; for just like the Normans, the Irish valued family continuity and advancement. My theory is reinforced by his willingness to bring Anglo-Normans into Ireland, together with his knowledge of how governments operated elsewhere, especially in England. Did Diarmait hope to revolutionise Ireland, turning it into a truly united kingdom under a dynastic monarch, sanctified by a coronation conducted by the Church? For there is a fundamental difference between a coronation and the inauguration ceremony of the Irish Kings.

His ally, Strongbow, was in a similar situation when they met, though his was not such a dire or desperate problem. Having been downgraded by Henry II, he was certainly open to offers, and the one provided by Mac Murchada was highly tempting. But what did Strongbow really hope to achieve from Diarmait's audacious plan? Was it the kingship of Leinster as a stepping stone to then becoming king of a united Ireland? After all, Strongbow was a Norman and would be well aware of the de Hauteville brothers' glorious achievements in creating the kingdom of Sicily: their success was helped because they operated at a distance from a controlling authority. Strongbow would not be allowed a free hand; Henry II and the might of his empire were far too close at hand and Henry, ever suspicious, would be watchful and ready to reel him in. He probably accepted that the best he could hope for was what he could conquer and what he would be allowed to keep for himself. But Strongbow had one profound achievement: he unlocked the door of Ireland, allowing access to its powerful neighbours. This 'Pandora's box' released consequences for both our islands with which we are still living in the twenty-first century.

For both Diarmait Mac Murchada and Strongbow, Ireland was of central importance. Not so William Marshal. Born a second son of a second marriage into a relatively modest knightly family, though one with connections, William Marshal had to make his own way in the world. The nineteenth-century statesman Benjamin Disraeli's graphic phrase aptly describes Marshal's progress: 'a man might climb to the top of the greasy pole', and climb William did, albeit with the help of three lucky breaks. The first was through the help of the talent-spotting abilities (or was it seizing the main chance?) of his mother, who managed to have him placed under the tutelage of William de Tancarville's *mesnie* of knights, an opportunity of which he made good use. On graduating, he built up a formidable personal reputation as a knightly warrior both in battle and on the tournament circuit. His second stroke of luck was coming to the notice of Queen Eleanor through his efforts in helping her escape from kidnap; this in turn enabled him to catch the eye of King Henry when in the queen's service, which ultimately brought him the greatest prize of all – his wife, Isabel de Clare, the daughter of Strongbow, who brought her Irish inheritance with her as well as a foothold in the province of Leinster.

Without any doubt, although he was only resident in Leinster for two brief periods, Marshal's work in Normanising the province was of utmost importance. But acquiring Leinster also made him a truly international figure with substantial landed interests that extended from Kilkenny in

Ireland through south Wales and southern England into Normandy. What he expected his heir, William Marshal II, to make of his Irish inheritance is not clear, but it is known that William II carried on the unfinished work started by his father, an example of which is St Mary's Church, New Ross. We also know that William did his second son, Richard, no favours when he bequeathed him his properties in Normandy, thereby requiring him to be a subject of the king of France – this ultimately caused Richard a deal of problems with his English and Irish inheritance.

So far, the characters mentioned have been men, yet all had wives, mothers and female relations. The role of women, certainly in this period of the past, is so often the dark side of the moon. About Diarmait's wife, Mór, we know next to nothing; we have no inkling of her influence (or lack of it) over her husband. And this is a very valid point, since it was their daughter, Aoife, he was prepared to use as a political pawn when he presented her as part of his deal with Strongbow. Similarly, Aoife acquiesed and accepted her wifely role; and indeed she enhanced it by producing two children, one of which was a male heir. She is thought to have given a piece of sage advice to her illegitimate half-brother, Domnal Kavanagh, when she persuaded him not to fight Strongbow for the kingship of Leinster but instead to settle for a position of oversight of the Irish inhabitants. After all, as she and Strongbow had a male heir, it meant that Leinster would eventually be returned to her paternal family. Thereafter, we know little of her life, other than that her widowhood was lengthy and spent quietly in England – probably on royal command and under King Henry's watchful eye, for after all, she was an Irish princess despite being known in England as 'the Irish countess'.

Fortunately for us, Aoife's daughter, Isabel de Clare, emerges from the shadows into enough light to show us that she was an interesting woman. What we do not have is knowlege of her very earliest years or where she was brought up, although we do know of her transfer to the Tower of London on becoming a ward of King Henry II. Notwithstanding this void of knowledge, one aspect of her upbringing shines through: she had certainly been made fully aware of her regal maternal Irish ancestry. In Irish terms she was a princess, while her paternal roots were pure Norman, being planted in one of the most prominent and wealthiest families to gain from the Norman Conquest of England. In marriage she was William Marshal's partner and wife: she was much involved with his plans to develop Leinster, which after all was her province. At other times, she proved to be a strong character, showing will and commitment to the interests of herself and her husband. This was no mean feat, considering she gave birth to and raised ten children to adulthood; even travelling with her husband on some occasions to his estates in Normandy (for we know that she gave birth there to at least one child).

The final question is one that can be posed but should not be explored by a historian: how would the liberty of Leinster have fared had one of William and Isabel's sons founded an enduring dynasty? I fear it is one for the novelist.

In writing this book, I have frequently asked myself the question: why was Ireland not completely conquered and united by 1245? The early success of the relatively small body of troops under Strongbow's command, and the massive display of forces brought to Ireland by both King Henry and Prince John when they visited, must surely have left the Irish in no doubt as to the military capability at the disposal of the Anglo-Norman invaders and the English crown. But then, on the face of it, things are never as easy as they seem. Though the Anglo-Normans had the military might to conquer all, Irish bravery was never in doubt, and they did have two advantages to help in defending their country. One was the terrain: mountainous, with large areas of wooded country and bog, which was tailor-made for guerrilla warfare. The other advantage, surprisingly, lay in the absence of political unity. Victory required the defeat of not one, but up to nine small independent states. Contrast that with William of Normandy's conquest of England, where one battle sufficed to remove the head of state and the rapid seizure of control of the two centres of govenment, London and Winchester, completed the task. Although English resistance continued for a while, it was without a leader of national focus and dynastic loyalty. But the basic reason for the English failure to conquer the whole of Ireland was the lack of state commitment. English kings were keen enough on foreign adventures, but all of them lay in opposite directions. Henry III's forlorn hope of regaining that which his father had lost in France, and his even more forlorn desire to place his second son, Edmund, on the throne of Sicily, were fantasy.[1] The situation got no better under Edward I, who sought to create an *imperium* in Britain and succeeded up to a point in Wales, but failed in Scotland, which remained England's running sore until 1346.[2] Edward III turned again to France, winning notable victories on the field of battle, which were perhaps the stuff of chivalry but not of practical politics.[3]

Throughout these years, Ireland was starved of the input that might have brought success. Conquest was by proxy: Anglo-Norman adventurers campaigning under royal license were willing to hold what they conquered on feudal terms. English government involvement was limited to a justiciar with a basic administrative staff operating from Dublin, usually with insufficient resources. One novel experiment was the appointment of Lionel, duke of Clarence, Edward III's young son, as governor of Ireland. He lasted five years (1361–6) and achieved little: the experiment was not repeated.[4] There was no further royal descent on Ireland until the arrival of King Richard II in 1394 and 1399, by which time the English colony was near collapse through the incessant, belligerent attentions of the Irish clans.

So the English governments would not abandon Ireland; nor were they willing to do what was necessary to regain full control of what had become a somewhat lawless place. It was not surprising that their lack of interest had a like effect on the motivation of their subjects, who appear to have lost interest in advancing their fortunes in Ireland. This is patently exposed in the conquest of Connacht, the last part of Ireland brought under English control before the sixteenth century.[5] Nor was it part of a wider plan for Ireland, but a piece of political opportunism that took advantage of Irish folly.

It was triggered in 1224 by the death of the king of Connacht, Cathal Crobhdearg (meaning 'red hand') Ua Conchobar, an effective ruler since 1189. Almost inevitably, there was a disputed succession. In 1226, Henry III's government, which was dominated by the justiciar Hubert de Burgh, decided to replace the Irish kingship with an Anglo-Norman baron: and lo and behold, the chosen baron was Hubert de Burgh's nephew Richard, who already had large interests in Ireland and even larger ambitions.

It took several years and three military campaigns to subjugate the province, but by 1237 Richard de Burgh was able to reward the men who fought with him by granting them land on feudal terms. The salient point here is that they were not newcomers from England, but a virtual roll-call of 'old Norman families' who had helped Strongbow win Leinster. Prominent amongst them were names like FitzGerald, Prendergast, de Lacy and de Riddlesford. Now increasingly linked by intermarriage, they had come to form a clique that did not welcome intruders or rivals – and they were not settlers but rentiers, seeking greater income and status.

By the time Connacht was settled and the liberty of Leinster broken up, the conquest and colonisation of Ireland was in its dying days, but leaving a divided country – as revealed in a map in the *Atlas of Irish History* drawn to show Ireland *c.* 1300.[6] It shows sixteen clearly delineated areas; some counties were under the direct jurisdiction of the government in

Dublin, while others were liberties in the hands of privileged Anglo-Normans. But something over 30 per cent of the country was held by fourteen Irish clans in five undefined areas, from smaller ones in the south to one huge one covering almost all of the present Northern Ireland, plus the border counties of the Irish Republic. Their chiefs may have sworn loyalty to the crown of England, but in everyday terms this meant little or nothing. For all practical purposes, a clan chief was king in his kingdom.

These Irish areas were not defined reservations but amorphous bases that could expand or contract in response to circumstances. By the time of the map, a Gaelic revival was under way that posed a threat for the former liberty of Leinster. This came from the area dominated by the troublesome, lawless (at least to the Anglo-Normans) MacMurrough Kavanaghs, which covered the southern part of Wicklow, the northern part of Wexford and the eastern part of Carlow. The power of this clan was exercised physically, but its authority was based on descent from Diarmait Mac Murchada. Gradually they exerted their dominance over the other Irish clans so that the MacMurrough Kavanaghs in effect, but unofficially, became kings of Leinster. By 1282, they were already sufficiently a problem for the Dublin government to arrange the assassination of Art and Murchad MacMurrough at Arklow.[7] It solved nothing. The earl of Norfolk, who had inherited a fifth share of the liberty of Leinster, adopted a more diplomatic approach, calling Art's successor 'my cousin' – which, distantly, he was – and paid him an annual 'retaining fee' along with gifts of wine and furs for good measure, no doubt in the hope of ensuring his good behaviour.

But the blatant bribery did not work either, for the cunning Mac-Murrough Kavanaghs continued harrying the local settlers and charging 'black rent' for passage up and down the river Barrow. By the early fourteenth century, the area under the clan's control had expanded thanks to the chaos and disruption caused by Bruce's invasions of Ireland in 1315 to 1318. Such was their power that by 1327, Donnell Óg Mac Art Kavanagh was elected king of Leinster.[8] To celebrate his elevation to kingship, he unfurled his standard (which was a known way of showing a state of hostilities existed) within two miles of Dublin, with the intention of parading it throughout Ireland: clearly, he was making a bid for the kingship of Ireland too. This act of bravado met the fate it, perhaps, deserved: Donnell was captured and locked up in Dublin Castle.

The story of Ireland is in many ways one of English failure and decline, particularly after the expeditions of Richard II in 1394 and 1399.[9] Blame for this lies exclusively with the crown because of its inattention and inadequate support for the Dublin government – who controlled an area of contracting size, so that by the beginning of the sixteenth century the Pale, as it had come to be known, was no more than Dublin and its immediate hinterland. Elsewhere, authority was exercised by the Irish clan chiefs or by the descendants of Anglo-Norman settlers, notably the Butlers and the FitzGeralds.

But the sixteenth century witnessed a transformation in England, the cause of which was the Reformation. The underlying effect of this caused a transformation in Ireland too. This began with two acts passed by the Irish parliament: one, in 1537, declared Henry VIII head of the church in Ireland, while the other, in 1541, made Henry king of Ireland. These acts lit a slow-burning fuse which finally triggered a massive explosion late in the reign of Elizabeth I (1558–1603).[10] This fuse was made up of three intertwining strands: the first was the continuing adherence of the majority of the population to pre-Reformation religious forms and practices, which was bolstered by the inflow of trained priests from continental seminaries; the second was Ireland's rising wish to be rid of English rule; and the third was the knowledge that the necessary help in achieving liberation would have to be supplied by Spain, England's enemy. By the last quarter of the sixteenth century, England could no longer ignore Ireland; it had become a serious threat to its own back-door security.

The issue was settled by Charles Blount, Lord Mountjoy, who found ways and means of defeating the uprising led by Hugh O'Neil, earl of Tyrone – whose aim was to end English rule in Ireland, an objective he might have achieved had Spain given him more vigorous support. Tyrone then made his final submission to Elizabeth I in 1603, shortly before she died. For the first time, the whole of Ireland was now under English control and subject to English law, which outlawed the settlement of disputes by private warfare.

In 1603, Diarmait Mac Murchada's gamble and dearest wish, if such he had, of a united Ireland under a dynastic monarchy was finally realised. But the monarch was not one of his Irish descendants – instead, it was one of Henry II's successors.

Glossary of Terms

Advowson: The right to nominate the new rector of a parish.

Appropriation: The transfer of the rectorship of a parish to the head of an ecclesiastical corporation so that the corporation secured the rector's income.

Baile: Usually rendered as 'Bally' or 'Balli', this is the commonest Irish place-name element. It generally indicates a settlement with associated land.

Borough: A defined area of land in which certain inhabitants, known as burgesses, enjoyed specified rights and privileges in respect of rent, commercial activity and local government.

Burgage: A building plot in a borough laid out with the use of a surveyor's rod. Burgage tenure confirmed burgess status.

Cantred: Derived from the Welsh *cantref* (one hundred farms/hamlets). It replaced the Middle Irish words *tricha cét* (thirty hundreds, presumably the number of warriors the district was expected to produce). The modern Irish is *Triocha céad*.

Caput: The administrative centre of a feudal lordship, which would usually be a castle; from the Latin *Caput* meaning head, chief or top.

Charter: A legal document which specified in detail the land, rights and privileges the donor was conveying to the recipient. In effect, a title deed.

Crannock: A measure of cereals and other dry goods comprising eight bushels. The term, which was used throughout Ireland, was not known in England, where its equivalent was a quarter. Both crannock and quarter comprised eight bushels.

Crossland: Land that belonged to the church from which lay administration arrangements were excluded.

Demesne: That part of an estate which its owner elected to retain under his direct control and from which he drew most of his income.

Distraint: Seizure of a property for repayment of debt.

Dower: The portion of a feudal or freehold estate assigned to a widow for life. It came to be fixed at one third.

Escheat: The repossession of a property by its lord following the death of its tenant; or because of his/her misdemeanour.

Extent: A survey of an estate to discover the size and nature of its constituent tenements, who held them and what rent and other obligations the tenants owed.

Famulus: A living-in servant. The term applied in particular to farm servants.

Farthing: A quarter of a penny, recorded in the documents in the Latin *quart*, expanded to *quarta*. A coin of that value was later minted, but withdrawn from circulation in 1971.

Fidus Achates: The quintessential loyal and faithful companion, as portrayed by the poet Virgil.

Fine: Comes from the Latin word *finis*, meaning end. It was not a pecuniary punishment, but rather a payment made to secure the conclusion to a dispute.

Forest: A defined area of land subject to Forest Law, the purpose of which was to preserve for royal use deer and wild boar and the natural conditions under which they could thrive.

Free Tenure: A non-military tenure granted to free men at a fixed rent, which was in most cases a low rent, and with it the rights of inheritance and free disposal guaranteed by English law.

Furlong: 220 yards (201 m), that is, one eighth of a mile of 1,760 yards (1,609 m). The maximum length of an open-field furrow.

Gressum: Same as relief, but for unfree tenants.

Haggard: A compound enclosed by a wall, adjacent to the farmstead, which was used for storage. It was an Irish term, not used in England.

Half-Penny: This is recorded in the documents in the Latin *ob*. expanded to *obolus*. A coin of that value was later minted, but withdrawn from circulation in 1985.

Hosting: An Irish term for raiding.

Hundred: In Ireland, a borough court; in England, a subdivision of a shire.

Justiciar: Originally the king's chief minister in charge of government during the king's absence; an office which very soon became permanent.

Keep: A fortified tower (usually of stone) that was the final redoubt of a castle. Also known as a *donjon*.

Knight's Fee: An estate granted in return for the military service of a fully trained and equipped knight. By 1200, this obligation had become limited to service in time of war for forty days at his own expense.

Manor: An area of land whose inhabitants were subject to the lord of the manor and the jurisdiction of his court.

Mesnie: A company of household knights retained by a lord, each member paid an annual fee.

Motte and Bailey: A basic castle comprising a conical mound of earth (motte) surmounted by a stockade and fronted by a compound (bailey) formed by a ditch, mound and stockade.

Mountain: An Irish term used to describe rough grazing for animals; in England, the equivalent term would be moor or fell.

Murrain: Appears in documents as a general term for diseases fatal to domestic animals. Identifying specific diseases is well-nigh impossible.

Prebend: A source of income attached to certain ecclesiastical offices, notably cathedral canonries.

Rath: An Irish word which describes an enclosure formed by a ditch and bank inside of which was a homestead.

Rector: A man in holy orders responsible for the spiritual welfare of a parish, for which service he was entitled to the income from the endowments of office.

Reeve: A manager of a property, in many cases a farm.

Relief: Money demanded of the heir to a feudal tenement as a condition of his succession to it. An inheritance charge.

Royal Service: This was known in England as scutage. In origin, it was money paid by a military tenant of the crown in lieu of service. It gradually became a fixed charge of forty shillings (£2) per knight's fee.

Seizin: The formal granting of possession to a tenancy of a feudal or freehold tenement.

Seneschal: A French word that translates as steward. It was the title held by the senior manager.

Sergeant: A sheriff's officer with powers of arrest and distraint. Also, a holder of land in return for a specified service, if military, of lower status than a knight.

Sheriff: The chief agent of the crown in a shire or county.

Tholsel: The office (in Britain known as a tollbooth) at which market tolls were paid and from which the market could be administered. In some places it came to serve as the town hall.

Tithe: The tenth part of a person's income owed to the rector of their parish. In most cases, it took the form of farm produce.

Vicar: A resident priest in a parish who performed the rector's duties as his deputy. From 1216, canon law required the sources of the rectorial income to be divided and assigned to the rector and the vicar.

Wapentake: A Norse word meaning weapontake. In areas of England that fell under Danish control, it was used instead of the word hundred.

Glossary of Irish Names

Middle Irish names of the twelfth century and their modern Irish equivalents.

Ailbe O' Maelmuídhe = Albi O'Molloy
an Robhar = The Rower
Aoife = Eva
Ard-Ri = High King of Ireland
Derbforgail = Dearbháile, Dervla
Diarmait Mac Murchada = Dermot MacMurrough
Dómhnall = Dónal
Domnal 'Caomhánach' = Donell, Donnel, Domnel Kavanagh
Domnal Mac Gilla Pátraic = Dónal Mac Giolla Phádraig (Son of the Servant
   of Patrick)
Donnchadh = Donough, Donaghy
Énna or Eanna = Enda
Felix Ua Dubhlaine = Felix O'Delaney
Lorcán Ua Tuathail = Laurence O'Toole
Máel Máedóc Ua Morgair = St Malachy
Muirchertach Ua Briain = Murtagh O'Brien
O'Dunlaing = O'Dowling, Dowling, Dolan, Doolin, Doolan
Osraige = Ossory
Ruaidri Ua Conchobair = Rory, Rodri, Roderick O'Connor
Tigernán Ua Ruairc = Tiernan O'Rourke
Toirdelbach Ua Briain = Turlough O'Brien
Uí Chennselaig = O'Kinsella
Uí Dúnlainge = O'Dunlaing

Notes

PART I: ROOTS

Chapter 1 Viking Eruptions

1. The treaty agreed at Verdun in August 843 enabled a pragmatic division based upon what each brother currently controlled. The imperial title went to Lothar, whose kingdom comprised an elongated corridor stretching from south of Rome to the North Sea. To the east, Louis took East Francia (basically western Germany), while Charles had West Francia (roughly France west of the Rhone). This division, which invited strife, was the product of failure to think of succession in imperial terms rather than treating Charlemagne's legacy as a patrimony to be divided between heirs. For the process of division see L. Halphen, *Charlemagne and the Carolingian Empire* (Amsterdam, 1977), pp. 215–227.
2. For the impact of the Viking raids on the West Frankish kingdom, see M. Deansley, *A History of Medieval Europe 476–911* (London, 1956), pp. 445–465.
3. The origins of Normandy are discussed in M. Chibnall, *The Normans* (Oxford, 2000), pp. 3–37; and D. Bates, *Normandy before 1066* (London, 1982).
4. F. M. Stenton, *Anglo-Saxon England*, 3rd edn (Oxford, 1971), pp. 1–73.
5. A. Woolf, *From Pictland to Alba 789–1070* (Edinburgh, 2007).
6. Stenton, *Anglo-Saxon England*, pp. 239–75 and 320–363.
7. Woolf, *From Pictland*, pp. 312–350.
8. M. A. Valante, *The Vikings in Ireland: Settlement, Trade and Urbanisation* (Dublin, 2008) is a concise and lucid account of the Viking impact on Ireland.

Chapter 2 Norman Eruptions

1. M. Chibnall, *The Normans* (Oxford, 2000) is a very good, up-to-date account of all aspects of the Norman phenomenon. More detailed accounts are to be found in D. C. Douglas, *The Norman Achievement* (London, 1969) and J. le Patourel, *The Norman Empire* (Oxford, 1976).
2. Chibnall, *Normans*, pp. 17–20 and 107–124.
3. Chibnall, *Normans*, pp. 75–93. For a more detailed account, J. J. Norwich, *The Normans in the South* (London, 1964).
4. J. Riley-Smith, *The Crusades: A Short History* (Yale, 1987), pp. 1–49.
5. C. Kleinhenz (ed.), *Medieval Italy: An Encyclopaedia A–K* (London, 2004), pp. 133–134. From this it is clear that Bohemond betrayed the idealism of the crusade by reneging on the promise he made to the Byzantine emperor, Alexius, that he would hand back any former imperial territory he conquered.
6. This basic account of events in England in the eleventh century is based upon Stenton, *Anglo-Saxon England*, pp. 384–431, 576–577 and 581–621. The Norman conquest of the far north of the country is dealt with in R. A. Lomas, *County of Conflict: Northumberland from Conquest to Civil War* (East Linton, 1996), pp. 9–15.
7. The Domesday Survey did not cover the north of England for the simple reason that it was not yet fully under Norman control. The transfer of land to Norman conquerors did not really begin until after 1100. Lomas, *County of Conflict*, pp. 15–25.
8. D. Walker, *Medieval Wales* (Cambridge, 1990), pp. 20–43. I. W. Rowlands, 'The Making of the March: Aspects of the Norman Settlement of Dyfed', *Anglo-Norman Studies III*, pp. 142–157.
9. For events in Scotland see R. Oram, *David I: The King Who Made Scotland* (Stroud, 2014), pp. 17–88, 121–144 and 167–190.

PART II: CONQUEST, CREATION AND CONTROL

Chapter 3 The Protagonists

1. For the sequence of events that stemmed from this tragedy see A. L. Poole, *From Domesday Book to Magna Carta* (Oxford, 1951), pp. 131–166.
2. L. Hilton, *Queens Consort: England's Medieval Queens* (London, 2008), pp. 68–92. Queen Matilda's career opens a window on the important, effective role women could and did play in political as well as family life. Ciphers they were not.

3. M. Altschul, *A Baronial Family in Medieval England: The de Clares 1217–1314* (Baltimore, 1965), pp. 17–29.

4. The political situation in Ireland in the decades before the Norman arrival, including the career of Diarmait Mac Murchada, is covered in F. J. Byrne, 'The Trembling Sod', in A. Cosgrove (ed.), *A New History of Ireland II* (Oxford, 1993), pp. 1–42; and C. Kostick, *Strongbow: The Norman Invasion of Ireland* (Dublin, 2013), pp. 58–99.

5. The following account is based upon my reading of three books: G. H. Orpen, *Ireland under the Normans 1169–1333*, reissued as a single volume with an introduction by Sean Duffy (Dublin, 2005), pp. 24–91; F. X. Martin, 'Diarmait Mac Murchada and the Coming of the Normans', in Cosgrove, *A New History*, pp. 98–155; Kostick, *Strongbow*.

6. See Geraldines, text p. 35.

7. H. Owen, 'The Flemings in Pembrokeshire', *Archaeologia Cambrensis* 5th series, 12 (1895), pp. 96–106.

8. Poole, *From Domesday*, pp. 302–318. Orpen, *Ireland*, pp. 91–106. M. T. Flanagan, 'Strongbow, Henry II and the Anglo-Norman Intervention in Ireland', in J. Gillingham and J. C. Holt (eds), *War and Government in the Middle Ages* (London, 1984), pp. 62–77. Martin, 'Diarmait Mac Murchada', pp. 98–110.

Chapter 4 Interlude in Leinster: 1176–1189

1. Le Poer is the origin of the Irish surname Power. It may derive from the Latin word *puer* (boy), i.e. junior. Alternatively, it is from the town of Poix in Picardy.

2. Orpen, *Ireland*, pp. 91–105. F. X. Martin, 'Allies and an Overlord', in Cosgrove, *A New History*, pp. 89–96. Poole, *From Domesday*, pp. 307–309.

3. This compromise was largely unavoidable as the only means of governing an extended empire.

4. Orpen, *Ireland*, pp. 153–180.

5. King Henry saw the kingship of Ireland serving two purposes. One was to provide for his youngest son, John. The other was to create a more regular and effective government for Ireland. If achieved, both would be to his advantage.

6. Orpen, *Ireland*, pp. 187–193; Martin, 'Overlord Becomes Feudal Lord', in Cosgrove, *A New History*, pp. 122–126.

7. Rich widows always attracted men who were in want of a fortune, and were prepared to pay money to buy them. For the crown, a second husband

could be expected to take better care of the estate's feudal and military obligations.

8. The importance of William Marshal is attested by the fact that seven full-scale studies of him have been published since 1930. The three I have made most use of are: S. Painter, *William Marshal* (Baltimore, 1933); D. Crouch, *William Marshal: Knighthood, War and Chivalry, 1147–1219* (Abingdon, 1990); T. Asbridge, *The Greatest Knight* (London, 2015).

9. Origins of the Marshal family are a matter of speculation. We are ignorant of how, why, from where, or when Gilbert was appointed master marshal of the king's court; or even when he was born and came to England from Normandy. There is no confirmation of him in the Domesday Book; and what became the family seat, Hamstead (later Hamstead Marshall) was held by a ship's captain, Hugolin the Steerman. A. Williams and G. H. Martin (eds), *Domesday Book: A Complete Translation* (London, 2003), p. 157.

10. The Marshal child and King Stephen whiled away their time in the royal camp, it is said, by playing games together; particularly a game of knights. There was a popular childhood game called 'Knights' and it was possible that this was the game young William played with the king; it is played by attempting to knock off the head of an opponent's plantain stalk. Plantain is a common weed with a tough stalk and a seeded head. Asbridge, *Greatest Knight*, p. 29.

11. D. Crouch, *The Image of Aristocracy in Britain, 1000–1300* (London, 1992), pp. 220–246.

12. On the knight, Crouch, *Aristocracy*, pp. 120–16; C. Gravett, *Knight: Noble Warrior of England 1200–1600* (Oxford, 2010), pp. 25–79.

13. Guy de Lusignan migrated to the kingdom of Jerusalem in the early 1180s, having been urged to do so by his two brothers, who had settled there in 1174. Not surprisingly, they had a scheme afoot to marry him off to Sibyl, heiress to the throne of the kingdom. They succeeded, and Guy de Lusignan became king of Jerusalem – but not for long. In 1187 he led his kingdom's army to a catastrophic defeat, the result of which was that Jerusalem fell into the hands of the famous Turkish leader Saladin. But Guy de Lusignan was not finished. He purchased the island of Cyprus from Richard I, who overran it during the Third Crusade. Although Richard was never paid, the de Lusignan family ruled Cyprus until 1489. Clearly, the Normans did not have a monopoly over political buccaneering: what they could do, so could the Poitevins. P. Lock, *The Routledge Companion to the Crusades* (London, 2006), p. 238.

14. D. Crouch, *Tournament* (London, 2005), pp. 19–105 . The sites for tourna-
    ments designated by Richard I were between Salisbury and Wilton, between
    Stamford and Wansford, between Brackley and Mixborough and between
    Blyth and Tickhill. Staines and Dunstable were added later (pp. 53–54).

Chapter 5 A Promise Fulfilled

1. G. Kenny, 'The Wife's Tale: Isabel Marshal and Ireland', in John Bradley et
   al. (eds), *William Marshal and Ireland* (Dublin, 2016), pp. 315–325. The fact
   that this is the shortest of the book's ten articles in no way diminishes Isabel's
   importance but is merely due to the paucity of evidence, as is so often the
   case with wives.
2. The Augustinian priory at Cartmel was founded in the early 1190s. W. Farrer
   and J. Brownbill (eds), *Victoria County History of Lancashire* II (London,
   1908), pp. 143–148. Its foundation community was brought from an earlier
   Augustinian house, Bradenstoke, in Wiltshire, founded *c.* 1142 by Walter of
   Salisbury, Sheriff of Wiltshire, the father of Patrick, earl of Salisbury and his
   sister Sibyl, John Marshal's second wife and mother of William Marshal. R.
   B. Pugh and E. Crittall (eds), *Victoria County History of Wiltshire* III
   (Oxford, 1956), p. 288. Marshal later granted to the canons of Cartmel the
   village of Kilrush, the advowson of the parish church, together with the
   parish of Ballysax and its chapel at Ballymadan. Cartmel's right was disputed
   by an Irish Augustinian house, St Thomas in Dublin. It was settled in
   Cartmel's favour by a papal commission in 1205. Farrer and Brownbill,
   Victoria County History, p. 144.
3. There is no doubt that Marshal bet that John would be Richard I's successor
   as king and acted accordingly. This can be seen in his refusal to do homage
   to Richard for Leinster, claiming that this was due to John as lord of
   Ireland, which elicited from the chancellor, William de Longchamp:
   'Planting vines, Marshal?' (Crouch, *William Marshal*, p. 79). This sardonic
   remark may contain much truth, but it must also be remembered that
   Marshal was a stickler for feudal protocol and Leinster was an Irish estate,
   a fact that Richard accepted with good grace. Feudal correctness also
   figured in the debate between Marshal and Hubert Walter immediately
   following the death of Richard I, as to whether John or Arthur of Brittany
   had the better claim to the throne. Marshal may indeed have favoured John
   as the better prospective monarch, but supporting John satisfied his loyalty
   and homage given to both men. It was a case of virtue and convenience
   happily coinciding.

4. The composition of Marshal's *mesnie* and household is analysed in Crouch, *William Marshal*, pp. 166–176; and in J. Bradley and B. Murtagh, 'William Marshal's Charter to Kilkenny, 1207, background, dating and witnesses', in Bradley et al., *William Marshal and Ireland*, pp. 225–244.

5. John's expedition to Ireland lasted nine weeks and is dealt with in Orpen, *Ireland*, pp. 245–261. It needs to be emphasised that this was not simply a demonstration of political might; rather it marked a step forward in the English government of Ireland, particularly in the matter of law, a subject in which John had a genuine interest.

6. The evolving opposition to John in terms of both personnel and ideas is analysed in D. Carpenter, *Magna Carta* (London, 2015), pp. 274–309, and W. L. Waren, *King John* (London, 1961), pp. 172–192 and 226–237.

7. Archbishop Langton's position as papal legate and at the same time a major figure in English politics and government became acutely embarrassing: he was now in the service of two masters in bitter conflict. Carpenter, *Magna Carta*, pp. 322–352.

8. The battle in Lincoln is described, with a helpful map, in J. W. F. Hill, *Medieval Lincoln* (Cambridge, 1948), pp. 201–205.

9. For the burial and subsequent disturbances to Marshal's tomb, see R. Griffith-Jones, *William Marshal: The Greatest Knight that Ever Lived* (London, 2019), pp. 30–31.

Chapter 6 Sons of William Marshal

1. M. Prestwich, *Plantagenet England 1225–1360* (Oxford, 2005), pp. 93–98.

2. A. Gwynn and R. N. Hadcock, *Medieval Religious Houses in Ireland* (London, 1970), p. 220. This was the first of the thirty-nine Dominican houses founded in Ireland, twenty-five of them before 1300.

3. M. Powicke, *Thirteenth-Century England 1216–1307* (Oxford, 1953), pp. 94–104.

4. A. J. Holden (ed.), *L'Histoire de Guillaume Le Marechal (History of William Marshal)* (London, 2002–6).

5. Prestwich, *Plantagenet*, pp. 83–87; Powicke, *Thirteenth-Century*, pp. 42–45; R. C. Stacey, *Politics, Policy and Finance under Henry III 1216–1245* (Oxford, 1987), pp. 12–29.

6. N. Vincent, *Peter des Roches: An Alien in English Politics 1205–1238* (Cambridge, 1996), pp. 334–339 and 456–464.

7. B. Smith, 'Irish Politics, 1220–1245', in *Thirteenth-Century England* VIII (1999), pp. 13–21. Orpen, *Ireland*, pp. 310–316.

8. Gwynn and Hadcock, *Medieval Religious Houses*, p. 38. Like the Dominicans, this was the first of the forty-eight Franciscan houses established in Ireland, thirty-two of them by 1300.

9. G. H. Orpen, 'Charters of the Forests of Ross and Taghmon', *Journal of the Royal Societies of Antiquaries of Ireland*, 7th series, 4, pp. 54–63.

10. D. Carpenter, *Magna Carta* (London, 2015), pp. 168–169, 176–177, 191–192, 195, 209–210.

11. Prestwich, *Plantagenet*, pp. 96–98; Powicke, *Thirteenth-Century*, pp. 75–77.

12. Orpen, *Ireland*, pp. 318–335.

PART III: IMPACT

Chapter 7 Imposition of a Feudal Structure

1. N. Saul, *For Honour and Fame: Chivalry in England 1066–1500* (London, 2011) is a detailed explanation of all aspects of the subject.

2. Stenton, *The First Century of English Feudalism 1066–1166* (Oxford, 1932) is, I believe, the best account of feudalism in England up to Henry II's Inquest of Knights 1166.

3. Stenton, *Anglo-Saxon England*, p. 618.

4. Carpenter, *Magna Carta*: text with parallel translation, pp. 36–65. For scutage, reliefs and disparagment, see clauses 12, 2 and 6.

5. On the changing numbers, status and functions of knights, see Prestwich, *Plantagenet*, pp. 390–402, and Powicke, *Thirteenth-Century*, pp. 535–542.

6. Orpen, *Ireland*, pp. 139–149, and J. Otway-Ruthven, 'The Medieval County of Kildare', *Irish Historical Studies*, 11.43, pp. 181–199.

7. For the de Riddlesfords, see below.

8. C. A. Empey, 'Conquest and Settlement: Patterns of Settlement in Munster and South Leinster', *Irish Social and Economic History*, 13 (1986), p. 15, and C. A. Empey, 'County Kilkenny in the Anglo-Norman period', in N. Nolan and K. Whelan (eds), *Kilkenny: History and Society* (Dublin, 1990), pp. 65.

9. This charter is printed, in Latin, in Orpen, *Ireland*, p. 149.

10. My calculations are based on evidence drawn from: J. Otway-Ruthven, 'Knight's Fees in Kildare, Leix and Offaly', *Journal of the Royal Society of Antiquaries of Ireland*, 91 (1961), pp. 163–181; E. St-J. Brooks, *Knight's Fees in Counties Wexford, Carlow and Kilkenny* (Dublin, 1950); B. Colfer, *Arrogant Trespass: Anglo-Normans in Wexford 1169–1400* (Cork, 2002). The figures are my own, based on the evidence I have seen, but I cannot claim their absolute accuracy.

11. B. Colfer, 'Anglo-Norman Settlement in County Wexford', in K. Whelan (ed.), *Wexford: History and Society* (Dublin, 1987), p. 73.

12. N. B. White (ed.), *Red Book of Ormond* (Dublin, 1932), pp. 34–45.

13. Williams and Martin, *Domesday*, pp. 1,235–1,236.

14. These figures, for which I do not claim absolute accuracy, are the outcome of my reading of T. McNeil, *Castles in Ireland* (Abingdon, 1997); T. McNeil, 'Early Castles in Leinster', *Journal of Irish Archaeology*, V (1989–90), pp. 37–64; K. O'Conor, 'Anglo-Norman Castles in Co. Laois', in P. G. Lane and W. Nolan (eds), *Laois: History and Society* (Dublin, 1999), pp. 160–168.

15. R. Avent, 'William Marshal's building works at Chepstow Castle', in J. R. Kenyon and K. O'Conor (eds), *The Medieval Castle in Ireland and Wales* (Dublin, 2002), pp. 50–71.

16. E. St-J. Brooks, 'The de Riddlesfords', *Journal of the Royal Society of Antiquaries of Ireland*, 81 (1951), pp. 115–138.

Chapter 8 Manors and Manorial Farms

1. E. Miller and J. Hatcher, *Medieval England: Rural Society and Economic Change 1086–1348* (London, 1978), pp. 184–239, gives a broad, overall view of the diversity of manors and changes in estate management during the years covered by this book.

2. J. Otway-Ruthven, 'The Organisation of Irish Agriculture in the Middle Ages', *Journal of the Royal Society of Antiquaries of Ireland*, 81 (1951), pp. 1–13.

3. R. Bartlett, *England 1075–1225* (Oxford, 2000), pp. 370–373.

4. Miller and Hatcher, *Medieval England*, pp. 64–69. Price inflation was more or less continuous for 150 years between 1170 and 1320, but was particularly acute between 1180 and 1220. The causes were multiple, but underlying everything was an expanding economy in response to the rising population. One particular cause, however, was the opening up of silver mines in the Harz Mountains in Germany.

5. M. Clyne, *Kells Priory, Co. Kilkenny: Archaeological Excavations by T. Fanning and M. Clyne* (Dublin, 2007), pp. 1–40; also, M. Clyne, 'Kells and its Priory', in J. Bradley et al., *William Marshal*, pp. 78–110.

6. M. C. Lyons, 'The Manor of Ballysax 1280–1288', *Retrospect, New Series 1* (1981), pp. 40–50. The text of the account is on pp. 45–50.

7. The earl of Norfolk's other manors were at Fenagh and Forth (Co. Carlow) and Old Ross (Co. Wexford).

8. Some of this is provided by M. C. Lyons on pp. 40–45, but see M. Murphy, 'The profits of lordship: Roger Bigod, earl of Norfolk, and the lordship of

Carlow, 1270–1306', in L. Doran and J. Lyttleton (eds), *Lordship in Medieval Ireland: Image and Reality* (Dublin, 2008), pp. 75–98.

Chapter 9 Boroughs

1. Stenton, *Anglo-Saxon England*, pp. 525–540; H. R. Loyn, *Anglo-Saxon England and the Norman Conquest* (London, 1962), pp. 132–140, 368–384.
2. Personal calculations based on Williams and Martin (eds), *Domesday Book*.
3. M. Beresford, *New Towns in the Middle Ages: Town Plantation in England, Wales and Gascony* (London, 1967), p. 330.
4. Beresford, *New Towns*, p. 341.
5. A. A. Duncan, *Scotland: The Making of the Kingdom* (Edinburgh, 1977), pp. 463–501.
6. Beresford, *New Towns*, pp. 652–655.
7. J. Lydon, 'The Impact of the Bruce Invasion', in Cosgrove, *A New History*, pp. 275–302, p. 449.
8. Prestwich, *Plantagenet*, pp. 529–533 is important for its recognition that, despite much historical and scientific research, we are still unable to say precisely what the disease was. The Irish evidence is pitifully sparse. It is accepted that the Black Death entered Ireland via Howth in the late summer of 1348 and that, as elsewhere, the overall death rate in Ireland was between 40 and 50 per cent. There is also some evidence that the native Irish, because they lived in small scattered settlements, may have been less severely affected than the immigrant settlers, who tended to live in more clustered communities. R. Frame, *Colonial Ireland 1169–1369* (Dublin, 2012), p. 129.
9. A. Thomas, *The Walled Towns of Ireland*, vol. 1 (Dublin, 1992).
10. Thomas, *Walled Towns*, vol. 2. The archaeological data is contained in the following sections: Athey, pp. 18–19; Callan, pp. 30–32; Carlow, pp. 34–37; Castledermot, pp. 49–51; Gowran, pp. 113–115; Inistioge, pp. 116–117; Kildare, pp. 113–115; Kilkenny, pp. 126–132; Naas, pp. 168–170; New Ross, pp. 175–179; Thomastown, pp. 190–192; Wexford, pp. 210–214. Thomas states that for the following three towns the evidence is uncertain: Ferns, pp. 227–228; Old Leighlin, pp. 229–230; Tullow, pp. 240–241.
11. J. Bradley, 'The Early Development of the Medieval Town of Kilkenny', in Nolan and Whelan, *Kilkenny: History and Society*, pp. 75–95.
12. G. Mac Niocaill, *Na Buirgéist XII–XV Aois* (Dublin, 1964), pp. 135–138.
13. J. Otway-Ruthven, *Liber Primus Kilkenniensis* (Kilkenny, 1961), pp. 2–3.

14. C. Ó'Drisceoill, 'Pons Novus, villa Willelmi Marescalle: New Ross, a town of William Marshal', in Bradley et al., *William Marshal and Ireland*, pp. 268–314.

15. K. Down, 'Colonial Society and Economy', in Cosgrove, *A New History*, pp. 482–514. See also p. 167, which shows that New Ross exported 60 per cent of the income of £3,517 raised from the wool customs arising from New Ross, Waterford and Wexford between 1275 and 1279.

16. H. Shields (ed.), 'The Walling of New Ross: a thirteenth century poem in French', *Long Room* 12–13 (1975–6), pp. 24–33.

17. C. O'Brien, *The Origins of Newcastle Quayside* (Newcastle-upon-Tyne, 1988).

18. P. F. Wallace (ed.), *Waterford Treasures* (Waterford, 2004), pp. 66–78.

19. C. Kenny, 'New Leighlin: An Anglo-Norman Settlement', in T. McGrath (ed.), *Carlow: History and Society* (Dublin, 2008), pp. 213–227.

20. G. Mac Niocaill, *Na Buirgéisí*, pp. 296–299.

21. M. Murphy, 'Tullow – from Medieval Manor to Market Town', in McGrath (ed.), *Carlow*, pp. 235–254.

22. C. O'Cléirigh, 'The Impact of the Anglo-Normans in Laois', in P. G. Lane and W. Nolan (eds), *Laois: History and Society* (Dublin, 1999), pp. 167–170; Orpen, *Ireland*, p. 332.

Chapter 10 Local Government

1. Stenton, *Anglo-Saxon England*, pp. 548–549.

2. J. D. Mackie, *The Earlier Tudors 1485–1558* (Oxford, 1952), pp. 366–369, 159–162, 168–170.

3. Duncan, *Scotland*, pp. 159–162, 168–170, 204–208, 596–599.

4. R. Nicholson, *Scotland: The Later Middle Ages* (Edinburgh, 1989), pp. 417–541.

5. Poole, *Domesday*, pp. 389–390.

6. J. Ruthven-Otway, 'Anglo-Irish Shire Government in the Thirteenth Century', *Irish Historical Studies* 5 (1946), pp. 1–28.

7. J. B. Black, *The Reign of Elizabeth 1558–1603* (Oxford, 1959), pp. 461–464, p. 491.

Chapter 11 Church Reform

1. Z. N. Brooke, *A History of Europe 911 to 1198* (London, 1947), pp. 143–203, 249–294, 373–379, 430–455.

2. D. Knowles, *The Religious Orders in England* I (Cambridge, 1962), pp. 114–179, 194–204.

3. J. A. Watt, *The Church in Medieval Ireland* (Dublin, 1998), pp. 1–40; M. T. Flanagan, *The Transformation of the Irish Church in the Twelfth Century* (Dublin, 2010).

4. Bede, *The Ecclesiastical History of the English People*, trans. L. Sherley-Price and R. E. Latham (London, 1990), pp. 90–91.

5. Gwynn and Hadcock, *Medieval Religious Houses*: Ferns, pp. 78–79; Kildare, pp. 82–84; Kilkenny, pp. 84–87; Leighlin, pp. 89–90.

6. K. W. Nichols, 'Medieval Irish Cathedral Chapters', *Archivium Hibernicum* 31 (1973), pp. 102–111.

7. R. Sharpe, 'Churches and Communities in early medieval Ireland: towards a pastoral model', in J. Blair and R. Sharpe (eds), *Pastoral Care before the Parish* (Leicester, 1992), pp. 81–109. J. Blair (ed.), *Minsters and Parish Churches 950–1200* (Oxford, 1988), pp. 1–19. E. FitzPatrick and R. Gillespie (eds), *The Parish in Medieval and Early Modern Ireland* (Dublin, 2006).

8. A. Hamilton Thompson, *The English Clergy and their Organisation in the Later Middle Ages* (Oxford, 1947), pp. 101–131.

9. My calculations are based on data from the following: Colfer, 'Anglo-Norman Settlement in County Wexford'; M. O'Neil, 'The Medieval Churches and Old Leighlin Cathedral', in McGrath (ed.), *Carlow*, p. 121; H. J. Lawlor, 'Calendar of the *Liber Ruber* of the Diocese of Ossory', *Proceedings of the Royal Irish Academy* 27 (1908/1909), pp. 159–208; W. Sweetman, *Calendar of the Ecclesiastical Taxation of Ireland 1302–1307* (Dublin, 1886), p. 40, pp. 242–251.

10. O. O'Kelly, *The Place Names of County Kilkenny* (Kilkenny, 1985).

11. White, *Red Book of Ormond*, p. 35, p. 38; O'Kelly, *Place Names*, p. 82, p. 89.

12. For St Malachy see S. Duffy (ed.), *Medieval Ireland: An Encyclopaedia* (London, 2005), pp. 312–314.

13. Gwynn and Hadcock, *Medieval Religious Houses*, pp. 114–152.

14. J. A. Watt, *The Church in Two Nations in Medieval Ireland* (Dublin, 1970), pp. 85–107; Gwynn and Hadcock, *Medieval Religious Houses*, pp. 146–200.

15. Gwynn and Hadcock, *Medieval Religious Houses*, pp. 146–198.

16. Gwynn and Hadcock, *Medieval Religious Houses*, pp. 208–216.

17. Gwynn and Hadcock, *Medieval Religious Houses*, pp. 343–345.

18. Gwynn and Hadcock, *Medieval Religious Houses*, pp. 307–325.

19. Gwynn and Hadcock, *Medieval Religious Houses*, pp. 327–342; E. Lord, *The Knights Templar in Britain* (Harlow, 2002): for Ireland, pp. 137–142, for London Temple Headquarters, pp. 22–37.

20. Gwynn and Hadcock, *Medieval Religious Houses*, pp. 218–234 (Dominicans), pp. 235–262 (Franciscans).

21. G. A. Lee, *Leper Hospitals in Medieval Ireland* (Dublin, 1996), pp. 11–20, 45, 50–53, 58–60.

Afterword

1. Powicke, *Thirteenth-Century*, pp. 84–117.
2. Prestwich, *Plantagenet*, Wales, pp. 141–157, Scotland, pp. 230–244. Brown, *Wars of Scotland*, pp. 179–254.
3. M. McKisack, *The Fourteenth Century 1307–1399* (Oxford, 1959), pp. 127–149.
4. J. A. Watt, 'The Anglo-Irish colony under strain', in Cosgrove, *A New History*, pp. 384–390.
5. Orpen, *Ireland*, pp. 361–393.
6. S. Duffy, *Atlas of Irish History* (Dublin, 2012), p. 41.
7. Lydon, 'The Impact of the Bruce Invasion', pp. 259–260.
8. Kavanagh private family archive.
9. A. Cosgrove, 'England and Ireland, 1399–1447', in Cosgrove, *A New History*, pp. 525–532.
10. Black, *Elizabeth*, pp. 480–491.

Bibliography

PRINTED PRIMARY SOURCES

Calendar of Documents relating to Ireland 1302–1307, ed. H. S. Sweetman (Dublin, 1886).

'Charters of Earl Richard Marshal of the Forests of Ross and Taghmon', *Journal of the Royal Society of Antiquaries of Ireland* 4 (Dublin, 1934), pp. 54–63.

Documents Relating to the Suppression of the Templars in Ireland, ed. G. Mac Niocaill (Dublin, 1967).

Expugnatio Hibernica (The Conquest of Ireland) by Giraldus Cambrensis, ed. and trans. A. B. Scott and F. X. Martin (Dublin, 1978).

Extents of Irish Monastic Possessions in *1540–41*, ed. N. B. White (Dublin, 1943).

Knights' Fees in the Counties of Wexford, Carlow and Kilkenny, ed. E. St-J. Brooks (Dublin, 1950).

L'Histoire de Guillaume Le Marechal (History of William Marshal), ed. A. J. Holden, trans. S. Gregory, notes D. Crouch, 3 vols (London, 2002, 2004, 2006).

Liber Primus Kilkenniensis, trans. J. Otway-Ruthven (Kilkenny, 1961).

Na Buirgéisí, xii–xv aois, ed. G. Mac Niocaill (Dublin, 1964).

Red Book of Ormond, ed. N. B. White (Dublin, 1932).

Red Book of the Earls of Kildare, ed. P. Flattisbury and G. Mac Niocaill (Dublin, 1964).

Song of Dermot and the Earl, ed. G. H. Orpen (Oxford, 1892).

'The Walling of New Ross': a thirteenth century poem in French, ed. H. Shields, *Long Room*, 12–13 (1975–6), pp. 24–33.

SECONDARY SOURCES

Altschul, M., *A Baronial Family in Medieval England: The Clares 1217–1314* (Baltimore, 1965).

Armstrong-Anthony, S., 'From Anglo-Norman Manor to Plantation Estate: An Archaeological Survey of Monasteroris, County Offaly', in J. Lyttleton and T. O'Keefe (eds), *The Manor in Medieval and Early Modern Ireland* (Dublin, 2005), pp. 105–119.

Asbridge, T., *The Greatest Knight* (London, 2015).

Barry, T. B., *The Archaeology of Medieval Ireland* (Dublin, 1987).

Barry, T. B. (ed.), *A History of Settlement in Ireland* (London, 2000).

Bartlett, R., *England Under the Norman and Angevin Kings 1075–1225* (Oxford, 2000).

Bartlett, R. and A. MacKay, *Medieval Frontier Societies* (Oxford, 1989).

Bates, D., *Normandy Before 1066* (London, 1982).

Bates, D., 'The Rise and Fall of Normandy', in D. Bates and A. Curry, *England and Normandy in the Middle Ages* (London, 1994), pp. 19–35.

Bhreathnach, E., *Ireland in the Medieval World ad 400–1000* (Dublin, 2014).

Black, J. B., *The Reign of Elizabeth 1558–1603* (Oxford, 1958), p. 473.

Blair, J., *Minsters and Parish Churches: The Local Church in Transition* (Oxford, 1988).

Bradley, J., C. Ó Drisceoil and M. Potterton (eds), *William Marshal in Ireland* (Dublin, 2017).

Brett, M., 'Canterbury Perspectives on Church Reform and Ireland 1070–1115', in D. Bracken and D. O'Briain-Raedel (eds), *Ireland and Europe in the Twelfth Century: Reform and Renewal* (Dublin, 2006), pp. 13–33.

Britnell, R., *The Commercialisation of English Society* (Cambridge, 1996).

Brookes, E. St-J., 'The de Ridelsfords', *Journal of the Royal Society of Antiquaries of Ireland* 81 (1951), pp. 115–138 and 82 (1952), pp. 45–61.

Brown, M., *The Wars in Scotland 1214–1371* (Edinburgh, 2004).

Byrne, F. J., *Irish Kings and High Kings* (Dublin, 1973).

Carpenter, D., *Magna Carta: With a New Commentary* (London, 2015).

Clyne, M., *Kells Priory, Co. Kilkenny: Archaeological Excavations by T. Fanning and M. Clyne* (Dublin, 2007).

Colfer, B., 'Anglo-Norman Settlement in County Wexford', in K. Whelan (ed.), *Wexford: History and Society* (1987), pp. 65–89.

Colfer, B., *An Arrogant Trespass: Anglo-Norman Wexford 1169–1400* (Enniscorthy, 2002).

Colfer, B., *Wexford Castles: Landscape, Context and Settlement* (Cork, 2013).

Cosgrove, A. (ed.), *A New History of Ireland: II Medieval Ireland 1169–1534* (Oxford, 1991).

Crouch, D., *The Image of Aristocracy in Britain 1000–1300* (London, 1992).

Crouch, D., *William Marshal: Knighthood, War and Chivalry 1147–1219* (London, 2002).

Crouch, D., *Tournament* (London, 2005).

Cullerton, E., *Celtic and Early Christian Wexford ad 400–1166* (Dublin, 1999).

Doran, L., 'Medieval Settlement Hierarchy in Carlow and the "Carlow Corridor" *1200–1550*', in T. McGrath (ed.), *Carlow: History and Society* (Dublin, 2008), pp. 173–207.

Down, K., 'Agriculture and Manorial Economy in County Carlow in the Late Thirteenth Century', in T. McGrath (ed.), *Carlow: History and Society* (Dublin, 2008), pp. 259–271.

Duffy, S., 'The Western Word's Tower of Honour and Dignity: The Career of Muirchertach Ua Briain in context', in D. Bracken and D. O'Briain-Raedel (eds), *Ireland and Europe in the Twelfth Century: Reform and Renewal* (Dublin, 2006), pp. 56–73.

Duffy, S. (ed.) *Atlas of Irish History*, 3rd edn (Dublin, 2012).

Duffy, S., 'The Welsh Conquest of Ireland', in E. Purcell, P. MacCotter, J. Nyhan and J. Sheehan (eds), *Clerics, Kings and Vikings* (Dublin, 2017), pp. 103–115.

Empey, C. A., 'Inistioge in the Middle Ages', in J. Kirwan (ed.), *Kilkenny Studies in Honour of Margaret M. Phelan* (Kilkenny, 1982), pp. 9–15.

Empey, C. A., 'Medieval Knocktopher: A Study in Manorial Settlement', *Old Kilkenny Review* 2 (1985), pp. 329–342.

Empey, C. A., 'Conquest and Settlement: Patterns of Anglo-Norman Settlement in North Munster and South Leinster', *Irish Economic and Social History* 13 (1986), pp. 5–31.

Empey, C. A., 'County Kilkenny in the Anglo-Norman Period', in W. Nolan and K. Whelan (eds), *Kilkenny: History and Society* (1990), pp. 75–95.

Empey, C. A., 'The Lay Person in the Parish: The Medieval Inheritance, 1169–1536', in R. Gillespie and W. G. Neely (eds), *The Laity and the Church of Ireland 1000–2000* (Dublin, 2002), pp. 7–25.

Empey, C. A., 'The Liberty and Counties of Carlow in the High Middle Ages', in T. McGrath (ed.), *Carlow: History and Society* (Dublin, 2008), pp. 153–168.

Etchingham, C., *Church Organisation in Ireland ad 650 to 1000* (Maynooth, 1999).

FitzPatrick, E. and C. O. O'Brien, *The Medieval Churches of County Offaly* (Dublin, 1998).

FitzPatrick, E. and R. Gillespie (eds), *The Parish in Medieval and Early Modern Ireland* (Dublin, 2006).

Flanagan, D. and L. Flanagan, *Irish Place Names* (Dublin, 1994).

Flanagan, M. T., 'Strongbow, Henry II and Anglo-Norman Intervention in Ireland', in J. Gillingham and J. C. Holt (eds), *War and Government in the Middle Ages* (London, 1984), pp. 62–77.

Flanagan, M. T., *Irish Royal Charters: Texts and Contexts* (Oxford, 2005).

Flanagan, M. T., *The Transformation of the Irish Church in the Twelfth Century* (Woodbridge, 2010).

Fleming, J., *Gille of Limerick (c. 1070–1145)* (Dublin, 2001).

Flori, J., *Richard the Lionheart: King and Knight*, trans. J. Birrell (Edinburgh, 1999).

Frame, R. F., *Colonial Ireland 1169–1369*, 2nd edn (Dublin, 2012).

Frame, R. F., 'Ireland after 1169: Barriers to Acculturation on an "English" Edge', in K. J. Stringer and A. Jotischky (eds), *Norman Expansion: Connections, Continuities and Contrasts* (London, 2013), pp. 115–141.

Gillingham, J., *The Angevin Empire* (London, 2001).

Gravett, C., *Knight: Noble Warrior of England* (Botley, Oxford, 2008).

Gwynn, A. and R. N. Hadcock, *Medieval Religious Houses in Ireland* (London, 1970).

Hartland, B., 'English Landholding in Ireland', in M. Prestwich, R. Britnell and R. Frame (eds), *Thirteenth Century England*, vol. 10 (2003), pp. 119–129.

Hore, P. H., *History of the Town and County of Wexford: Old and New Ross* (London, 1900).

Kenny, C., 'New Leighlin: An Anglo-Norman Settlement', in T. McGrath (ed.), *Carlow: History and Society* (Dublin, 2008), pp. 213–227.

Kenyon, J. R. and K. O'Conor (eds), *The Medieval Castle in Ireland and Wales* (Dublin, 2002).

Knowles, D. and R. N. Hadcock, *Medieval Religious Houses in England and Wales* (London, 1973).

Kostick, C., *Strongbow: The Norman Invasion of Ireland* (Dublin, 2013).

Lawlor, H. J., 'Calendar of the Liber Ruber of the Diocese of Ossory', *Proceedings of The Royal Irish Academy* 27 (1908/1909), pp. 159–208.

Lee, G. A., *Leper Hospitals in Medieval Ireland* (Dublin, 1996).

Leroux-Dhuys, J.-F. and H. Gaud, *Cistercian Abbeys: History and Architecture*, trans. E. Clegg, C. Higgitt and M-N. Ryan (Paris, 1998).

Lomas, R. A., *County of Conflict: Northumberland from Conquest to Civil War* (East Linton, 1996).

Lord, E., *The Knights Templar in Britain* (Harlow, 2002).

Lydon, J. F., 'Medieval Wicklow – A Land of War', in K. Hannigan and W. Nolan (eds), *Wicklow: History and Society* (1994), pp. 150–182.

Lyons, M. C., 'The Manor of Ballysax 1280–1288', *Retrospect* n.s. 1 (1981), pp. 40–50.

Lyons, M. C., 'An Account for the Manor of Old Ross, September 1284 to September 1285', *Decies* 28 (1981), pp. 33–40 and 29 (1982), pp. 18–31.

MacCotter, P., *Medieval Ireland: Territorial Political and Economic Divisions* (Dublin, 2008).

MacCotter, P., 'The Medieval Rural Dean and Deanery in Ireland', in E. Purcell, P. MacCotter, J. Nyhan and J. Sheehan (eds), *Clerics, Kings and Vikings* (Dublin, 2017), pp. 25–40.

MacEnearney, E. and R. Ryan, *Waterford Treasures* (Waterford, 2004).

MacKie, J. D., *The Early Tudors 1485–1558* (Oxford, 1952).

McKisack, M., *The Fourteenth Century 1307–1399* (Oxford, 1959).

McNeil, T. E., 'Early Castles in Leinster', *Journal of Irish Archaeology* 5 (Dublin, 1990).

Miller, E. and J. Hatcher, *Medieval England: Rural Society and Economic Change 1086–1348* (London, 1978).

Morris, M., *The Bigod Earls of Norfolk in the Thirteenth Century* (Woodbridge, 2005).

Morris, M., *King John: Treachery, Tyranny and the Road to Magna Carta* (London, 2015).

Mortimer, R., 'The Beginnings of the Honour of Clare', in R. Allen Brown (ed.), *Anglo-Norman Studies II: Proceedings of the Battle Conference 1980* (Woodbridge, 1980), pp. 119–141.

Morton, N., *The Medieval Military Orders 1120–1314* (Harlow, 2013).

Murphy, M., 'The Profits of Lordship: Roger Bigod, earl of Norfolk, and the Lordship of Carlow, 1270–1306', in L. Doran and J. Lyttleton (eds), *Lordship in Medieval Ireland* (Dublin, 2008), pp. 75–98.

Murphy, M., 'Tullow – From Medieval Manor to Market Town', in T. McGrath (ed.), *Carlow: History and Society* (Dublin, 2008), pp. 235–254.

Nichols, K. W., 'Medieval Irish Cathedral Chapters', *Archivium Hibernicum* 31 (Dublin, 1973), pp. 102–111.

Nicholson, H., *The Knights Hospitaller* (London, 2001).

O'Brien, C., *The Origins of Newcastle Quayside* (Newcastle upon Tyne, 1988).

O'Byrne, E., *War, Politics and the Irish of Leinster* (Dublin, 2003).

O'Cléirigh, C., 'The Impact of the Anglo-Normans in Laois', in P. G. Lane and W. Nolan (eds), *Laois: History and Society* (1999), pp. 160–182.

O'Conor, K., 'Anglo-Norman Castles in Co. Laois', in P. G. Land and W. Nolan (eds), *Laois: History and Society* (1990), pp. 183–211.

O'Keefe, T., *Medieval Ireland: An Archaeology* (Stroud, 2001).

O'Kelly, O., *The Place-Names of County Kilkenny* (Kilkenny, 1985).

O'Neil, M., 'The Medieval Churches and Old Leighlin Cathedral in County Carlow', in T. McGrath (ed.), *Carlow: History and Society* (Dublin, 2008), pp. 121–136.

O'Neil, T., *Castles in Ireland: Feudal Power in a Gaelic World* (Abingdon, 1997).

Oram, R., *David I: The King Who Made Scotland* (Stroud, 2004).

Orpen, G. H., *Ireland Under the Normans, 1169–1333* (Dublin, 2005).

Otway-Ruthven, A. J., 'Anglo-Irish Shire Government in the Thirteenth Century', *Irish Historical Studies* 5 (1946), pp. 1–28.

Otway-Ruthven, A. J., 'The Organisation of Anglo-Irish Agriculture in the Middle Ages', *Journal of the Royal Society of Antiquaries of Ireland* 81 (1951), pp. 1–13.

Otway-Ruthven, A. J., 'The Medieval County of Kildare', *Irish Historical Studies* 11 (1959), pp. 181–199.

Otway-Ruthven, A. J., 'Knight's Fees in Kildare, Leix and Offaly', *Journal of the Royal Society of Antiquaries of Ireland* 91 (1961), pp. 163–181.

Otway-Ruthven, A. J., *A History of Medieval Ireland* (London, 1968).

Otway-Ruthven, A. J., 'The Character of Norman Settlement in Ireland', in P. Crookes (ed.), *Government, War and Society in Medieval Ireland* (Dublin, 2008), pp. 263–274.

Painter, S., *William Marshal: Knight Errant, Baron and Regent of England* (Baltimore, 1933).

Prestwich, M., *Plantagenet England 1225–1360* (Oxford, 2005).

Roche, R., 'The Normans', in K. Whelan (ed.), *Wexford: History and Society* (1987), pp. 106–109.

Rowlands, I. W., 'The Making of the March: Aspects of the Norman Settlement of Dyfed', in R. A. Brown (ed.), *Anglo-Norman Studies III* (1981), pp. 142–157.

Rowley, T., *The Origins of Open Field Agriculture* (London, 1981).

Saul, N., *For Honour and Fame: Chivalry in England 1066–1500* (London, 2011).

Sharpe, R., 'Churches and Communities in Early Medieval Ireland: Towards a Pastoral Model', in J. Blair and R. Sharpe (eds), *Pastoral Care before the Parish* (1992), pp. 81–109.

Shine, L., 'The Manor of Earlstown, County Kilkenny: An Interdisciplinary Approach', in J. Lyttleton and T. O'Keefe (eds), *The Manor in Medieval and Early Modern Ireland* (2005), pp. 40–57.

Shine, L., 'On the Edge of the Colony: Overk and the Carlow Corridor', in V. McAllister and T. Barry (eds), *Space and Settlement in Medieval Ireland* (2015), pp. 64–85.

Smith, B., 'Irish Politics 1220–1245', in *Thirteenth Century England III* (1999), pp. 13–21.

Stacey, R. C., *Politics, Policy and Finance under Henry III 1216–1245* (Oxford, 1981).

Stalley, R. (ed.), *Irish Gothic Architecture: Construction, Decay and Restoration* (Dublin, 2012).

Stenton, F. M., *The First Century of English Feudalism 1066–1166* (Oxford, 1932).

Stenton, F. M., *Anglo-Saxon England*, 3rd edn (Oxford, 1971).

Swift, C., 'Follow the Money: The Financial Resources of Diarmait Mac Murchada', in E. Purcell, P. MacCotter, J. Nyhan and J. Sheehan (eds), *Clerics, Kings and Vikings* (Dublin, 2017), pp. 91–103.

Thacker, A. and R. Sharpe, *Local Saints and Local Churches in the Early Medieval West* (Oxford, 2002).

Thomas, A., *The Walled Towns of Ireland*, 2 vols (Dublin, 1992).

Valante, M. A., *Vikings in Ireland: Settlement, Trade and Urbanisation* (Dublin, 2008).

Vincent, N., *Peter Des Roches: An Alien in English Politics 1205–1238* (Cambridge, 1990).

Watt, J. A., *The Church and the Two Nations in Medieval Ireland* (Dublin, 1970).

Watt, J. A., *The Church in Medieval Ireland* (Dublin, 1998).

Williams, A. and G. H. Martin, *Domesday Book: A Complete Translation* (London, 2003).

Woolf, A., *From Pictland to Alba 789–1070* (Edinburgh, 2007).

Index